D1416988

Recruiting Confidential

Recruiting Confidential

A Father, a Son, and Big-Time
College Football

David Claerbaut

Taylor Trade Publishing

Lanham New York Toronto Oxford

Published by Taylor Trade Publishing
An imprint of The Rowman & Littlefield Publishing Group, Inc.
4501 Forbes Boulevard, Suite 200
Lanham, Maryland 20706

Distributed by National Book Network

Design and composition: Barbara Werden Design

Library of Congress Cataloging-in-Publication Data

Claerbaut, David.
    Recruiting confidential : a father, a son, and big time college football / David Claerbaut.— 1st Taylor Trade Publishing ed.
        p.   cm.
    ISBN 1-58979-025-1 (hardcover : alk. paper) 1. Football—Scouting.
    2. Football players—United States—Recruiting. 3. College sports—United States—Recruiting. 4. Velissaris, James. 5. Claerbaut, David. I. Title.
GV953.4 .C53 2003
796.332'63—dc22

                                                                          2003015507

∞ The paper used in this publication meets the minimum requirements of American National Standard for Information Sciences—Permanence of Paper for Printed Library Materials, ANSI/NISO Z39.48–1992.

Manufactured in the United States of America.

To Chris and Mike, Rachel and Christine, Rae and Rochelle—but most of all to Rita, the heart and soul of all that is good in our family.

Contents

Acknowledgments

No book is written in a vacuum. There are many to thank, and I will mention ten key people here. A special thanks to my editor, Mike Emmerich, for believing in this project. A word of sincere appreciation to Rita, Chris, Rochelle, and Nina, along with Ivan and Ann Eernisse and Ed Zbikowski, for their faithful support of James' athletic endeavors. Finally, a word of gratitude to Steve Helminiak and Mike Herbert for their guidance through the football recruiting jungle.

The ultimate acknowledgment is to James. This is his story, and his inviting me into his life, of which this is a part, is something for which I can never thank him enough.

Recruiting Confidential

1.

Iowa vs. Michigan

It was a magic autumn night—cool, crisp, and exciting. Glenbrook North was opening the 2001 7A playoffs against Machesney Park of Harlem, Illinois. It was the third straight postseason for the Spartans, after spending twenty-four straight seasons (1975–1998) in the high school football wilderness. For Glenbrook North and James, now a junior, it was a night to remember. The Spartans smashed their opponents by a whopping 34–6 margin, and James had a banner night. Things could not have been better.

There are few pleasures in life that run deeper than a gridiron win. A happy air fills the lungs, the injuries are scarcely felt, and the food tastes good. Team cleavages melt, all coaching decisions seem sound, and mistakes during the game pale to nothingness amid the excitement and satisfaction that comes with victory. A no-one-can-beat-us aura of invincibility envelops a team after a lopsided playoff triumph. Such was the case at William Lutz Stadium in Northbrook, Illinois, on that exhilarating fall evening.

I had to wait for James, as a number of high school sportswriters from major and local papers wanted to talk with him about his eye-popping night. His mother and I waited with joy in the car as he showered and dressed with his teammates. I hoped he wouldn't linger because I wanted to drive while still wide awake. While waiting, Rita and I enthused about the game and James' personal success. "I'm so happy for him; it's been a difficult year," was the kind of statement tossed back and forth. I wondered what the *Chicago Tribune* and *Sun-Times* would have to say about James Velissaris and his team in the morning papers.

Soon the conversation moved to the drive we were about to make to Iowa City, home of the University of Iowa Hawkeyes.

"It's a three-plus-hour drive so I'm going to go as far as I can tonight. That way we don't have to get up early tomorrow," I explained. "I hope James stays awake for a good bit of it. It will keep me alert."

"Make sure to call me when you settle in for the night," Rita requested.

Eventually a quiet but happy James emerged. Hugs and kisses were exchanged with his mother, and we were off to Iowa City.

The drive from the northern suburbs of Chicago to Iowa City is usually not an interesting one. It is about a four-hour jaunt over flat interstate land down I-80 in the direction of the Quad Cities (Rock Island and Moline, Illinois, in addition to Davenport and Bettendorf, Iowa). That night it was different. There was a victory to celebrate and an exciting new experience to anticipate. And James was talkative.

Talkative is not a word that would customarily describe James. In fact, James dispenses words about as liberally as the nineteenth-century robber barons dispensed raises to their employees. This has been a matter of some mirth between us. Occasionally I enjoyed mimicking one of his typical voice-mail messages, like the one he left upon arriving at a football camp the previous summer.

"Hello. This is James. I'm here. I'm checked in. I'm OK. Love you. Bye."

In any case, this night was different. The conversation centered early on the Spartan team and the prospects for the rest of the playoffs. The questions and comments flowed back and forth. How did this year's team compare with the 2000 squad? "I think we're better," said James, as almost anyone would reasonably expect from a sixteen-year-old. "We are really quick on defense now and our offensive line is coming together at the right time."

How did Kevin Kaspers compare with "the great Matt Haggis," last year's quarterback? (The modifier I used preceding Haggis' name was a part of our shtick, ribbing James as I had the previous season that Haggis was truly "the man.") "Kevin is really throwing well and he really fits in with the rest of the guys," was James' summation.

An ever more amplified discussion rolled on as the miles flew by.

"I feel so alive playing football, I don't know how to explain it.

I just feel complete, in touch with myself. I don't know what I would do if I couldn't play," James shared.

Did Machesney's defense key on James? Would James be returning punts now that the team was in the playoffs, or would he continue to be on the line in quest of stuffing a kick? How would the team's man-to-man pass defense do against future throwing opponents? What kind of offense and defense would be the most difficult for the Spartans to contend with? Those were some of the items of discussion as the minutes and hours passed. Soon we were flying past the Quad Cities with the gas gauge getting low.

"If you see an exit, James, don't let me miss it. Pushing a car in this darkness is not something I want to do."

"There's an exit sign a mile away."

We got off and drove warily through the dark of the Iowa night until we found a bleary-looking service station that took credit cards at the pump.

I knew Iowa City was an hour past the Quad Cities, with Davenport at roughly the halfway point. I wanted to find a place to stay for the night that was clean and reasonable, so when we got to Davenport that became the objective.

"We better find something here," I said, "because the next stop is Iowa City. And with a home game tomorrow the hotels and motels will really smoke us."

Seeing nothing from the highway we went past Davenport and had to turn around, exit, and look for what was available. We were fortunate. Just off the highway was the right place, and better yet for James, an all-night restaurant was perched on the corner of the block.

"You hungry?" I asked, knowing the answer in advance.

After James devoured as many carbs and calories as possible while I carefully reviewed my less satisfying dietary options and ate lightly, we turned in for the night. Neither of us talked much of the next day's events, perhaps because this was our maiden recruiting voyage together.

We left at 9:30 the next morning for a short breakfast. That the *Tribune* featured James as one of its "Friday Night Heroes," something that would ordinarily be a major highlight, did not stimulate much conversation. The fish in Iowa City were bigger.

We were heading for Big Ten country. The excitement was palpable, although as it is with most men, neither of us acknowledged his anticipation.

Traffic had a near convoy-like nature as we came within fifteen miles of Iowa City. I observed the license plates and noticed a sizable number of Michigan vehicles as we drove. Wolverine fans are notorious for their loyalty and fanaticism. Clearly, many of them were on a pilgrimage to this Big Ten site. Time became a factor, as the sprawl of vehicles was not moving swiftly.

Iowa City is a typical university town—clean, proud, and not very large. Finding and getting to the stadium soon became the challenge. We had exited properly but the southbound traffic was grinding along so slowly that I despaired of making it to our initial goal—the distant intersection—any time soon. A veteran of many accelerated trips to Wrigley Field from our Chicago home, I began thinking of shortcuts. I took a right turn off the main street, hoping I could save time using less-traveled, residential streets. It didn't work, and soon we were back on another main drag, this time heading east toward the same intersection. Once through the intersection, a bit of anxiety and a good bit of indecision set in.

"I know we're close. Do we turn here?" I asked James as we began encountering police directing cars toward the stadium.

"I think it's the next right turn, according to the directions."

Kinnick Stadium is plunked in the center of the university community. We had been sent a pass to park, but the designated lot was full. We then had to negotiate our way into a multilevel hospital structure down the street.

Every time I attend a major sporting event I find my pulse quicken once the stadium is in sight. This was no different. I even looked for shortcuts down the parking levels and then across the lot to the street running near the stadium. To James' annoyance I did stop him once as we were walking to take his picture. His mother wanted some snaps and, truth be told, so did I. To James this recruiting trek was a new experience. To me, it was a soon-to-be banked memory. So it is across the generations.

Gold and black were everywhere as we walked down the ramp toward the Hayden Fry complex, following the signs for football recruits. We were on time. James signed in his usual nonchalant style and I registered as his parent, making sure to grab two copies of *Hawkeyes*, the 108-page official game program. James' nonchalance was evident when greeted upon entry by a graduate assistant.

"How did you do last night?" said the Iowa representative.

"We won," said James in his usual long-winded style.

"No, how did *you* do?"

James answered, quietly reciting his rather incredible stats for the evening.

"Wow! Aren't you excited about that? Not every guy puts up numbers like that."

"I guess," said James politely, as we moved on.

Right from the start, I found it interesting to observe many of the potential student-athletes. Many of the young men appeared drunk on their celebrity, cavorting around in their high school letter jackets as if they were already scholarship recipients. I was proud of James' demeanor; he was adorned in a nondescript jacket and stood quietly and followed directions unobtrusively.

The first event, the lunch, was held in Iowa's indoor practice field. Major universities customarily have these football-field-size, astro-turf practice facilities. They make big-time college football truly year-round enterprises for players and coaches alike. I took little notice of this practice monstrosity what with the inviting luncheon buffet set before us. It was the usual high school jock fare—hamburgers, hot dogs, chips, cookies, and lots of water and soft drinks. There was the usual salad bowl and cold pasta choices for parents able to restrain their desires to stuff themselves with the fat-laden food typically consumed by fans.

That I rarely eat desserts and that this was a special occasion were what I used as permission-givers to attack the melt-in-your-mouth chocolate chip cookies over and over again. They were temptingly displayed near the end of the buffet. I watched closely for gaps in the line and times when no one was serving him or herself for opportunities to seize additional cookies. I fed my well-developed sense of denial by drinking only diet soft drinks.

People sat where they wished as they ate, and coaches stopped to chat with groups of prospects and parents. Among the more memorable was Ron Aiken, the defensive line coach. The hand-

some, forty-five-year-old African American Aiken had left San
Diego State to join Head Coach Kirk Ferentz, who left his assistant coaching post with the NFL's Baltimore Ravens after the
1998 season to rebuild the Iowa football program. Ferentz's task
was a daunting one. He succeeded legendary mentor Hayden Fry,
who had had a twenty-two-year run at the Hawkeye helm. Fry's
teams contended for the Big Ten title throughout the 1980s, when
Ferentz was an assistant on his staff, and they continued to win
up until Hayden's last few years. Then Fry began suffering from
the Joe Paterno syndrome—up in years—and recruiting became
more difficult as other schools attempted to scare would-be
Hawkeye recruits away by saying aging Fry wouldn't persist
through the youths' full college tenure.

Wins were few for Ferentz in his first two years, but progress
had indeed been made. The Hawkeyes entered the Michigan game
4–2 and pointing toward a bowl. The charming Aiken brimmed
with enthusiasm as he described the upward slope of the program.
He summoned running backs coach Carl Jackson over to greet us.
Jackson, in his sixteenth year at Iowa gave the program continuity
with the glory years under Fry. Having been an athletic director at
a small college, I sensed good things ahead for Hawkeye football.
Enthusiasm and pride were evident everywhere one looked in the
gold and black drenched environment.

Lunch was followed by brief but informative academically ori-
ented presentations by nonfootball staff, conducted on a
makeshift stage in the front. The presentations were well-done,
thinly disguised promos for the university. From there the throng
of one hundred–plus was broken into groups for tours of the rest
of the football facilities conducted by what I assumed to be Iowa
student volunteers.

All football facility tours are pretty much the same. There are
stops in the equipment, locker, weight, and training rooms. Each
stop includes a brief synopsis of the room's functions and how it
contributes to the overall success of the football program. Unique
designs or features, awards won by faculty or staff, and any other
distinguishing characteristics are sure to be mentioned.

Every room was modern, organized, pleasing to the eye, and
state of the art. The weight room was typical. A jungle of shiny
weight machines dotted the floor, with the walls filled with

plaques and charts indicating the individual training achievements of its football inhabitants. The group was addressed by Strength and Conditioning Coach Chris Doyle. Doyle—a thirty-four-year-old billiard-headed, Palooka-looking man, who had been the Big Ten Strength Coach of the Year in 2000, spoke forcefully of the importance of conditioning and how Iowa gridders had gone from among the weakest to among the strongest in the Big Ten over the past several seasons.

Because college football teams have rosters of about a hundred players, all the rooms are large. The equipment room presentation featured more than just helmets and shoulder pads, but how the equipment is distributed, cleaned daily, and returned. The visit to the training room, an impressive expanse of tables and technology, included information about the prevention and rehabilitation of injuries and the many up-to-the-minute methods employed at the university.

The players' locker room is always a selling point on any tour. Whether wood or metal, the individual equipment containers are always highly attractive, with the player's name and number prominently displayed on an attached name sign. It all but cries out for the high school aspirant to imagine his name proudly in evidence on one of the cubicle doors. The walls are usually adorned with signage, often containing various when-the-going-gets-tough clichés, along with photos and stirring mementos. Player locker rooms are spacious and well-carpeted, rather than the dingy, claustrophobic entities of previous eras. Showers, once almost staring a visitor in the face, are not even visible in the up-scale expanse. In short, the room looks more like an elite country club gold room than a place where sweaty football players dress.

Promotional signage was everywhere as we walked the corridors and toured the various rooms. Just outside the weight room was a life-size bust of Hayden Fry. Nile Kinnick, the great 1939 Heisman Trophy winner who died a war hero in 1943, and after whom the stadium is named, was honored with a number of items on display devoted to his memory. Plaques commemorating Iowa's participation in bowl games, no matter how minor, were brazenly evident. Another area was comprised of photos and synopses of Hawkeyes in the NFL. In addition, prominent toutings of All-Americans, All–Big Ten selections, Academic All-Americans, and all-conference picks from Iowa were in evidence. Indeed, there was precious little "white space" in the facilities. It seemed any excess square footage was devoted to the school's official proclamation: "It's Great to Be a Hawkeye." In short, the entire black and gold complex was suffused with items and information pointing to past, present, or future Hawkeye gridiron success.

The tour was well-crafted and ended with a sense of drama. When it seemed as though there was no room left to visit, we were herded down yet another corridor. This one, however, took us not just outdoors, but directly into the end zone on the floor of Kinnick Stadium. Typical of a running back, James' first reaction was to the playing surface. "This is really great turf." he said. "Even though it's grass it's as firm as artificial turf."

I, however, had been looking up, and all that I could see were rows and rows of Iowa fans stretching to the sky. Immediately in front of us were the Hawkeyes doing their pregame drills. On the other side of the field were the mighty Wolverines of the University of Michigan.

I decided to seize the moment.

Twenty-three years ago I had met Michigan coach Lloyd Carr at Wrigley Field. Carr, then in his mid-thirties, had been hired by Gary Moeller as the defensive coordinator at the University of Illinois. Carr was in Chicago to speak at Baseball Chapel. I was a sociology and psychology professor in Chicago, and had been involved in Christian work with professional athletes, conducting a Bible study with Cubs and White Sox players among other things. Baseball Chapel Coordinator Sam Bender had asked me to accompany Lloyd on his visit to speak to the teams. Baseball Chapel services are nondenominational, voluntary worship services held each Sunday in clubhouses throughout the major leagues. Attendance may run from three to twenty, depending on the composition of the team. In any case, an immediate rapport developed between Carr and me. His presentation to the players was personal, authentic, and powerful, and the conversation flowed freely between us when we left the clubhouse.

At the conclusion of the day, Lloyd suggested we keep in touch and that perhaps I could come down to Champaign-Urbana that fall to catch a game. Not long later, at the outset of the football season, my phone rang. It was Lloyd.

"We're having some friends over this Saturday after the game. It would be great if you could make it down here and stop by afterward."

It was good to hear from him, but I had a touch of ambivalence regarding the invitation. Champaign-Urbana was two hours away, and the University of Illinois was no football juggernaut. The major attraction would be to see Lloyd and his family, a good enough reason to go, but it would be among a crowd of people and likely after a defeat.

"Sure," I said, nonetheless fully intending to go.

I didn't.

The Saturday in question was a boiler and I got detained. I felt badly about not following through on the invitation and worse, I never called to explain and apologize.

In any case, things did not work out for Gary Moeller and his staff at Illnois. They were launched after several losing seasons. Moeller returned to his pre-Illinois role of defensive coordinator on Bo Schembechler's Michigan staff, and Lloyd Carr continued to work under Moeller there. Nearly a decade later, after the 1989 season, Carr's career took the first of two dramatic upswings. Moeller became the coach at Michigan—named by the retiring Bo Schembechler to succeed him—and Carr was once again a defensive coordinator, this time on a national power. My warm spot for Carr had never cooled and I was overjoyed for his success.

Perhaps I should have called or written him then, but I didn't. I did, however, become an ardent fan of the Wolverine defense and riveted my eyes to the screen every time a Michigan game was televised, hoping to catch a glimpse of Carr. But more was still ahead. Five seasons later Moeller was forced to resign after an unfortunate alcohol-related incident in a Michigan bar. With insufficient time to conduct a national search for a head coach, Carr was advanced to the head coaching position for at least the 1995 season.

The rest is commonly known and well-documented history. Carr went on to great success at the University of Michigan, including an undefeated national championship in 1997, and he had no greater fan than I. He entered the game at Iowa with a 63–17 record, an estimable mark to be sure. Throughout Carr's Michigan tenure I had thought of contacting him, but I felt very uncomfortable about it. I didn't want to appear a glad-handing front-runner, trading on his celebrity rather than a genuine good feeling about him and his success.

Then, during the Thanksgiving holiday of 2000, I decided enough time had passed to contact him. I sent him an overnight letter. In it I recounted his speech of 1978, congratulated him on his success, and wished him Godspeed in the future. I encouraged him to respond and told him I would try to stop by next time I was in Ann Arbor on my consulting business. When I next arrived in Ann Arbor, I drove to his office, hoping to catch him in. He was out of town.

I never heard from him.

Now was the time to reconnect with Carr and get closure. As the two teams continued to warm up I headed down the sidelines into the end zone on the Michigan side of the field. Because I was wearing an official Iowa pass, no one questioned my presence. I waited for Carr, then in the middle of the field. I hoped to catch him briefly as he headed off the field with his team for the final pregame preparations.

My moment finally came.

At about the twenty I walked toward him, met his eye, and said: "Do you remember me?"

A friendly look came over his face, but no name came to his consciousness. "You look very familiar," he said.

"David Claerbaut," I stated.

"Hey," he said, as we shook hands warmly, "I think I got a note from you some time ago. But what are you doing wearing an Iowa tag?"

"They're recruiting my son," I replied.

"Who is your son?" he asked instantly, perhaps wondering how a prize recruit could be at Iowa, having slipped through the seemingly omniscient Michigan net.

"James Velissaris," I said. "He's a running back."

Whether real or feigned, a look of familiarity became evident. "He's your son? We're going to be calling him."

Time was fleeting. He said he had to go. Our clasped hands parted, and we shouted our farewells as he walked backward facing me while making his way to the tunnel to join his team.

"God bless you, man. I'll be in touch."

"Thanks, and we'll be calling your kid," he said as he disappeared into the tunnel.

I crossed to the Iowa side and stayed on the field to soak up the throbbing pregame energy, so much a part of D-1 (Division I), major college football. The cheerleaders romped and chanted in front of the seventy-thousand–plus throng as they anticipated the teams' return to the gridiron. I looked and watched the clock clicking off the seconds to kickoff as the stirring and anticipation built. I stood near the Iowa tunnel with my camera poised to catch the Hawkeyes as they entered the field.

While I was waiting outside, James was inside with the other recruits, being addressed briefly by Head Coach Ferentz. Ferentz struck James as calm, cool, and friendly, able to create a comfortable ambience. The coach congratulated the group collectively on its achievements and then said, "I know some of you guys' seasons may be over, but I wish you guys still left in the playoffs all the best. Enjoy the game, and always think Iowa."

As usual, Michigan—the visitors—returned first, recipients of at best a mixed reaction from the inhabitants of the teeming stadium. Then I saw the Iowa players, lining up just inside their tunnel. I snapped some pictures when, as one, the Hawkeyes poured back onto the field amid the deafening roar of the crowd. The roar continued, the chants went up, and the stage was set. Now I had to find my seat.

All the guests were seated in the same section, about thirty rows above the field in the northeast corner of the end zone. I finally spotted James in the middle of a row and made my way next to him. The view was fine as end zone seats go. Not lost on James was the size of the Iowa running backs. "Look at number 2 out there," he said, "that's Fred Russell and he's only 180."

Originally named Iowa Stadium, Kinnick Stadium opened on October 5, in the Depression year of 1929. It has been marvelously maintained and currently seats 70,397. On this November day, the structure was jammed. I ran my eyes around the top brim of the stadium and could see heads silhouetted against the blue sky all around. The atmosphere was exploding in black and gold colors, and the energy was intense.

Hopes were high as Iowa entered the game undefeated in its first four home contests. The Hawkeyes got out of the gate auspiciously and held a precarious halftime lead, much to the pleasure of the fiercely partisan masses. In the second half Michigan restored order and won the contest, 32–26. The fans booed lustily as the Wolverine defense throttled the Kirk McCann–led Iowa offense. Right from the start, McCann was singled out for particular fan abuse. The senior's very jaunt onto the field elicited hoots from the crowd. Conversely, junior Brad Banks was the fans' darling. The styles of the two T-men could not have been more stereotypically different. McCann was the quintessential white pocket passer, while Banks displayed the daring run-and-throw mien typical of black signal callers. Despite the crowd's noisy referendum, Ferentz stayed with his senior. Although the temperature dropped sharply as the sun headed downward, James and I stayed until the end of the game, actually losing track of each other as we filed out among the murmuring denizens.

As we made our way out of Iowa City we tuned in to the postgame show on the radio. It was open season on Kirk Ferentz. James and I laughed openly as caller after caller excoriated Ferentz's decisions, particular his quarterback choice. I wondered if he wouldn't have been wiser not to play Banks at all, given the firestorm that developed. Sometimes coaches inadvertently create quarterback controversies. In any case, the most memorable call came from a woman listener.

"It's just obvious," she said with quiet but maximum disdain, "that Coach Ferentz doesn't have the experience the Michigan coaching staff has in close games." Her comment was typical of the less than knowledgeable fan. Despite Carr's big-game acumen, Ferentz had spent the six seasons prior to Iowa coaching in the NFL.

"We've got to find a Steak 'n Shake on the way home," I said to James, referring to a fast-food chain heavily concentrated in the downstate Illinois area. We had fun playing detective. Exit after exit was dominated by Burger King, Wendy's, and McDonald's restaurants. We, however, would have nothing but Steak 'n Shake.

"There's one," James called out, pointing in the distance. Indeed it was, and soon we were seated as I watched him crunch through his steak sandwich and eat his fries. "The flavor of the vanilla in their (Steak 'n Shake) shakes is really good," said James as he drained the final drops.

The interlude was sweet, but for much of the trip a happy James had rolled back his seat and gone to sleep. The silence was comfortable for me. I amused myself listening to the Notre Dame–Boston College game and replaying memories of the day.

2.

Chris, Mike, and James

It was a warm August night in 1997, shortly after I had met Rita for the first time on a train in from the O'Hare Airport. She and I went for a walk in one of the trendy areas of Chicago. As we held hands, she said, "I have a son who is a thousand-yard rusher."

I was stunned. A thousand-yard rusher. These were words not likely uttered by a person whose football knowledge was pretty much limited to the test she had to pass some decades previous as the only black cheerleader for Zion-Benton High School's "Fighting Zeebees."

"My son, James, plays junior Spartan football, and he has rushed for a thousand yards in a season."

Junior Spartan football, roughly akin to Pop Warner football, was where I first saw James play football. And it was a treat. Soon to enter the seventh grade, he was simply faster and more elusive than any other player on the field. On weekend afternoons Rita and I would find our way to Northbrook or one of the surrounding suburbs to watch James simply dominate the gridiron. Although he played in the secondary on defense, standing out as a pass defender and tackler, carrying the ball was his forte as he routinely broke punts, kickoffs, and runs from scrimmage for touchdowns. I didn't bother to keep track of his yardage or number of touchdowns. I simply marveled at his incredible speed and agility, in addition to the hunger and joy with which he played the game.

Curiously, I became much closer to his older brother Chris. Chris, embarking on his sophomore season at Glenbrook North, is almost impossible to dislike. Warm, talkative, and engaging, instantly I felt a bond with him. I was delighted whenever he would join Rita and me, because the sports conversation flowed smoothly between us. The younger and quieter James was far more difficult to get to know. Never impolite or contrary, he kept his own counsel most of the time. By the fall, Rita and I were thick and "the boys," as she called them, were often with us on weekends.

Although I was much closer with Chris, the athletic focus in the early going was on James. Chris was a very good athlete, but because he was still on the junior varsity of Glenbrook North football team I tended not to look at him as a first-rate performer. James was already a talked-about star, even though he was still two years away from high school.

"James is the best football player his age I have ever seen," I told Rita.

Rita, not one to boast of either herself or her five children, took it in stride, making "that's kind of you to say" remarks in response.

I meant it. I simply had not seen any youngster even remotely as quick, elusive, and fast as James. Though small, he simply overwhelmed every defense against which he played. Over and over teams would try to hem him in, and occasionally they would be able to hold him in check for a while. Invariably, and not unlike his favorite Barry Sanders of the Detroit Lions, however, he would break one, then another long run, averaging three touchdowns an outing. Whenever he got a step on the defense he was simply gone, easily outrunning every other player on the field. He was so fast that opponents simply miscalculated his speed. On end sweeps opposing players would have an angle on him, only to discover James was two steps ahead of where they had expected him to be, as they reached the point at which they planned to collide with him.

More than that, he loved contact and coaching. "I'm not doing something right on defense to stop guys from catching passes. I'm not approaching them right," he once said in search of advice.

"When you see that pass receiver about to catch the ball," I said, "run right through him as if he were not there." That was easy for me to *say*. When I was a freshman in high school, 125 pounds of rompin' stompin' dynamite, I was terrified of the hitting. I had gone to a school with 124 students, only about 30 of which came out for football. As such, we freshmen were hamburger for the varsity in intrateam scrimmages. I hated it. The very thought of *running through* someone had all the appeal of being mugged.

Not so James. The next game he immediately put my advice into practice.

Chris supported James loyally, faithfully showing up for each of his games even though he was already in high school. Rita explained to me how important Chris and older brother Mike had been to James' athletic development.

"I would watch the three of them playing together and James—so much smaller than Chris and Mike—would always get the short end of it. Sometimes, I would hear James chanting 'Yea, Jimmy' to himself to keep going against his older brothers."

Quickly it became clear. Chris, though affable in nature, was lean and fast. He was extremely quick and lithe. He excelled in basketball and baseball, in addition to throwing and catching a football. Mike (five years older than Chris and seven years the senior of James) was bigger and stockier than Chris. Intensely competitive and fearless, he was a forceful football player, a baseball power hitter, and a self-taught, college-level golfer. This is what James went up against daily. There is no overestimating the impact of a youngster having to compete with older, stronger kids early in life. It has a Nietzsche-like—"that which does not destroy makes stronger"—effect.

I saw it in my own neighborhood as a youngster. Three houses west of me lived three boys separated by not seven, but four years. When we were in our grade school and junior high years the younger, Kenny, took a merciless pounding in any sports competition. We all but dismissed him as a force for athletic good, what with his physical immaturity limiting his value. Two years after I graduated from high school I discovered to what great benefit Kenny had put those poundings. He was the top basketball player in the Eastern Wisconsin conference in both his junior and senior seasons, leading the league in scoring, and probably rebounding both years, had they kept those stats. Kenny went on to play in one of the member schools in the Wisconsin State University conference. Neither of his brothers, nor I for that matter, even approached his athletic success in our high school careers.

By the time I met James and Chris, Mike was largely out of the picture, though ever loyal to his two younger brothers. Chris, however, emerged very quickly as a star in his own right. As junior in 1998–1999, he came into his own on the gridiron, as did his high school football team. Glenbrook North, or GBN as it refers to itself, had won the Illinois High School football championship back in 1974. In recent years, however, the program had fallen on the hardest of times. The Spartans of Chris' junior year were entering the campaign at the dead bottom of the prep football heap. GBN was on what was essentially a two-year losing streak. Its lone win was due to a teacher-strike-driven forfeit during the 1996 season. The team's last actual, on-the-field triumph had been on October 21, 1995. From 1992–1997, the Spartans were 9–45 (4–32 in the last four seasons), and that's counting the forfeit of 1996 as a win.

To get fortunes turned after the dismal 1996 season, GBN had hired Bob Pieper, a young coach who had previously worked football wonders in south suburban Crete-Monee. Pieper, a small intense former running back, suffered through an all-losing 1997 campaign without losing his vision or drive. His perseverance paid off when on opening night of the 1998 season the Spartans defeated Rolling Meadows by a 32–27 count. Three games later GBN was 3–1, and talk was of conference contention and a play-off appearance, the school's first in eighteen years. In the season's third game, Chris picked off three opposing aerials (returning one for a touchdown) and recovered two fumbles in a 37–14 swamping of Maine East. He was cited as one of Chicagoland's "Athletes of the Week" in a major paper. The game had added meaning for Chris and his teammates' coming as it did on the heels of a stroke suffered by youthful assistant coach Brad LaMie.

After winning the Central Suburban North (CSN) opener in their fifth game, misfortune struck the Spartans in the next contest. Junior running back Sean Brandt, who had rolled up 1,192 yards on just 156 carries, broke his ankle and was out for the season. The team did not win another game, finishing 4–5 on the year, 1–4 on the CSN. For Chris, however, it was a breakthrough season. Playing end on offense, he averaged a school record 25.8 yards per catch. In addition, he returned kickoffs at better than twenty yards per attempt, along with intercepting five passes from his spot in the defensive secondary. His exploits resulted in his selection to the CSN all-conference team, despite the team's weak finish.

As Chris' athletic star suddenly went into ascendancy—he played hoops and baseball as well—James, now an eighth grader, continued to dominate junior football.

Spirits were high and talk was of a bright football future that Christmas as Chris, James, and Rita headed for South Bend. I wanted the boys to see Notre Dame and visit the College Football Hall of Fame.

"I predict we get through the first two rounds of the playoffs next season," announced the extroverted Chris from the back seat. The playoffs are what it's all about in Illinois high school football. At the time there were six divisions in the state, determined by total school enrollment, with thirty-two playoff entrants in each division. The rule of thumb was that teams had to go 6–3 to get in. They were then seeded by record and strength of schedule. Clearly, winning two playoff games and getting to the round of eight in a large school division would be a rather heady accomplishment.

The banter went back and forth, with James challenging Chris' predictions in good fun. Chris then turned it on James. "I expect you to gain 1,500 next year on the sophomore [freshman/sophomore junior varsity] team."

"No way." James, intense and eager, did not like lofty expectations attached to his performance, something the mischievous Chris was well aware of. What was clear was that the pads may have been put away for 1998, but the months could not move swiftly enough for the two boys, as they awaited their first year in high school together.

And that year was a good one. Chris was rather prescient. The Spartans rolled through the CSN undefeated at 5–0, and closed the regular season at 8–1. Chris repeated his all-conference designation, while Sean Brandt ran wild in the GBN backfield. The sophomore team—on which freshman James was the running star—went undefeated. For Chris, however, the season ended bitterly. GBN drew Marian Catholic (from south suburban Chicago Heights) at home in their Class 5A playoff opener. The weather was perfect and the stands were packed with passionate Spartan rooters. With the scored tied at 10 in the second quarter, the incomparable Brandt swept right end to send the team into the intermission up 17–10. And so it was until with 4:49 left in the contest, Marian Catholic scored, leaving them but a PAT away from knotting the score. Marian coach, Dave Mattio, remembering that in the regular season finale a week previous his team had botched a potentially game-tying extra point, elected to lay the chips on the table right then and there. His team lined up for the kick. Holder Tom Raczka took the snap, then suddenly rose up and chucked a game-winning toss to Luke Carreras.

Ever game, the Spartans decided to use the last four-plus minutes constructively. They drove sixty yards to the Marian twenty-three. There on first down, future Spartan star Matt Haggis threw a backbreaking pick to end the game, the season, and Chris' high school football career.

How good had the Spartans been in 1999? Very. Marian Catholic went on to lose the state championship game.

Chris and Sean headed for Division III powerhouse Augustana in the fall.

James' time now had come.

3.

Sophomore Sensation

"Honey, we have a problem." It was Rita on the day of James' first varsity game.

"James just called and he doesn't have any football shoes," she said with understandable anxiety permeating her voice.

"How is that possible?"

"Last night he ran with them on the sidewalk and damaged the cleats."

"I'll pick him up right away." I left my office at the Argus Press and drove north to GBN, picking him up outside the athletic entrance. There James was—about four hours before his first varsity game—with no serviceable shoes. Off we went to a nearby sporting goods store with which James was familiar. The shoes were on shelves going all the way up near the ceiling. We got a teetering ladder, and with me holding it, James clambered to the top and found the shoes he wanted.

On the way back to Glenbrook North, James was very quiet. No doubt he was ruminating over being the heir apparent to Sean Brandt as a varsity running back in this, his sophomore year. Coach Pieper obviously expected big things from James. A former running back himself, he had given James his old number, 22. Wanting to break the palpable tension I felt with his debut game but a few hours away, "Just remember, you've got to relax," I said with a joking sound to my voice. "Because if you don't relax you could fumble and lose the game."

He laughed, and I silently congratulated myself for engineering this psychological breakthrough. James is kind; too kind to tell me the remark disturbed him. Later, his mother told me that he had only felt more tight after my quip.

Well, not too tight. The first time he touched the ball, James broke a kickoff return for an eighty-eight-yard touchdown. But that wasn't all. He also scooted through the Mundelein defenders for a 60-yard touchdown jaunt in the fourth quarter. Shades of Sean Brandt. Overall, James ran for 127 yards on 21 carries in this, his first varsity game. A star was born. It must have been the shoes. GBN won the opener convincingly, 23–9 over the Mustangs on the road. I was jubilant for James, yet not surprised. Given his 4.4 (on the forty) speed, what I had seen going back to junior football—and that as a sophomore none of his at least early opponents figured to be prepared for what he could bring to the gridiron table—it did not seem shocking that he would explode on the football scene.

The home opener was a 33–7 rout of Peoria Woodruff. Though not a statistically dominating night, James did tally a score in the fourth quarter. A visit to Waukegan and 27–8 romp was next. Two more touchdowns—one on a 40-yard punt return—to go with 165 rushing yards on 23 attempts was James' considerable output. The *Chicago Sun-Times* took note, placing Glenbrook North in twenty-fifth position on "The Super 25," with its comment being, "Watch soph James Velissaris."

At the high school, college, and pro levels, certain teams seem to own others. For GBN, New Trier High School had proven itself to be a recent nemesis. Such was the case in game four as the Spartans were dominated to the tune of 24–7. Though scoring the team's lone touchdown, James was held in check. The GBN team rushing total was just seventy-nine yards.

No longer undefeated and out of "The Super 25," GBN opened the conference season at Maine West the following Friday night. If there is one game that put James on the prep football map it was this one, as he broke loose for 193 rushing yards and 2 touchdowns on just 19 carries in a 41–7 blowout. Described by Alan Sutton of the *Chicago Tribune* as 5-10, 155 pounds (about two inches and fifteen pounds too optimistic), James dazzled the fans with a ninety-two- and fifty-two-yard scoring run. For his performance, James was one of just nine area players from the Chicago metro area to make the newspaper's "Friday Night Heroes" list.

The pattern was becoming evident. Given James' scant size and blazing speed, if an opponent did not stop him by wrapping him up at the line of scrimmage, he was a good bet to find daylight and make it into the foes' secondary with six GBN points in the offing. As with junior Spartan football, again and again defenders would approach him at an angle in the open field only to discover that James was several yards beyond their anticipated point of collision. No one could believe his speed.

It was more of the same in game six, as GBN pounded Niles North 43–14 with James amassing another 119 yards from scrimmage on just 15 carries. Again, he turned in another highlight: a thirty-four-yard touchdown sprint in the first quarter. The Spartans then moved on to defeat Highland Park 28–14 in a game in which James was "held" to eighty-four yards on nineteen efforts. In the 48–21 crushing of Maine East that followed, however, James returned to the main stage rushing, for a whopping 212 yards on only 20 carries and hitting paydirt three times.

I was excited. James had already had a breakout season, on a playoff-bound team that was having as good a year as the '99 squad of which Chris was a star member. Each game I kept mental track of his rushing yards, realizing that at any point James could break a big one. He might grind along with relatively few yards on a number of carries, then suddenly find an opening and win the dash to the end zone fifty–sixty–seventy yards away, suddenly swelling his yardage total.

Making it all the more exciting, was that from the team standpoint the stage was now set for a year-end confrontation for the conference title. Both 7–1 Glenbrook North and the 6–2 Deerfield Warriors were a perfect 4–0 in the CSN, and the two squads would collide the following Friday night for all the conference marbles in Northbrook.

"Sophomore carried Glenbrook North," was the headline of the *Tribune* article with a photo of James, and "Spartans clinch crown with Velissaris and 'D,'" was the lead in the *Sun-Times*, as GBN buried Deerfield 31–0. Not surprisingly, given the night he had, James was the first of ten Chicagoland stars named to the "Friday Night Heroes" honor roll by the *Tribune*: he had 4 touchdowns, and 214 rushing yards on 27 carries. The spectacular night on the ground pushed James' rushing total for the season to over 1,200 yards.

Life was good for turnaround wizard Bob Pieper and his troops. The team had turned in another 8–1 regular sparkler to go with a second successive 5–0 CSN championship. Perhaps better yet, these accomplishments put the Spartans back in the state playoffs in which they would host a first-round game.

Glenbrook North was in the 6A class. In 2000, the state play-off system was a six-class entity (with 6A comprised of the largest schools), again with thirty-two teams in each class. Teams with 6–3 or better records got bids, and seeding was done according to overall record, in addition to a point system based on opponents' wins in the cases of teams with identical records. Hence, no 7–2 team would be seeded above an 8–1 squad, but the point system would be applied for seeding purposes among all the 7–2 and 8–1 teams to determine their placement. In reality, however, the seed-ings were often misleading. Teams with say 6–3 records that played in powerful conferences were often even with schools with better records from weaker conferences. The 1999 Marian Catholic team was such an example.

GBN (number 13) drew a tough 7–2 (number 20) Willow-brook team in the opener. On the face of it, the Spartans would rate the edge. Willowbrook, however, was from Chicago's western suburbs, where prep football is played for keeps. Moreover, with no Spartan team having recorded a single playoff win since the state championship 1974 season along with the bitter memory of the last-minute loss to Marian Catholic a year ago, there was am-ple reason for apprehension. There was one more reason. The Spartans were facing the most celebrated defender in the state, Matt Roth. Roth, who went on to Iowa, was the Player-of-the-Year in Illinois and ranked by ESPN as the third best linebacker in the country.

No apprehension was necessary, however, as GBN defeated highly talented Willowbrook comfortably by a 26–17 margin on a windy autumn evening. Before the game, Willowbrook's coach, Chuck Tassio, had claimed that no defense had shut down his team's running game that season. GBN, led by ace middle line-backer Mike Pearson, did just that. Aaron Burns, the Willow-brook tailback who had rolled up 1,253 yards during the regular season, was held to 52 yards on 14 attempts.

For James, it was another big night—this time in the air. He threw two option passes for scores to junior Sebastian Klosowiak, one of fifty-three the other forty-seven yards. The strategy was clever and effective. Because James had been pretty much confined to running from scrimmage and returning kicks, while star quarterback Matt Haggis (who finished the season with a 107.6 NFL rating in the air, much due to his thirteen touchdowns against just three picks) did the throwing, the option tosses caught Willowbrook by surprise.

What a year. GBN was now 9–1, a conference champion, and had broken the 26-year playoff hex in the process. The major dailies took note of the Spartan triumph. The *Sun-Times* returned GBN to its Super 25, placing them twenty-third, while the *Tribune* ranked them eighteenth. With but sixteen teams left to fight for the state crown, attention turned to round two.

The opponent was to be a 7–3 team with a similar sounding name, Glenbard North from Carol Stream. The good news was that the Panthers were seeded a lowly twenty-ninth. The bad news was that they played in the powerful western suburban DuPage Valley Conference, a loop that still had three of its members alive among the state's sweet sixteen. Both major papers offered previews of the game, with *Tribune* scribe Bob Sakamoto picking Glenbard North to emerge.

"Here we are attending the final game of the season," I quipped to Rita as we walked into the game. Ever the optimist, Rita rebuked me lovingly for my statement. Deep down, however, I meant it. I had a sense that this was as far as the Spartans, though very good but playing in a less than daunting conference, could go. Though I was bracing myself to ward off any impending disappointment, I was ready to root hard.

There is something magic about single-elimination playoffs, or tournaments at any level. Perhaps due to the all-or-nothing pressure, crazy, bizarre things happen regularly. GBN had been a victim of such a happenstance the previous year against eventual state contender, Marian Catholic. I didn't know what to expect from the Carol Stream squad, but I figured they would be big and physical. Nonetheless, if James could find an early crack in their defense the Spartans could stun the Panthers by jumping out to a quick lead.

Sakamoto was right. The powerful Panthers disposed of GBN 26–7. Obviously, they knew about and focused on James. Now down to about 140 pounds, he picked up but five rushing yards, repeatedly being gang tackled and tossed backward like a sack of potatoes. GBN was forced to throw and they did—thirty-four times with only eleven completions to go with 2 interceptions. Although the total yardage differential was just thirty-six, the Spartans never scored after a game-tying fifty-two-yard Haggis-to-Klosowiak aerial in the first quarter. Despite James' near shutout evening, he got his due. Both major papers cited comments by Panther Coach Dale Evans, in which he lauded his troops for stopping James.

Despite its unhappy ending, the season had been nothing short of sensational.

The team had posted nine wins, and James' sophomore numbers were eye-popping: 17 touchdowns and 1,290 yards rushing on 218 carries; 5 for 5 passing for 173 yards and 2 more touchdowns. He was named offensive player of the year in the CSN, leading the conference in rushing and scoring. The *Pioneer Press* (a suburban paper affiliated with the larger *Chicago Sun-Times*) selected him to its second all-area team—a region that includes the better part of one hundred high schools running from the north side of the city into the suburbs.

As I had anticipated, James was now a major presence in Illinois high school football with two years of high school football still ahead. Little did I realize that the off-season would be just as exciting.

4.

An Answer to a Prayer

Life was not complete for Rita. Despite separating from James' father on the heels of an indescribably traumatic incident, she had allowed James and Chris to spend summers with their father in Northbrook, a highly affluent suburb of about forty thousand, located twenty-five miles north of Chicago's downtown. Life for them in Northbrook was rather comfortable. It was where they spent time growing up, going to school, and developing friendships. It was a community they knew. The alternative was life in a cramped city apartment with Rita and Mike. One year, owing a series of manipulations, the summer stretched into the early fall, and Rita learned that their father had enrolled them in school. Possession often being 100 percent of the law in custody cases, Rita suddenly realized she may have lost "the boys," as she called them.

Not yet divorced, she knew she could regain custody legally if she moved quickly, but that would be expensive—beyond her means. She had been working two jobs to provide for her brood as it was. Slowly she began realizing her boys were gone. It was a wrenching, cruel experience for her, one filled with guilt over letting them move back even for the summers, tragic memories, and great pain. By the time we married, several years had passed. Her daughters, Rachel and Christine, were married, and Mike also was on his own. The boys were well ensconced in school and moving them now meant crossing district lines. Clearly, their father had the edge. And control. After we were married, many nights she would grow somber and quiet, and then express her pain and regret. She felt powerless.

Rita is a strong believer. One winter day in early 2001 she got down on the floor and literally begged God in anguish to give the boys back to her. About a week later, with absolutely no warning,

James called. He wanted to move in with his mother and me. We were jubilant. With Chris away at college, it was the only half loaf available, but God had answered in the affirmative.

Immediately I spent as much time with James as possible. I got up early and made the half-hour drive to GBN, then returned at 5:00 p.m. to take him home. The addition of James was no problem for me. "Blood means nothing to me James," I told him early in his stay. "I am adopted and so that kind of link makes no difference." And I meant it. I told him I would treat him no differently from my own daughter, Rochelle.

A flight attendant at the time, Rochelle had long been the jewel of my life. I was blessed with a father/daughter closeness that so many parents do not enjoy with their children. Whenever I was in New York I would stay with her in her apartment in Brooklyn. We had our own sweet pattern. I would come over after my consulting assignment at the R.S. Rosenbaum Co. in Manhattan and we would go out and eat, often at a favorite Jamaican restaurant. We would eat and talk, talk and eat, and then walk back to her apartment in the night. There was always room for me at her place, because she made room and insisted I stay. The latter was so important, because I didn't want my being there to become an obligatory event. Later, when she bought her co-op in Brooklyn, she had more room, and the monthly visits continued unabated.

"You know you're getting old," I would often say to Rochelle, "when you look forward to seeing your kids more than they look forward to seeing you." And indeed I looked forward to seeing her. Her mother and I divorced when she was not yet three, something I have felt guilty about and regretted for decades. I had remained in Chicago and visited Rochelle weekly as she grew up, but it wasn't the same. I often asked myself all the familiar questions: How could I have handled that time in my life differently? Why couldn't I have been more mature? If I had trusted God and done the right thing, would it have worked out better?

I had failed and I knew it. That I had retained my relationship with Rochelle—even strengthened it—was an unmerited blessing for which I continue to be deeply grateful. When I assured James of his status in my eyes, he seemed calmed and pleased. From the outset he was polite and respectful. An early highlight occurred in late February. Rita, James, and I celebrated my birthday at a popular restaurant. James ate heartily and had a good time. "Thank you for taking me along," he said quietly during the evening.

"Hey, you're one of the family, James; of course you should be here," I said eagerly.

Rochelle and James—both biracial—were good for each other. Rochelle, an only child, was in the middle of writing a book on the subject, *Seeing with Both Eyes*. She enjoyed regaling James with her experiences. "What gets me is how people are so curious about you, and what race you are. After they look at you for a while they just can't stand it and then it will come out. Every once in a while someone on a plane will ask, 'What are you anyway?'" Rochelle once began relating in her own dramatic way. "I just play dumb to it. 'I'm an American. I grew up in Chicago.' 'You know what I mean,' the person will say, 'are you Spanish?' And I will just go on focusing on my being an American."

I reminded her that race, being the third rail of American culture, invites that sort of curiosity and that no harm is meant by those inquiries. Rochelle knew that all too well, yet the repetitive nature of the experience had become tedious. "People just got to know if you're black. That's what it's all about."

James, darker skinned than Rochelle and his brother Chris, grinned through the narrative. He, too, was often an object of curiosity in Northbrook, and had gotten similar treatment by people who were unsure of his lineage. For me, the conversation was beneficial if only because it put the issue of race on the table for James and me. Navigating around racial edges was common for me. Early in my marriage to Rochelle's mother we lived in Michigan. Wanting to avoid paying rent, we went looking for a place to buy in a motor home park. I found a good opportunity, and wanting the approval of my bride, took her and one of my white friends' fiancée out to see it, giving the seller the impression that he was turning his trailer over to a white couple. Once the ink was dry, it was ours and there was nothing anyone could do. All that was left was to endure some of the stares.

As for James and me, night after night we would sit up and watch games on ESPN together. Some nights we would go into the kitchen and talk. He would tell me what had been going on and how he had been feeling before he moved in. I felt a healthy bond develop between us.

On weekends he would stay in Northbrook with his father, less because of any custodial arrangement than that his high school friends were there. Often Rita would worry that he'd change his mind and remain there. Based on our evening talks, I had an inner sense that he would not. James is, if anything, resolute. I believed he had made up his mind as to his life's course now, and that would be with his mother. Indeed he had. We would see him again at church where I spoke each Sunday, and the week would resume. Scarcely a cross word passed between us. There was very little tension between us, and I am sure he was even more careful than I was at keeping it that way. Since James was so serious, I constantly joked with him, told him amusing (by my standards, anyway) stories, and kept things light.

I now had a son, and I was overjoyed about it. At first he was uncomfortable with my hugging him and telling him I loved him. Perhaps it was too much too soon. Anyway, I was unrelenting. "James," I said, "I grew up with as wonderful a father as anyone could ask for, but he was a man of his generation, not given to emotional expressions. I decided early on if I ever had a child that child would never doubt that I loved him or her. I tell Rochelle I love her after every conversation, and I won't treat you any differently."

James said little in reply, but seemed OK with it. In any case, I have never stopped telling him how dear he is to me.

5.

The Loyola Experience

Mike Herbert, a young man in his early thirties, is a wildly successful print salesperson at Argus Press, and a sports junkie. The son of a Chicago policeman who now scouts a bit for the White Sox, he is very well connected. We talked at length about James, and Herbert was eager to offer advice.

"If you want to give James the best possible shot at a Division I scholarship, you need to get him into the Catholic league," Herbert asserted. Herbert, a graduate of Loyola Academy and Loras College, knew whereof he spoke. The unvarnished reality is that the Catholic league plays a much better grade of football than the public schools. Marian Catholic, despite having a weaker won/lost mark than GBN, had come within a game of the state crown. Joliet Catholic and Chicago's Mt. Carmel were perennial state contenders, the latter counting NFL star Donovan McNabb among its recent graduates.

"Look," said Herbert, "the Catholic league is where the scouts are—where the connections are. You want James to develop against the best, and I don't want to offend you, but the CSN is not considered a very good conference, even by public school standards."

He was right on that count as well. The CSN was comprised of students that were generally rich and white. The survival hunger one sees among lower income and minority students was not there. James was the only black player on his team, and other than Evanston and Waukegan, I saw almost exclusively white skin when I looked at the teams GBN played. Among Catholic schools, however, football seemed to rank right behind the Baltimore catechism in import.

I told Rita about my talk with Mike Herbert, and she was eager to pursue the matter. I was convinced. "Let's face it, James has a gift," I told her, "no different from a concert pianist, and we need to put him into the best possible environment to develop that gift."

Rita not only agreed with the football argument, but was concerned about meatier issues. "James needs to be in a school with some racial diversity," she explained, "plus he needs a Christian environment."

The racial point merits comment. The previous summer he had gone to a football camp at college in the western suburbs. He had been racially hazed by some white youngsters there. In addition, a teammate uttered the dreaded "n" word once, not realizing James was nearby. The incidents troubled James and he had told a coach at GBN about it, but the coach had tried to minimize the events, telling him nothing was meant and to forget about them. This was absolutely the wrong thing to say to a victim of racial hazing. Such taunting is unspeakably painful to the recipient, something few whites ever experience and therefore are unable to imagine. In short, James' personhood had been attacked and it hurt badly. The response by his coach only made him feel psychologically unsafe at GBN, a school located in a suburb—Northbrook—that was less than 1 percent black.

Nonetheless, GBN is where James went to school. It was where all his friends were. As such, I wondered just how receptive James would be to transferring. I approached him on it and suggested he meet Herbert himself and hear what he had to say. He agreed.

We met at Graziano's, a favorite restaurant of ours between Northbrook and Chicago, not far from Argus. Herbert was at his diplomatic best and James listened intently. The next day I asked Herbert what he thought. "He is just a very nice young man, really a good kid," Herbert enthused. "I heard how good he is, and he would probably start next year at Loyola. Let me call Les Sietsinger; he's the admissions director and a good buddy of mine. Then give him a call and see if James, you, and his mom can meet with him. He's also a football assistant, so maybe he can get James in to meet Coach Hoerster."

Herbert was sensitive to our concerns about Loyola's racial climate. "I can't promise that he will never encounter some unpleasant incidents. You know, that stuff is everywhere. Even though the school has a fairly sizable black population, it is predominantly white. I can tell you Hoerster won't put up with something like that. He would fight a kid who used the 'n' word at a black student.

"The time to transfer is now. If James' grades are good he should get into Loyola with no problem. And if you emphasize the racial angle, the IHSA will almost certainly declare him eligible immediately."

Herbert did have one major concern. "One thing about James. He isn't very big, only about 150 pounds. He's going to have to put on some bulk if he is going to run in the Catholic league, especially at Loyola. Hoerster runs the ball constantly. I don't know if James can carry twenty-five–thirty times a game at his size. It won't be easy for him to put on weight. Look at him carefully with his moustache and facial hair; James is not a boy. He's a young man."

James was willing to take the next step and visit Loyola. With Herbert blazing the trail we set up an after-school visit with Les Sietsinger, the admissions director. Loyola Academy is just off Interstate 94 north of the city. As such it was closer to our house than GBN, yet within ten minutes of James' high school. The buildings are not new, but sturdy and well kept. We met Les in his office.

Typical of admissions directors, he was courteous and friendly. In pitching Loyola, he placed almost the entire emphasis on the academic focus of the school, along with the religious flavor. He steered clear of references to athletics. In short, he wanted us to look at Loyola as the best choice, irrespective of James' football prowess. On one hand, that was good. Too many schools see a kid of James' athletic caliber and cannot hide their watering mouths for a minute. On the other, it seemed strange. Indeed, Mike had told Les of James' football ability and interest, so I thought he would mention it.

In any case, Les offered a very complete presentation of the key features of the school and gave us a thorough tour of its facilities. The experience was relaxed, informative, and impressive. Clearly, Loyola's commitment was to the student and his or her development, and Loyola was appropriately proud of how it had lived out that mission over the years.

We eventually did get a chance to meet Coach and Athletic Director John Hoerster. Sitting amid a sea of plaques and memorabilia, Hoerster has presence. In his sixties, he had a strong vital look, with the face and hands of a football coach. Although tall and fit, he had been a lineman at Northwestern University as an undergraduate, and he bled Rambler blood. James and I later found his voice-mail message particularly amusing. After stating that the caller had reached Head Football Coach and Athletic Director John Hoerster, and requesting that the caller leave a message, it ended with "Go Ramblers."

In step with Sietsinger, Hoerster spoke authoritatively, highlighting academics. Rita and I were very receptive to the academic and spiritual advantages of Loyola, but we were also interested in James' singular gift—football. Hoerster made nothing approaching a football recruiting pitch. In a very attractive, old-school, believable way he simply stressed that James would be evaluated fairly, along with every other Rambler player, and the chips would fall from there. "I'm not promising anything, except that James will get a fair look, no different from our other players." Furthermore, he would offer no assurances that James would play running back. Hoerster did emphasize the importance of attending the team's summer camp. "It's not mandatory, but no one has started here who hasn't attended our camp."

Summer camps are a routine staple among schools with a quality football program. They are not and cannot be mandatory because they are not an official function of the school's football program. They are important, however, because there coaches can get a glimpse of the talent level of the coming season's players, get them in shape, and teach skills and systems. Above all, the rigors of summer camp constitute a discipline. It is through these intense, several-week experiences that the values and expectations of the coaching staff are instilled. Schools with weak football programs often have either no summer camps or poorly attended ones. A football program without a summer camp is high risk, leaving too much to be done too soon during double sessions in the August heat.

I could feel Hoerster dominating the room such that it felt uncomfortable to challenge him with a question. Nonetheless, I did. "Coach, I wouldn't be James' stepfather if I didn't ask about the running back position. Is it open or do you have someone already slotted in for it?" Hoerster was candid. He did have someone who had the inside track among the players currently there, but the youngster most certainly had not laid claim to it. There was a question of size, strength, and commitment to working out in the youngster's case. No, the position was not at all sewed up. James would get a fair shot at it.

Sometimes assurances of that nature ring hollow, when the coach, knowing the position the youngster wants to play is filled, simply desires to get the player into the program. Once in his control, that coach will use him at any position—offense or defense— he sees fit. Hoerster did not strike me as such a person. There was, however, one major concern, one that perhaps explained Sietsinger and Hoerster's assiduous avoidance of football talk: eligibility. It would not be as easy as Mike Herbert had thought.

Rita had joint custody of her boys with James' father, who lived in Northbrook. As such, we could not claim that James no longer lived in the Glenbrook North school district, something that would make a request for transfer cleaner. With James' father remaining in Northbrook the case would hang on nonresidential issues. Moreover, the joint custody matter raised an additional issue, the value of having James' father also favor his transferring. Approaching James' father raised two additional concerns. He might oppose the transfer, all but killing it, or by telling him about the idea, word of James' possibly leaving GBN may get out, making life very uncomfortable for James. The issue of secrecy was very important. James was now a genuine area prep star and any of a number of well-heeled ardent Spartan fans may have cried foul to the IHSA should they hear of their star running back moving on. Perhaps worse, if James' transfer did not go through, he could be subject to a great deal of negativity from teammates, coaches, and fans, all of whom would feel betrayed by his effort to leave.

James' case did not look at all ironclad, particularly in view of another of Hoerster's comments. "I can't be certain how the IHSA will respond; they are very concerned about any possibility of a young man being recruited by a Catholic school for football reasons." And they had a point. Under the radar, athletic recruiting had been going on at the high school level for many years. It was hard to imagine, for example, that Catholic school students in the Mt. Carmel area, on the south side of Chicago, just happened to be blessed with more students with highly developed football skills than those living elsewhere; or that the boys living near King High School, a public school, just happened to possess more and better basketball-specific genes than those from other parts of the city. Sports powerhouses like these, however, tried to identify skilled youngsters before they reached high school age to avoid being seen openly soliciting youngsters to transfer.

The Catholic schools, however, had an added problem. They were private institutions taking kids from the public schools. And they were elite football schools.

"The worst thing that can happen is for James to transfer in and have to sit out his junior year. He would definitely be eligible as a senior," Hoerster explained.

Sietsinger and Hoerster suggested James consider transferring before the beginning of the upcoming second term in February. Having James in Loyola would probably strengthen his case with the IHSA. Hoerster buttressed their position by telling the story of a young man from Florida, who, having transferred to Loyola, was ineligible for the first eight games of his first season there. "In the first game he did play," related Hoerster, "he broke a sixty-yard touchdown on his first carry. That kid went on to play at Western Michigan as a receiver, where he broke a number of their receiving records." All that was missing from the story was the "and he lived happily ever after" tag. Such a risk was completely unacceptable, I explained. It would be devastating should James have to sit out a year for no good reason. Besides, it was not as if Glenbrook North was deficient academically or that its football program had slipped into the tank.

"What should we do?" I asked.

"Write me a letter explaining everything as honestly and completely as possible," Hoerster said. "I will run it by one of my contacts at the IHSA to see what he says."

Morally, Rita and I were on high ground. We had not been recruited by Loyola Academy. It was the other way around. In addition, our interests in Loyola were not driven by a desire to power

up our favorite Catholic school. We wanted James there because
we felt it would be the best environment for him—academically,
socially, athletically, and spiritually. Feeling we had right on our
side, we talked of setting up a date for James to spend a "shadow
visit day" there, to experience firsthand what student life was like,
while at the same time exploring the situation with the IHSA.

James was concerned about keeping the lid on the Loyola venture. "What should I say if people find out I visited there? There
are kids from Northbrook that go to Loyola and they are friends
with students at Glenbrook North. The word will get out."

"Lay it off on me," I told him. "Tell them that your stepfather
is pushing you to look into Loyola. Don't make it look as if it was
your idea."

James liked Loyola and Hoerster. He appreciated the coach's
non-manipulative approach. After weighing the risks against his
desire to look into the school further, James set up a day to visit.
Meanwhile, nothing definitive emerged from the IHSA.

James' interest increased after a spring visit, as did ours. "You
didn't get that 'there's a black person' stare at Loyola," James
noted. Hoerster was also helpful on the visit. "James, you can't
play here for two years to get a scholarship. You've got to play for
the fun of the experience," the veteran mentor counseled. "I've
seen kids do that—go to the Catholic league just to get noticed
and offered—and often it impairs what could have been a much
more successful experience."

No progress, however, had been made on the eligibility front.
In April James got a signed letter from his father supporting the
request for transfer. Hoerster was not sounding optimistic. "All
we can do is submit our case and pray," he stated after one telephone conversation. After dawdling, the IHSA responded with re-
quests for more information, including a copy of the divorce de-
cree. The tape was getting redder and redder and summer
workouts were not far away. In retrospect, James' case would indeed have been stronger had he transferred in February, but neither Rita, James, nor I wanted to take such a risk.

Hoerster was a well-known and highly respected high school
coach statewide. If someone of his stature could not elicit a favorable judgment from the IHSA, taking any further risks seemed un-

wise. In addition, with James' shadow visit our cover had been partially blown. There were rumblings around GBN about James' possible transfer to Loyola. With his low-key demeanor, he handled it well, defusing the rumors.

James would remain a Spartan.

6.

Getting Ready for 2001

Talk of college football began in earnest in the summer prior to James' junior year. Now settled in with Rita and I, he was developing set patterns. Conscious of his diminutive size, James was eating regularly and well, in addition to working out intensely.

He also got his first taste of big-time college football, having been invited to a summer camp at the University of Illinois. It was a less than rapturous experience. Of the approximately three hundred skill position players there, he was the fastest player, winning the sprint competition. Nonetheless, the coaches all but ignored him, focusing on the larger boys about to enter their senior seasons. Not only were they better developed physically, they were the kids that could help the Illini most immediately.

Still it was a good experience if only because it challenged James to reach a performance level that would demand attention after his junior season. Perhaps because of his athletically formative experience playing against his older brothers, adversity and challenge seemed to motivate James. So often that is not the case. When a kid hears he is too small, too slow, or too unskilled, it has an immobilizing effect. James had spent his entire short life being regarded as "too small." Instead of being defeated by the tag, he simply ate more, worked out more intensely, and tried harder.

That was evident in his sophomore season. When he was at what I suspect was barely over 140 pounds, James had carried the ball just under 22 times a game from the tailback position without injury. What's more, he hadn't worn down, saving perhaps his finest game for the regular season finale against Deerfield, the one that won the conference championship. As for Glenbrook North's football fortunes, things were clearly on the upswing. After going 4–5 in 1998, the Spartans had posted a 17–4 log over the past two seasons; this after winning but four (and losing thirty-two) games in the four years previous to 1998. In addition, the two-time CSN champions were riding a ten-game conference winning streak. In short, Bob Pieper had turned it around. He had not only put together winning teams, he had built a winning program.

The change was visible. Prior to the turnaround, players were not spending the off-season in the weight room pumping iron, and they most certainly were not sacrificing summer work and fun to attend captain-led team workouts. Now they were. And this, perhaps more than anything else, is what separated the winning programs from the rest of the pack. This is also a major reason why suburban and Catholic league programs have an advantage. Students from many of these schools enjoy among the best of facilities, and because they often come from affluent families, they have the luxury of spending their summers heavily engaged in football conditioning rather than working a job.

Big-time high school football is a year-round sport. The coming season started essentially with doubles in August in my high school days. Now it starts in the weight room as early as the Monday after the current season ends. Football players like James may participate in track, but not necessarily because they are passionate about track and field events. Often its because track practice can augment football skills. Sprint events build speed, while working with the shot put can increase coordination and strength.

In no sport is the concept of program more important than in football. I knew this from my own two-year experience as athletic director at the college level. When I took over as athletic director in the 1985–1986 school year at North Park College the basketball team had already won four NCAA Division III championships in eight years (1978–1985) and had posted a flock of winning seasons in the years before that. Football, however, was another matter. The school had won less than 20 percent of its games from the 1960 to the 1980.

People are also correct when they speak of basketball programs. Indeed, Dan McCarrell and Bosko Djurickovic were truly excellent coaches and put together a consistent basketball juggernaut, capable of playing with any Division III college, most Division II schools, and some Division I squads. But the game of hoops is played by just five players at a time, not eleven or twenty-two as is the case with two-platoon football. A basketball team with two outstanding players, among its eight players that play the bulk of the team's minutes, can be a contender. A third star can push that same team over the top, to a championship level. Several excellent coaches coupled with conscientious, effective recruiting (at the college level) can take a school a long way.

Not so with football. Not only do you need many more players, but because of the team nature of the sport, a few porous spots on either side of the line of scrimmage will have you staring defeat in the face. As such, an individual superstar here or there may make little difference in a team's fortunes if the rank-and-file players are deficient. Further, even at the high school level, you need a coaching staff, not several good coaches.

In my two years at the North Park helm, both basketball and football proved to be an adventure. The basketball team, riding a winning tradition, claimed its fifth NCAA crown in 1987. The championship ring still looks good on my finger.

The football team was a much greater challenge. The school was coming off seventeen straight losing seasons when I took over prior to the 1986 season. After an exhaustive search, one that included interviews with people with high school, small college, and even major college coaching experience, I settled on Ron Ellett. Though devoid of college experience, I wanted Ellett because he was a stone winner in Illinois. Not only had he put together a string of winning squads, Ellett had won one IHSA championship and finished second another season. "I don't know much about losing, and I don't want to learn either," said Ellett in a well-received address to the Viking Club, the boosters of the athletic program.

Filled with enthusiasm, Ellett pulled together a staff, rolled up his professional sleeves, and went to work. He spent the winter on a scavenger hunt through the state looking for prospects, and preaching the evangel of an impending North Park football turnaround. When practice opened in August, he had brought in a bevy of new recruits, teeming with energy and optimism. I remember addressing the team one summer night during doubles at what turned out to be a combination chapel service and pep rally. The team was committed. Focused. Mentally ready.

The season opened at home against heavily favored Elmhurst College. After leading at the intermission much to the joy of the crowd, the offense sputtered in the second half, eventually losing on a late turnover. Despite the defeat Ellett had put his stamp on the team. His energetic presence was evident in the team's play. After the game, the Elmhurst coach was visibly impressed by the unanticipated upsurge in the North Park program. The team then went to Augustana College, playing perhaps the best Division III team in the country, and lost by a lopsided margin as most Augie opponents did. Ellett, however, was undaunted by the drubbing. After all, there was no shame in losing to Augustana, and if nothing else, it gave North Park a yardstick against which to measure itself.

Seven games later the team completed an unblemished, 0–9 season.

By the spring of 1987 Ellett resigned. Problems were everywhere. From the field to the weight room, the facilities were dreadfully substandard. Not only was Ellett forced to keep several coaches from the previous football regime, he could not retain a solid, full-time staff of his own, losing his defensive coordinator when the school would no longer allow the assistant and his family to live in the dorm where he was the resident adviser. In addition, the coach was faced with a less than cooperative admissions office, headed by a former coach who was one of Ellett's major critics (and not coincidentally this same director of admissions became his immediate though no more successful successor).

In brief, Ellett saw no hope for the program. The school was simply unwilling to pay the price necessary to build a quality football program. I was equally disgusted. After writing an angry letter to the acting president, I decided to leave the college to go into my consulting business full-time. Over the years, Ellett's words stayed with me, "You can put together a winning team or two, but what you want is a winning program."

Though faced with far different challenges than Ron Ellett's at the college level, after years in the football wilderness, Bob Pieper had succeeded in building a winning program at Glenbrook North. Only he was no longer its head coach. Pieper had been promoted to athletic director for the 2000–2001 academic year, and because the CSN had a league rule preventing athletic directors from serving as head coaches (at least in the major sports), Pieper turned the reins over to his assistant, Frank Whalen.

A former small-college defensive line star, Whalen was a huge man, with a jovial spirit. Far more extroverted than Pieper, James liked Whalen. There was pressure on the new mentor to keep adding to the recent Spartan tradition of winning football, but with GBN stocked with returnees from the previous championship campaign, optimism abounded as the season approached.

The *Chicago Tribune*, in its Preps Plus preseason edition, picked Glenbrook North to win its third consecutive CSN crown. The *Chicago Sun-Times* did the same.

James, himself, was now drawing attention. The *Tribune*, in the same preseason edition, listed twenty-four running backs among its "Top Players." James was one of just five juniors to be cited. The *Tribune* also featured James as the top player in its preview of the CSN race. The *Sun-Times* went even further. Steve Tucker and Taylor Bell named James as one of the area's top one hundred players, and one of its best nineteen running backs. James, though just 155 pounds (the *Sun-Times* listed him at 170), was about 15 pounds heavier than a year ago. But it was his blazing speed that set him apart. He had been timed on the forty at 4.4 flat. To put that in perspective, he was faster than any wide receiver then playing for the Kansas City Chiefs.

In any case, James was on the football map. I was delighted. Just a junior, he had yet to step on the field with a player demonstrably better than he was, at least on offense. As with any father, I wanted James to get his due. Also, I knew that the more recognition he received, the less likely he would escape the attention of college recruiters. Had he been in the Catholic league, or playing in one of the power conferences west of the city, I would have been less concerned about this. But the CSN was no main stage football loop. It had not exactly peppered the major college football scene with talent. As such, a player had to make some rather large waves to be taken seriously as having major college potential.

For James, that no longer loomed as a problem. He had made those waves as a sophomore and now was prominently situated on the prep radar screen. With the outlook bright, I don't know who was looking more forward to the coming season, James or me. I found myself talking high school football with friends, relatives, and many of my consulting clients around the country.

Despite having to replace quarterback star Matt Haggis, the

team's signal caller the past two seasons, James saw a potentially big year ahead for the team. He was unconcerned about the change at quarterback, with junior Kevin Kaspers taking over. "Kaspers is not as fast as Haggis," he said, "but he has a stronger arm and he is accurate." Though disinclined to give the envelope a shove with his predictions, James saw no team on the GBN schedule as out of the Spartans' league.

The season was slated to open August 24 at home against Mundelein. Despite the rainy weather, there was excitement in the Northbrook air enveloping William Lutz Stadium. After two banner seasons the fans now anticipated gridiron success. The night had an added touch for us, because James' new sister, Rochelle, had flown in from New York, especially to see him play.

7

Junior Highs and Lows

Frank Whalen won his coaching debut rather comfortably, 24–12. Only two fourth-quarter scores kept Mundelein from being blown out. Much to my delight and that of Rochelle and Rita, James got out of the gate quickly, scoring all three Spartan touchdowns and running for 122 yards on 26 carries. Rochelle rooted hard and was very impressed.

James really felt at home with this group of teammates. It was the group with which he had played two years previous on the sophomore team (as a freshman). Playing on the varsity as a sophomore did have its drawbacks. The price James paid for his celebrity was having to endure the poorly concealed resentment of some of his teammates two years his senior. It was painful enough that he told me he would never dole out that kind of treatment to a younger team member, should he be placed in leadership later in his career. That he felt more at home with this group was evident in his words to *Pioneer Press* writer Jim Coffman after the game. "I'm back with my age group again and that's great," he said. Furthermore he saw better things to come. "Everyone will see later this season, when everyone gets comfortable, we really can click."

James was in good spirits when he went out with Rochelle, Rita, and me to eat later on in the evening. I was very happy. On one hand, I had my daughter with us, and on the other, there was clear evidence of a new family forming.

The Spartans, who went into their second game ranked twenty-fifth in the area by the *Sun-Times*, did nothing to hurt their rating, smashing Taft High School from the city 56–6. James piled up 159 more yards to go with 4 touchdowns. Evanston lay ahead now for the twenty-third-ranked Spartans, and James was going into the contest with a full head of steam. Through two games he had rushed for nearly three hundred yards and scored seven touchdowns. At his present pace, it was conceivable that he could shatter Sean Brandt's single touchdown mark of thirty.

Just as things appeared unable to get much better, they did. GBN put Evanston away 31–20, and James was better than ever. He rolled up 199 yards on the ground (including runs of 35 and 56 yards) and went into the end zone three more times. His name was really up in lights now. He was one of but seven Chicago area players listed in the "Friday Night's Heroes" bracket in the *Chicago Tribune*. Now ranked twenty-first, the Spartans would take to the road to face another 3–0 team, Niles West, in a game highlighted as a key area game in the city's major papers.

I did not see the Niles West game. I was out of town.

The car service picked me up at Rochelle's Brooklyn co-op at 8:00 a.m. and headed over the Brooklyn Bridge in Lower Manhattan not far from the World Trade Center on the morning of September 11, 2001. Although the ride was uneventful for me, little did I know how tragic that Tuesday already had been for thousands of people perhaps a half mile from the car in which I was riding. When I reached the R.S. Rosenbaum Company at 435 Hudson, the police were already cordoning off the streets. Because the Big Apple is forever crackling with activity, particularly in areas like that of Greenwich Village, I paid little attention to their efforts.

When I got inside, people were huddled around a television. "A plane has just crashed into the side of one of the World Trade Center towers," someone said. Although no one seemed to think the event was purposeful, it was nonetheless so novel that the television networks had interrupted their regular programming to cover the event live. Then, as millions including those at R.S. Rosenbaum were watching, another plane was televised live as it crashed into the other tower. Slowly it dawned on New Yorkers that their city may be under attack. News reports, some factual, others speculative, began flooding in, and one of the most tragic yet memorable chapters in this nation's history was well under way.

The phone lines were jammed, making it nearly impossible to call Rita to let her know I was safe. Later she told me that James, knowing I was in New York, had called from school concerned about my well-being. The employees were allowed to leave the Rosenbaum Company about noon, yet there was great apprehension as to the safety of the subways. The specter of a bomb going off there, sealing masses of humanity in a concrete grave, was almost unthinkable, yet within the realm of possible reality.

"You're not getting out of Manhattan today," said Bob Rosenbaum, who had long ago become more a friend than a client. "You will have to stay with me." It was a kind and gracious gesture. I eventually did get a hold of Rita, and in midafternoon Bob and I walked out onto Hudson Street en route to his apartment on the Upper East Side. Once out of the building we could smell the smoke coming from Ground Zero about a mile south. Ashes floated through the air. The Lower Manhattan area that once included the twin towers now looked like a set of human teeth with the front two missing.

The charred smell in the air, the ashes, and the absence of traffic created an eerie atmosphere. The psychological sensation was not unlike that following the assassination of JFK thirty-eight years previous. The normal boundaries of race, age, gender, and income level seemed to evaporate among the pedestrians. People were bonded—united as one by this larger than life experience. With the car service not available, Bob and I took a less than comfortable ride on the subway to his apartment. As we reached the building's elevator a young man who appeared to be a bicycle messenger was talking anxiously. He had been on one of the upper floors of the World Trade Center when the events occurred. Though almost certainly in shock, he told of seeing a fire wall develop quickly on one side of the tower, forcing the inhabitants of what would soon become an inferno to move swiftly across the floor to the opposite stairwell. People had been rather orderly, he said, as they descended the eighty-plus floors as quickly as possible. "I saw things I will never forget," the young man said, likely referring to people who dove head down to their death rather than perish in the blaze.

The apocalyptic event seemed to bring the best out of many people. The young man witnessed people helping impaired or disabled victims escape the soon to collapse tower. To hear such an eyewitness description within hours of the event was both mesmerizing and disturbing. Trapped as I was in New York, the reality of the anguish was driven home within days as Bob and I walked down the streets to do errands or get something to eat. People were missing. I remember seeing the very same "Have You Seen My Son?" black-and-white computer-generated picture poster attached to every light pole block after block. I could only imagine the indescribable anguish the parent who developed these posters must have been experiencing.

Throughout the week, planes did not fly, trains were overbooked, and rental cars were not available. I didn't get out of the city until Friday evening, and then not by flying out of LaGuardia or Newark, but on a smaller carrier out of Islip airport, well into Long Island. The anxiety was palpable, as passengers eyed one another suspiciously, paying extra attention to anyone who may appear to be of Middle Eastern descent.

By the time the plane landed and the relieved passengers exited the aircraft, it was too late to get to Niles West. The game, itself, drew particular attention since high school football was pretty much the only extracurricular event held throughout the metropolitan area in the wake of the attack on the World Trade Center. "I never played in an atmosphere like that before," said James later. "There was a crazy mix of high school intensity with two undefeated teams playing, and yet all the tragedy and patriotism in the air. Guys were saying, 'We aren't just playing for our schools, we are playing to honor the country,' things like that."

James most definitely did play and left his calling card. "Velissaris does job for Glenbrook North," and "Velissaris, defense key to Spartans' victory," were the titles of the *Sun-Times* and *Tribune* articles covering the team's 28–21 win. James now had it turned up all the way as the team was truly clicking as he predicted. The holes were there, and James ran through them again to the tune of 167 yards and three scores.

As for football, if James was high, I was higher. Going to the games was now an absolute delight, something I now appreciated all the more in the wake of September 11th. Wins were all but taken for granted as Rita and I would go to the GBN games focused largely on what wonders James might perform. It seemed too easy, too good to be true.

And it was.

Drinking is the drug of choice among teenagers in Chicago's northern suburbs. It was certainly the drug of choice in James' peer group, the fifteen or so kids—teammates and nonteam-mates—he went out with the following evening. There were more than soft drinks being consumed when the police entered the sub-urban park where they were hanging out. Alcohol was visibly present. Seeing the police, James panicked and ran, abandoning his father's car in the process. When the drama ended he was charged with underage drinking.

I found out Sunday morning as I left church to fly to a consult-ing assignment due to begin the next day. It was sickening. Not forty-eight hours previous James' star was in full ascendancy. Now his season, perhaps his career, was in doubt. I was hurt, an-gry, disgusted. How could things turn so quickly? I talked with him briefly on the phone in the evening. Remaining calm, I told him he and I would talk when I returned.

It was evident upon my return that he certainly needed no ad-ditional punishment. When I came in the house he was watching a film his mother had picked out. Even though several days had passed he looked dazed, in shock. I hugged him empathically, say-ing sincerely, "You mean the world to me." He seemed relieved. He was probably anticipating my anger.

His football fortunes now hung in the balance. He was at the mercy of Coach Whalen's decision. I thought about what might have happened had he gone to Loyola. "There's a lot of drinking there, just like everywhere else," Mike Herbert told me, "but if you get caught, you know your season is over. That's the way Hoerster is." I remembered back to similar instances in my high school days in which area players were found "breaking train-ing." Punishments were severe. Two players at a nearby school were suspended for the entire regular season when they were caught drinking early in the year. One sure-shot all-conference basketball player was actually dropped for the remainder of the year after being caught smoking in midseason.

I had mixed feelings. On one hand, I wanted James to learn there are consequences for one's behavior. Sparing him by giving him another chance could well be done at the cost of learning that law of reality. On the other hand, having had a less than idyllic childhood and having been traumatized by the break in his family, he was severely depressed over the loss of his lone outlet—football.

Was Whalen like the coaches of my youth? Was he like Hoerster? We would know soon.

8.

The Rest of the Season

"Are we going to talk?" James asked a few days after I got home.

"Sure, when can we get together?" I was pleasantly surprised at his request. I thought he would want to avoid a serious discussion at virtually any cost.

Fortunately for James, Coach Whalen tempered justice with mercy. After mulling it over, James was allowed to practice with the team but would have to serve just a two-game suspension. It was the mildest punishment possible, but probably enough for James, given what he shared with me about his life a few nights later.

He told me of how deep his depression went in his freshman year. "I stopped attending school in the spring. With football over, I didn't care about anything." He missed his mother. But even more, he missed his family severely, eight years after his mother and father separated.

"If you don't have family, you don't have anything," he said softly, in a clear statement of his values. He explained why he hit bottom in the spring. "Football was all I had. When that was over, life was empty."

For several years his life had been careening back and forth, often on a secret downward spiral. Margaret Sullivan, a conscientious school counselor, had been concerned about James. Unlike Chris' more relaxed wanderings, she felt that once set firmly in motion, James was capable of moving in a regressive direction as fast as he could run the forty. Rita, praying faithfully for her children, had sensed things were not right. Yet she was powerless, owing to her limited access to Chris and James. James moved in with us when he realized he wanted to turn his life around from one in which his relationships were little more "than feeding on one another's destructiveness."

For several hours James and I sat outside and talked about reality. It was a difficult yet wonderful conversation, and I appreciated deeply his trust in me as someone who loved him. Moving in with us had been a difficult decision for James.

"We both are intense and felt it may be difficult for me," he said. "If you remember, when I began spending time with you and my mother (in 1997), I wasn't very open with you."

Ever polite, James had never given me any indication that he was uncomfortable with me then, but in retrospect, I recall feeling much more connected to Chris—really liking him. I didn't dislike James; he simply hadn't given me much to like. Now he was telling me why.

The conversation flowed smoothly. We agreed to continue our dialogue. Realizing James needed emotional space, I asked him to let me know if he felt crowded by me. When we returned home that September evening, I had a newfound respect for James' depth of insight and courage.

Fortunately, GBN won the two games James missed. The first, at highly competitive Deerfield, was arguably the most exciting game played during his tenure with the Spartans. Trailing 29–21 with 1:40 left, and having lost ace receiver Sebastian Klosowiak to a neck injury in the second quarter, Kevin Kaspers led the Spartans down the field, hitting 5–5 flanker Danny Schaecter in the end zone with less than twenty-five ticks left. A barely successful conversion run sent the contest into double overtime from which GBN emerged 32–29. John Hoppe moved to running back for the contest and ground out 190 yards in a whopping 32 carries.

I was relieved for James. A loss to Deerfield almost certainly (and understandably) would have been pinned on him. Now only a winless Maine West stood between James and his return to the field.

The undefeated (6–0) and now eighteenth ranked Spartans took to the field against Niles North, fresh from vanquishing Maine West 40–6 a week earlier. For the first time in three weeks James was back on the field with his mates. The game was a 46–6 blowout in which James played sparingly, picking up 110 yards and 2 touchdowns on just 10 carries. Now 7–0 (and 3–0 in the CSN) the Spartans remained number 18 in the *Sun-Times* Super

25, and a notch higher in the *Tribune* Top 20. Just two winnable conference games separated the Glenbrook North Spartans from an undefeated regular season.

They both proved to be easy wins. The Spartans downed Highland Park on the road in a driving rain, 17–0, and then pounded Maine East 53–21 a week later. I admired Rita. She sat through the monsoon at Highland Park while I spent most of the soggy Saturday afternoon in the car, keeping an eye on the scoreboard while listening to college games on the radio. James slogged through the Highland Park mud for 147 yards on 26 carries; then picked up 192 more (on 21 attempts) against Maine East.

That was it. The Spartans had run out the season a perfect 9–0. James, coming on strong in the last two games, hurdled the 1,000-yard barrier, picking up 1,115 yards on 175 carries in just 7 games.

It was now playoff time. Illinois had added two classes for the 2001 season, bringing the total to eight. Running in order of school size from 8A to 1A there remained thirty-two teams making the playoffs in each class. Glenbrook North, with an enrollment of 1,992, was in the 7A class with five games separating them from a state championship. The Spartans drew the Harlem Huskies from Machesney Park, near Rockford, in the opener in Northbrook. Though only 5–4, the Huskies had defeated two playoff teams during the season and were coming off a one-point loss to undefeated Freeport.

The only thing more perfect than the delightful autumn weather was the performance James and his teammates turned in, as they walloped Harlem 34–6. It is difficult to exaggerate the night James had. It seemed that James had exorcised all the demons of his suspension in one incredible evening. He rushed for over three hundred yards and five touchdowns. "Velissaris, who piled up 344 yards on 28 carries and now has almost 1,500 yards on the season," wrote Jim Coffman of the *Pioneer Press*, "piled up 211 yards on touchdown runs (69, 15, 80, 9, and 38 yards) alone. His efforts added up to arguably the top individual performance state-wide in the first round of the playoffs."

Coffman wasn't the only one noticing. The *Tribune* put James on its six-player "Friday Night's Heroes" honor roll, and Edgy

Tim (O'Halloran), who had the top Illinois high school football website, named him "Illinois Prep Spotlight Week 10 Offensive Player of the Week."

As if the game were not enough, this was also the night James and I headed for Iowa City, on his first recruiting visit, one that included the game with mighty Michigan the following afternoon.

Now 10–0, the next game loomed large. It would pit the sixteenth or seventeenth-ranked Spartans (depending on which paper you read) against the Buffalo Grove Bison, and their celebrated quarterback, Tom Zbikowski. The media made much of the individual as well as the team matchup. The *Tribune*, spotlighting the contest as one of its "Games of the Week," got right to the point. "What to watch: The two most dynamic athletes on the field— No. 22 James Velissaris for Glenbrook North (10–0) and No. 9 Tom Zbikowski for Buffalo Grove (9–1). Velissaris is one of the most dangerous game-breakers in the Chicago area, having rushed for 346 yards, and five touchdowns last week, including scoring runs of 69 and 80 yards. The junior RB has gained nearly 1,500 yards in eight games and scored 21 TDs. Zbikowski is the junior QB who has rushed for 895 yards and 16 touchdowns and passed for 1,103 yards and 11 TDs."

Tribune writer Bob Sakomoto picked the Spartans, while Edgy Tim waxed poetic in his noncommittal prognostication. "Jimmy V vs. Tommy Z, looks like a toss-up to me," I recall his website reporting.

The game was everything Edgy Tim thought it would be. The Spartans hit pay dirt on their first possession on a quarterback keeper by Kevin Kaspers, but the Bison knotted it up at seven. In the second quarter a John Hoppe interception resulted in a score when, on fourth down, the Spartans faked a field goal as Sebastian Klosowiak sprinted for a touchdown. It was 14–7 at the half. James scored on a fifteen-yard scamper early in the third quarter, giving GBN a seemingly comfortable 21–7 lead. But Buffalo Grove answered with a score, and the game went into the fourth quarter 21–14.

After grudging defensive play on the part of both teams, Tommy Z and his mates went to work, driving down to the GBN twenty-four. With but 1:19 to play, Zbikowski hit Scott Harrington with a touchdown strike to pull the Bison within one. It looked like overtime, but Buffalo Grove had other plans. Unlike Marian Catholic who faked the PAT as they went for two, the Bison lined up in their standard offensive set ready to go for broke. Off a flea-flicker Zbikowski hit Pete Karamitos for what appeared to be the win. It also appeared that the Spartans had been robbed. Karamitos had landed with one foot on the chalk line but the officials did not see it.

But wait. The refs did see an ineligible receiver downfield and flagged the Bison for the infraction. The good news was that the two-point conversion was waved off. The bad tidings were that, because the officials did not see Karamitos' foot on the sideline, the Spartans could not decline the penalty and hold on to their 21–20 lead. The Bison were bold and played for all the marbles again. This time Karamitos was in bounds as he gathered in a Zbikowski aerial to put his team in the lead.

Zbikowski, whose total offense for the game fell 4 yards short of James' 168 rushing yards (on a hefty 34 carries), was not through with his heroics. With nineteen seconds left in the contest he picked off a fourth down pass to clinch the Bison victory.

Shades of Marian Catholic. Another last-minute one-point playoff heartbreaker. Tears flowed freely among the Spartans after the bitter defeat.

Rita's side of the family had come out in force for the game. Now in her eighties, James' grandmother Rae came up from the south suburbs. Chris made a four-hour drive from Rock Island to see the game, while James' sisters Rachel and Christine attended with their husbands, Kevin and Dennis. Uncles, aunts, and cousins were also there to root for him. We all waited to greet him after Coach Whalen addressed the team in the south end zone, as was his custom.

"I'll be home all weekend if you need me," I whispered in the tearful running back's ear as I hugged him. With the field cleared, the family went out to eat at a nearby restaurant. It was good to have an impromptu family gathering, albeit under less than the best of circumstances. Quite understandably, James, dealing with the stunning nature of this end of the road loss, did not attend.

Thanksgiving and another family get-together was right around the corner.

The season was over, and the recruiting letters were beginning to come in.

9.

The Recruiting Game

It was little consolation to talk with Mike Herbert after the 2001 campaign when he spoke of Loyola's 7–2 regular season. "If Loyola would have had James there's no doubt they would go undefeated and win the state championship. They would have been the best team in the state, period."

Herbert knew whereof he spoke. Not only did he see Loyola Academy play often that season, he also saw James. In addition, at the end of the year Herbert and his friends made their annual pilgrimage downstate to see the state title games in the various divisions.

"I think so, too," I said. I had visions of Loyola making *The USA Today* high school top 25 with James prominently featured.

Nonetheless, GBN had turned in a strong year, and had James been apprehended for an alcohol episode at Loyola, his transfer might have been moot in terms of state championship runs. For the record, at the end of his junior season, James' highlight sheet read as follows.

YEAR

- Junior Running Back for 10–1 Glenbrook North Spartans
- 1,629 Yards Rushing, 234 Carries, 7.0 Average
- 22 Touchdowns (21 Rushing, 1 Receiving)
- Rushed for 100 Yards in Nine Games

Games

- Rushed for 159 Yards and 4 TDs in 56–6 Win over Taft
- Rushed for 167 Yards in 28–21 Win at Niles West
- Rushed for 168 Yards in 22–21 PLAYOFF Loss to Buffalo Grove
- Rushed for 192 Yards in 53–21 Win over Maine East
- Rushed for 199 Yards in 31–20 Win over Evanston

- Rushed for 346 Yards in 34–6 and 5 TDs in PLAYOFF WIN over Machesney Park

Honors

- Twice *Chicago Tribune* Friday Night Hero
- All-Conference Central Suburban North
- First Team All-Area, Running Back, *Pioneer Press*

Career

- Team Record: 19–3 (playoffs: 2–2)
- 2,919 Yards Rushing, 452 Carries, 6.5 Average
- 39 Total TDs
- 15 Games over 100 Yards Rushing
- 10 Games over 150 Yards Rushing
- 3 Games over 200 Yards Rushing
- 1 Game over 300 Yards Rushing
- Two-time All-Central Suburban North Running Back
- Two-time All-Area Running Back (first team in 2001), *Pioneer Press*
- Four-time *Chicago Tribune* Friday Night Hero

For me the attention now turned to recruiting.

In football, the National Collegiate Athletic Association (NCAA) is divided into four divisions: IA, IAA, II, and III. From a scholarship standpoint, each IA school is allowed to have no more than eighty-five football student-athletes on scholarship at any one time. In addition, a IA school may grant no more than twenty-five scholarships in any one year. Division IAA schools are permitted a maximum of sixty-five scholarship students in football at any one time. The number drops to thirty-five at the Division II. Division III is entirely nonscholarship, though need-based grants are permissible.

There is no simple way to explain the football recruiting process at the Division IA level of the NCAA. Every school has its own methods. Nevertheless, there are some general points of import. At a Division IA school, there are several key figures in recruiting. These include the head coach, who of course has the final say on who is to be offered a scholarship. Under him is an assistant who carries the title of recruiting coordinator. The recruiting coordinator is exactly that, the one-man clearinghouse through whom all the pertinent recruiting information flows en route to the head coach. (Form letters sent out to prospects commonly go out over the signature of the head coach or the recruiting coordinator.) There are also position coaches—running backs coach, linebackers coach, and so on. These assistants are assigned recruiting areas on which to focus—Chicagoland, Michigan, Indiana, Ohio, and so on. They are charged with the task of identifying and evaluating youngsters within their assigned regions. Impressing an area recruiter is often a key first step to being offered a scholarship. James' case, for example, would be looked at by whatever coach handles the Chicago area. Hence, should I call a school, the receptionist would ask almost immediately what high school my son attended. The geographic location of the high school dictates to which coach the call will be directed.

The scholarship limits mentioned above are critical to a team's recruiting strategy, because a IA school has to stretch its eighty-five scholarships across a four-year—or in the case of redshirting—five-year span as well as all the offensive and defensive positions. Redshirting is a practice usually reserved for freshman in which the youngster practices but does not appear on the official playing roster. Many schools redshirt to give the players a year to adjust to college and the athletic program. In any case, different teams will be looking to recruit at different positions. A given college may, for example, be filled with good, young running backs. As a result, in James' case, the fact that he may be "good enough" to run the ball at that university is irrelevant. The school is already set at running back.

Furthermore, coaching staffs develop recruiting depth charts for each position. For example, they may have ten running backs on the board. Based on videotape, conversations with coaches, first hand scouting, and other pertinent information, the head coach, the recruiting coordinator, and the position coach (in this case, the running backs coach) will rank these players one through ten. These rankings may be revised periodically as additional information or (positive or negative) conditions emerge. Positive conditions may include unexpected physical development or increased speed, for example. Injuries, misconduct, or academic problems are negatives that can drive a youngster down the chart.

Schools start the recruiting process with a huge national database. There are a number of national scouting services that programs subscribe to. The name of virtually every player in the nation is in those databases. From there coaches begin whittling down the numbers to manageable size by looking at Top 100 lists in the various states, all-conference and all-area teams, as well as published preseason analyses of various teams and conferences. From there the sifting process continues. A given prospect may be tracked from his sophomore or junior year, and in tournament-like fashion, he will go through a series of eliminations by coaching staffs around the country until he is either dropped from consideration or offered (a scholarship).

The best way to conceptualize this process is to look at the national pool of high school football prospects as a triangle. At the top of the triangle is the relatively small number of "blue chippers," the can't-miss, no-doubt-about-it prospects. These kids are identified early and easily and will be pursued by the national powers. They will get the most attention from the recruiters at the various schools, and that attention will go beyond the regional recruiter. Offensive and defensive coordinators, even head coaches, will recruit these top-shelf prospects directly. As you move down from the apex, the triangle widens and the talent level drops. In short, there is an inverse relationship to width of the triangle and the amount of attention a youngster receives. The closer a kid is to the narrow top, the more the elite football schools will recruit him, and the more intensely he will be pursued.

The recruiting process for a junior like James follows a fairly set pattern. Some schools hold varying forms of Iowa's "Outstanding Junior Day." These may be held late in a youngster's junior year or after the season. A school will send a letter to a number of junior prospects and invite them for an unofficial visit to the campus. The key word here is *unofficial* in that the prospect travels to the university entirely at his own expense. If there is an overnight, the player (or his family) must find a place to stay and pay. Meals are also the prospect's responsibility. What the player does receive is an opportunity to visit a campus, see the sports facilities, meet the coaches, and be the school's guest at a football or basketball game. The expenses associated with these unofficial visits serve to make the recruiting process regional, since few youngsters have the time or finances to travel across the country on unofficial visits.

Below are portions of a typical junior day invitation letter—this one from Eastern Michigan University. It was signed by Mike Cummings, an assistant coach.

> *Dear James,*
>
> *Eastern Michigan Football Program will host its annual "Outstanding Junior Day" on Saturday, February 9, at 11:00 a.m. We would like to extend an invitation to you and your family. This is a day that allows outstanding junior prospects, like you, to visit Eastern Michigan University on an "unofficial" basis.*
>
> *The event includes meeting the football staff, touring the football complex, Offensive and Defensive presentations by the staff, Academic presentations, and video of the previous season. There will also be a men's basketball game beginning at 7:00 p.m. We will provide each prospect three complimentary admissions to the game.*
>
> *There will be a campus tour at 2:45 p.m. from Hoyt Conference Center. The tour will last approximately an hour and a half.*
>
> *In order to attend we ask that you call into our office and leave your name and the names of anyone else that will be accompanying you on your trip. If you reach the voice mail, leave your information as a message.*
>
> *We look forward to seeing you and the rest of the outstanding juniors at Eastern Michigan!*
>
>

Mike Cummings
Assistant Football Coach

>
> *P.S. Please see your coach and get a copy of your videotape from your previous (junior) season. We would like to have a tape of you on hand in our office.*

Holding a junior day is wise for a school because it provides the football staff the opportunity to strut its stuff. Note well the P.S. Every school wants a videotape of every prospect in action. Coaches will prevail on the youngster's high school coach for a tape of his star in action. These tapes form the basis for much decision making. For example, a tape of a running back will show his size and speed, as well as provide an indication of his quickness, moves, and general running style.

Does he hit the hole quickly? Does he use his blockers wisely? Can he take a hit? How good is he in the open field? A highlight tape can help answer those questions such that the prospect can be placed on a team's recruiting depth chart.

In any case, unless a youngster is in the blue chip class, making an effort to attend a junior day is wise. Showing up provides the football staff at the school an indication that the player is willing to consider playing at that school.

There is also mail. Stacks and stacks of mail. Most of it is of a form variety, over the signature of the staff's recruiting coordinator or head coach. Often an early letter will contain questionnaires for the prospect to fill out, again a clue to the football staff of possible interest. Schools are not allowed to initiate contact directly—by phone or in person—with a prospect until after April 15. Nevertheless, the letter sending has real potential, because it is perfectly legal by NCAA standards for a player or parent to call a coach in response to some correspondence. The key is that the prospect or parent initiates the call. This is why the letters are quite clear as to a given coach's direct dial or extension. Many football offices have 800 numbers, making it all the easier for the more indigent kids to call. Once connected, the receptionist asks the caller his name and—if he is on their prospect list—puts him through to the coach in question.

Spring practices and the annual spring intrasquad game provide another recruiting opportunity. Letters clearly spell out spring dates and urge the prospect to contact the school and let the staff know when he can attend.

Here is a portion of a typical letter, this one over the signature of Bob Stoops, head football coach at Oklahoma.

Dear James,
This is always an exciting time of the year because the spring is when your team for next season is formed and developed. We are working equally as hard here at The University of Oklahoma to prepare our team for Big XII championship.

The major part of our work in developing a championship team is recruiting. We spend countless hours in the research and evaluation of student-athletes. We are excited about you as a prospective student-athlete at Oklahoma. We have a strong interest in you and we will continue to correspond and keep track of your progress.

*It is our hope that you are equally as interested in the football program here at OU. We would love to have you stop by our office and visit with us if you are ever in Norman. We also hope that you will be able to attend our **Spring Game** on Saturday, April 20. Let me also personally invite you to attend the **Oklahoma Football Camp** this summer. You can choose from two dates—June 3–5 or **June 9–11**. A brochure that provides more information is enclosed.*

I hope you enjoy your Spring Break and return to school ready to finish the year strong.

Very Best Wishes,
Bob Stoops
Head Football Coach

Note the "We would love to have you stop by our office" line. This is a coach's way of encouraging a campus visit during a blackout period while keeping that visit safely positioned inside the NCAA guidelines. In addition, hardly a single prospect-initiated phone conversation does not include the highlighting of a spring practice or game. "You really got to come down this spring for a practice," or "Can you make it down for our spring game?" or "Just let us know in advance, and we'll set you up for a spring visit," are common coach-to-parent statements.

As with the junior days, these are unofficial visits and provide ways for schools to get more face contact with key prospects without going over any NCAA boundaries. They enable coaches to look recruits over, talk with them in order to gauge their interest and aptitude, and form relationships with prospects and parents. Without fail, the coach who is in charge of recruiting the area from which a given prospect comes will be certain to give the youngster his card and a "feel free to call me any time." Again, because the coaches are not permitted by NCAA rules to initiate personal contact, every effort is made to entice the youngster and/or his parent(s) to stay in consistent contact.

The only thing the schools can do in the case of junior prospects is use the mail. Schools vary greatly in the use of mail. Some of the major schools, with large budgets, will send mail with mind-numbing regularity—often a letter a week. Iowa, Wisconsin, and Penn State were heavy correspondents. Other schools use the mail less frequently, or begin later than others. Again, most of it is computer-driven, or may contain some famous quote from Vince Lombardi on the school's stationery, but it is an evidence of that school's interest. Some are careful to have the student's name carefully computer typed on the envelope. Others will use gummed labels. As of April 15, coaches are allowed to make one phone call to the home of the prospect, in addition to making one visit to the student's high school. The school visit usually involves talking and perhaps looking at game tape with the prospect's high school coach. The recruiter, however, is not allowed to initiate conversation with the prospect on that visit.

Clearly, one of the best things for a prospect (and especially his parents) to do is to exploit the pre-April advantages of unofficial visits and phone contacts. Conversations with college coaches at that time can yield valuable information, provided the right questions are asked. Moreover, it is perfectly appropriate for a parent or prospect to contact a school he or she feels might be interested in him or her. Such was the case for James. In discussions with Herbert, we determined that Purdue may be a very good football fit for him. The Boilermakers played a wide open passing style and used smaller than usual backs like Vinny Sutherland to great advantage. I contacted Purdue and James quickly received a handwritten note from Mark Hagen in which the coach alluded to my call.

Beyond junior days and spring practices, there are also summer coaching camps. These serve two purposes for a school. They are an income source because high school players pay to attend what is often a week of instruction by a head coach and members of his staff. More important, however, is that it gives coaching staffs an up close look at prospects. These thinly disguised tryouts are intensely promoted by the schools. James, for example, was invited to countless numbers of summer camps. "Have James come to our camp, even if it's for just a day," was a common statement.

Coaches almost never fail to invite a recruit to the team's summer camp. Stoops' rather official letter above, for example, makes mention of the "Oklahoma Football Camp." In a "Dear James" handwritten note dated March 8, Coach Hagen of Purdue tucked the invitation in by writing, "Just a quick note to say hello from the staff at Purdue. Congrats on an outstanding career to date! We look forward to following your progress closely during the next few months. I hope you can make it down for a Spring Practice and to camp this summer. Keep up the hard work and Go Boilers!"

Spring practices and summer camps prove a problem for a heavily recruited youngster. Because these events take place concurrently, it is simply impossible for a kid to attend even a single day of spring practice and summer camp at all the schools inviting him. Choices have to be made.

This is where the strategizing comes in.

10.

Strategizing

If there is one thing you learn when you are on the consumer end of the recruiting game it is this: no matter how charming, how understanding, or how seemingly altruistic a recruiting coach may be, he is working in the best interests of himself and the institution he represents rather than the recruit's.

It's just that simple. This is not to say that the process is adversarial—that the recruiting coach is not of good character, or that he does not care about the kids he is recruiting. On the contrary, in many, many cases the recruiting experience is a truly win-win endeavor. The school gets an excellent young athlete, and the athlete has a positive experience academically, socially, and athletically. The story often has a happy ending. Nonetheless, the prospect would not be sitting in the recruiting coach's office if he (or she) were not regarded as a person who could benefit that school's athletic program. In other words, as much as Coach X may like James personally, he would not be talking to him, much less be offering him a scholarship, if James were a second slower on the forty. Also, as much as Coach X may laud the program that now employs him, the minute he moves on to another school he will be lauding another new program. It is a business, and it is about sales.

Amid all the happy endings, there are many bitter experiences for recruits each year. Most of them involve deception. For example, mail can be tricky. Although consistent contact through the mail does indicate interest, it guarantees nothing. Mike Herbert told me about one of his teammates back in his days at Loyola Academy. "The guy must have gotten two, three letters a week from Notre Dame for months," he said. "I told my dad, 'Hey, my buddy is going to get a full ride to Notre Dame.' My dad told me it wouldn't happen. I wouldn't believe him; the contact was just so consistent.

"My dad was right. Never got a bite from the Irish. Didn't even get an official visit. Nothing. You can't conclude anything from that type of contact."

Steve Helminiak is a former small-college football recruiter. He knows the war stories inside and out. He confirmed Herbert's point, telling me the story of a Chicago high school star that received 180 letters from Nebraska, yet was never seriously recruited by the Cornhuskers. "It is always a good sign when a school is in regular contact," says Helminiak. "It's a lot better than if a kid is getting nothing. But a lot of early interest is not a certain indicator of what that school will do. You really can't predict whether the kid will be offered by the school or not. They may change their mind about him. They may suddenly like another kid better. They may have other needs in terms of positions . . . anything. So it is a good sign to get mail, but you don't want to get your hopes up."

Helminiak urged me to ask direct questions when speaking with coaches. "Don't be afraid to ask a recruiting coach, 'Where is James on your depth chart?' 'Do you have him as a running back or on defense?' Remember, they are trying to get something from you in the form of James for their team. If you are respectful you have every right to try to determine how interested they are in your son—where he fits into their plans. He may be their number one pick at running back. He also may be number five, and you don't know how many running backs they are going to recruit."

Beyond his advice regarding how to talk with a recruiting coach, Helminiak was making the point with which this chapter began. He is saying that the prospect and his loved ones have to protect the youngster's best interests first, and not be swayed by the charm and persuasive skills of the person attempting to bring him into a given university's program. So for us, the question is and always must be: What is best for James?

Prior to our strategizing, James and I were not excited about visiting schools like Eastern Michigan as we did on its junior day. EMU was really not on our list of favorite colleges. First, after the heady taste of the Iowa and the Big Ten, the idea of a Mid-

American Conference (MAC) school was not particularly daz-
zling.

A discussion with Helminiak resolved the matter for me.
"Doc," he said, "I strongly recommend going. They play outstanding football in the MAC, and it will show interest on James'
part in case things don't work out in the Big Ten. Plus, it will give
him more experience in deciding what he wants."

Sage counsel, I thought after hearing Helminiak's reasons for
visiting schools like Eastern Michigan, and I decided to pass his
insights along to James.

The matter raises an important point—the distinction between
the major and what is called the mid-major within Division I football. Big Ten schools—Iowa, Wisconsin, Penn State—play in huge
stadiums, are on national television, and have long-running tra-
ditions of playing top-level competition. They are majors. Mid-
majors are schools that play in less-publicized conferences, are not
consistently televised nationally or even regionally, and often play
in stadiums with seating capacities closer to thirty than eighty
thousand.

Make no mistake. Mid-majors are Division I schools and send
players into the NFL. In addition, they occasionally experience
success against majors. Bowling Green, for example, has defeated
Missouri, Northwestern, and Kansas over the past two years.
Northern Illinois fell to Wisconsin 24–21, Western Michigan was
edged 28–24 by Purdue, and Cincinnati lost to mighty Ohio State
23–19 during the 2002 season. Toledo, Marshall, and Boise State
are national powers. In short, some first-rate Division I football is
played at the mid-major level; therefore, a prospect needs to keep
the door open at these schools. In reality, any NCAA 1A program
has to be taken seriously, given how comparatively few football
scholarships are granted each year. Illinois, for example, is a major industrial state that plays top flight high school football. Yet
only about forty-five youngsters in the entire state will be offered
an NCAA 1A football scholarship.

There is no better way to distinguish a major from a mid-major
than to relate an experience I had in a coach's office at Bowling
Green. Looking at the high school film of an immensely talented
but incredibly raw quarterback from Florida, the coach said,

"Michigan would never even look at a guy like this, never look at him. Not polished. When we look at him, however, we look at the athleticism. [The film showed the youngster throwing a pass across his body that traveled thirty yards on a line for a touchdown.] You just can't teach that.

"Good coaching can provide the polish. Here, look, there's no carrying out of the fake," said the coach, pointing to a game videotape of the quarterback.

"He doesn't go downfield to block, either," another observer pointed out.

"That's just bad coaching," said the coach. "He can learn to do that. The question is: Does he have the patience and the desire to learn the proper techniques? If he does, he can be outstanding. That's the question."

The coach then went on to explain his role. "Let me tell you how a head coach will look at this kid's development. The kid can practice all day and use all the right techniques in drills, but when the head coach looks at the tape of a scrimmage and the kid doesn't follow through correctly, he will be all over me. Obviously I didn't really do my job teaching him if that kid does not implement in live action what he has been coached to do."

There were finer points. "Obviously this kid has arm strength. Let me tell you this, though. You see a guy throw a ball sixty–seventy yards and guys will rave about the player's arm strength. That has nothing to do with arm strength, that is all about style and technique. The question is can the guy fire it on the line thirty–forty yards with something on it. This kid can.

"When it comes to recruiting, the difference between and among majors is this. We look for athleticism here, so we need to do the job coaching them. Let's face it, in the Big Ten, Michigan and Ohio State get all the first picks. That's why it's so hard for teams to beat them. They have the best players. In the Big Ten it's really Michigan and Ohio State. Iowa is coming on; Michigan State is close. Still, Michigan State takes what Michigan doesn't want in Michigan athletes.

"Now when it comes to scheduling, you don't want to play Michigan or Ohio State. You'll play Indiana, Minnesota, teams like that. In the Big Twelve, you don't want to see Nebraska, Oklahoma, or Kansas State. You'll play Missouri, Kansas, or Iowa State. In the ACC you'll play Duke or Wake Forest, but you stay away from Florida State, North Carolina, and Virginia."

I presented Helminiak's position to James. "Tell me if you disagree, son," I said, "but I talked with Helminiak and here is what I think we should do. You may very likely get a full boat from a Big Ten school. There's lots of action out of Iowa, and Wisconsin, and you're hearing from Penn State, Purdue, Minnesota—schools like that. My concern, though, is that we don't pass over the MAC schools. If we give them the impression that you're not willing to play at that level, and the Big Ten doesn't come through, we may have a problem."

James agreed.

"Look, if a Big Ten school wants you," I went on, "they will be right there. The mail tells you that you are definitely on their radar screen, so even if you don't make it to their camps and spring practices, if they think you can help them they will come calling. My fear is that if you skip the mid-majors like MAC teams, they will assume you will not consider them and they will take you off their lists."

In fact, I believed a MAC-type school could very well be an ideal place for James, even though I felt James would probably get an offer from several Big Ten–level schools and would be able to play well there. I was very confident that James could run the ball at the Big Ten level for three reasons. First, his commitment to excellence, including putting on muscle weight, ensured he would be ready mentally and physically to meet any challenge. Second, his intelligence is such that he will catch on to any system in which he has to play. Third, his work ethic and humility make him optimally coachable, so sooner or later he was bound to catch the eye of a staff looking for players they can count on.

All that notwithstanding, I felt a Big Ten school could well offer him (a scholarship), but it may do so as a long-shot because of his size, such that he may well have to wait for his opportunity. I wanted him to get a good look early. I'd seen high quality players be victimized by early dismissals on the part of coaches that simply did not assess them carefully. In the 1980s, when the NBA draft went ten rounds, four North Park players were selected from our Division III national championship program. None of them went earlier than round three, and only one made it in the league.

I asked then–Head Coach, Dan McCarrell about two of the players who were cut, whether they had the stuff to play at the highest professional level. In both cases, his answer was almost identical. "He's better than some of the players in the NBA," he said referring to one of the players, "but because he's from a small school he went down in the draft, and because he is not a big name and they didn't have big money or hopes invested in him, he would have had to pop their eyes in the very first workout to get any real look at all. In the case of a long shot like that, unless he really had lit up the gym the first time he hit the floor, they would write him off and let him go in a day or two."

James was not trying to make a pro team, but I didn't want him to get little more of a look than a walk-on (a nonscholarship athlete who tries out for the team) might get. Being near the bottom of the depth chart entailed that risk. At a MAC school he would be much more likely to be at the top of the board, ensuring that he would be assessed carefully and given a chance to play early in his career. Beyond the issue of opportunity there was the matter of position. Were James to go to a major and they wanted him to play in the secondary as a defensive back or wanted to spot him on offense, rather than give him a shot at running back, he would have little leverage in the matter. At a MAC school his chances to play his position of choice would likely be much better.

That then became the strategy. Of course we would be responsive to the majors, which for us were usually Big Ten teams because of our Chicago location, but we would make abundantly clear to any mid-major that we were very interested in playing at one of their schools. We would project no arrogance. We would shoo no one away. We wanted to create as large a pool as possible.

Employing that strategy, conversations with mid-major coaches tended to go as follows.

"Hi, I'm Coach X from [mid-major school] calling about James."

"Great to hear from you, coach. I'm his dad and he and I have been working together on this recruiting business," I would respond.

"Really? Well, how's it going? Who is he hearing from?"

"We're hearing from a lot of Big Ten schools, Big Twelve, schools like that," I would explain, "but we are well aware that the MAC plays topflight football and that may be the best place for him."

And I was telling the truth.

11.

EMU

Ypsilanti is a long drive from the Windy City, and even among MAC schools EMU had hardly distinguished itself as a football power in recent years. In some respects, however, the experience at Iowa whetted my appetite for the visit to Eastern Michigan, more because it would give me time with James than visiting the school itself. Few experiences encourage bonding with another person more than a long car ride. It seems that the psychological effect of being sealed together closely in this moving container creates a special emotional openness. We left Chicago after school, intending to reach Ypsi in four or five hours and find a place to stay. Losing an hour to the Eastern time zone meant getting in fairly late.

As we drove out of Chicago on the famous Skyway and then connected with I-94 toward Detroit, the ride was smooth and enjoyable. We laughed and talked freely, with James tilted toward me leaning on the armrest separating us. I felt an inner compulsion to say something to him that I had been feeling for a long time. Somewhere in the Michigan night I found the words.

"James, I need to tell you something. I don't know if I will say it the way I want to, but here it is," I began. "I have no reason to believe there is anything wrong with your mother, but I want you to know this. If anything ever happens to her, nothing changes between us."

There, I had said it. James' response was immediate.

"You mean I'll always be your son?" he asked with searching eyes.

"Yes, you will always be my son."

I had a feeling of both resolution and exhilaration. Our bond was sealed.

At about midnight we passed through Ann Arbor and followed the signs to Ypsilanti. Ypsi, at least the part through which we drove, has an industrial quality typical of the larger rust belt cities of the Northeast. It felt like driving through the smoky, factory districts of Chicago. Not surprisingly, James was hungry. As we approached a main intersection we saw an all-night greasy spoon on the corner. I parked the car, and James and I went in.

Though a largely youthful assemblage of both blacks and whites populated this rather noisy, Formica-top establishment—typical of race relations in the United States—James and I were the only mixed pair at a table. I sensed the low-level racial alienation typical among customers in restaurants like this. Boisterous inner-city youth ate and talked loudly across the tables as what passed for a jukebox rang out its sounds, while white customers talked quietly and focused their attention on fellow whites at their own table.

James enjoyed the hearty late-night fare and we left in search of lodging. I quickly noted there were no motel chains anywhere nearby, so we drove around in search of something livable. On the corner of town was a dreary "Gil's Motel," the kind of motel that is usually either a very good bargain or simply very bad. A police car was next to us at a nearby intersection, and I rolled down my window.

"Excuse me, sir (a term almost every citizen uses to address a policeman when in need), could you tell me if that motel is a good place to stay?"

"In a word, no," the officer replied succinctly. He then went on to give us directions to an area on the outskirts of Ypsilanti in which better choices were located.

The next morning we made our way to Eastern Michigan. The stadium is located on the fringe of town on a winding road. Because it was winter, it did indeed feel like basketball rather than football season. When we arrived, we entered a huge room, not unlike a large hotel lobby, with a spiral staircase on the far end. Chairs and tables were being set up, and there were a number of rather well-dressed adults milling around in the area. The reason soon became obvious. There was to be a meeting involving the EMU Athletic Hall of Fame in the afternoon, as a prelude to the men's basketball game vs. Northern Illinois University that night.

"Dr. Claerbaut, I thought that was you." The voice belonged to Paul Saad, a fellow I once worked extensively with in a consulting assignment in nearby Detroit. Saad is impossible to dislike. "My son is being recruited by Eastern," I said proudly. "How about you?"

"So is mine."

"What position does he play?"

"Running back," replied Saad.

The world is always smaller than one thinks. I had mixed feelings about the interaction. I was happy for Saad but, of course, hardly wanted James to have to vie with Saad's son for one of the university's precious scholarships. After registering, the group was directed to the field house where the recruits were to be addressed en masse before being broken into touring groups. The basketball arena had a typical major college look: a bright, shiny wooden floor with the school mascot—the eagle—emblazoned in the center circle, with the playing area surrounded by rows and decks of seats. As the various members of the coaching staff were introduced I noted that the coaching group was both racially diverse and from major university football programs. Eventually, Jeff Woodruff, the head coach, got up to speak. Although Woodruff looks more like a chemistry professor than a major college football mentor, he has an excellent pedigree. He served as a right-hand man to legendary Don James at the University of Washington, and sports a huge NCAA championship ring commemorating the great 1991 season there.

As with Iowa, the import of academics was highlighted from the outset. I wondered if this was simply the politically correct thing to do or whether we had happened to encounter two institutions that truly made high graduation rates a priority. That Woodruff came from the lineage of Don James gave him the benefit of the doubt on that matter.

Woodruff honed in on academics using an apocryphal story. "Once when we were playing Nebraska I was walking down a hallway coming out from the dressing room," he said. "Suddenly I came face-to-face with an absolute giant of a player with a huge N on his jersey. He was a Nebraska lineman. We greeted each other briefly, and he said how proud he was of Nebraska and what he was studying there. 'And by the way, coach,' he said, 'do you know what this N stands for? Knowledge,' he said.

"Well, if that's where you are with academics," Woodruff concluded, "head for Central Michigan (a major EMU rival)."

The crowd of youngsters guffawed with delight at the harmless but cute story, and with that the facilities tour was under way.

What James found particularly impressive were the credentials of the coaching staff. The EMU coaches hailed largely from Big Ten schools, giving the entire program a powerful air. What became clear was that the MAC was clearly big league. And the coaches talked it.

I skipped the tour, knowing pretty well what James would see, and wormed my way into the area of the coaches' offices. There I ran into Jeff Woodruff. "Excuse me," I said, "but my son is being rather heavily recruited at running back. What are you looking for at that position?" I was hoping for some information on desired size.

"Come in here," Woodruff beckoned. I entered a room swimming with cassettes and VCR equipment. "Let me show you something," he went on. "When we look at film we look at how a back runs. Here, let's say you have a young man and he cuts into a hole right here," said the coach as he drew up a diagram with a gaping running chasm between right guard and right tackle. "Now 90 percent of the guys who hit a hole like that will enter it right in the center, where the space is the largest. But that's not where we want our runner to go, because that is the exact spot the defender will rush to in order to plug the hole. Instead, we want that runner to run as close to the butt of the inside blocker as possible, almost brushing his uniform and then cut straight through the middle away from the defenders expecting him to go through the center of the hole.

"That's how we evaluate kids. And when we evaluate kids we use the Washington method. Each coach looks at the tape and puts down a number. For example, a one-one means the kid will play in the first game of his freshman year. A two-three would mean he would be a key player in the third game of his sophomore season. After getting all the input we make a final determination of the youngster. We only take ones and twos when it comes to scholarships."

Lunch was not served by the university, so James and I headed off to a nearby pizzeria. "The facilities are top-notch," James said, "pretty much like Iowa's."

I couldn't wait to tell him of my visit with Woodruff. He, of course, was anxious to hear about it. After I painstakingly but eagerly broke down the nuances of Woodruff's disquisition on running to daylight, James unintentionally squelched my enthusiasm.

"I know," he said, "that's how they taught us to run at GBN."

From there the discussion led to more fruitful matters. "There are three criteria, son, that I think are key as you make your decision on where you want to go. First, you need to pick a school at which you will be happy even if you don't play football. That way, if for any reason things don't work out in football, you know you are still going to be happy there. Second, is how much you will play, and third, where you will play.

"You could play in the Big Ten but wind up waiting until your junior or senior year before you set foot on the field. Also, you could play at that level, but be moved to d-back or wide receiver. You have to decide how important it will be for you to play running back."

We returned to EMU for the afternoon session. "I played three years at linebacker for Iowa, made All-Big Ten, and was a semi–finalist for the Butkus Award," proclaimed Assistant Coach Bob Diaco, a handsome, intense, twenty-five-ish young man. Diaco is one of those guys that is a tad full of himself, yet at the same time charming and charismatic. After his rousing address I had him meet James. Clearly, Diaco knew who he was.

"I am really glad you made the trip all the way up here," said the young coach, looking James in the eye with what appeared to be maximum sincerity. "I've talked with some of the coaches in your area and they've spoken highly of you. We really like you and will be recruiting you. I will be at your high school in May. Again, it's really great you came."

For James, the moment was magic. Diaco was young, able to relate to a student-athlete of the new millennium, and oozing self-confidence and certainty in the future of EMU Eagle football. What made it particularly special is that Diaco recruited the Chicagoland area. We did not stay for the basketball game that evening. After hearing an impressive presentation regarding the import of academics, in addition to EMU's support program for student-athletes, we took off for home very happy we visited Ypsilanti.

James was impressed with EMU. When I asked if he was glad that we made the trek, he said yes.

"I was really surprised at the overall quality of the program, particularly how their coaching staff was almost all Big Ten people," he remarked.

"Remember, Eastern has been down, James. Now that Woodruff has been here for two years he should begin to turn the program around. Sometimes programs that are down like this (EMU was 3–8 the previous season) are preferable, because winning sometimes goes in cycles and by the time you get here it could be a winner."

James wanted to win, and Eastern was now on the list.

12.

It's Great to Be a Hawkeye

Iowa took the early lead in the recruiting derby. The first-class handling of junior day, coupled with faithful mailings and solicitous conversations ("We're really interested in James") with Eric Johnson in particular, put the Hawkeyes out front. You could just feel that the Iowa program was coming on. It went beyond the steady uphill climb of the program in the win-loss column under Kirk Ferentz. That in itself was most impressive. The Hawkeyes went a desultory 1–10 in 1999, Ferentz's maiden season. The team registered a 3–9 log the following year, and then jumped to 7–5 (4–4 in the Big Ten) in 2001, including a bowl win against Texas Tech. Larger than the ever-improving record, however, there was just this special energy around the program, a feeling of anticipation of even better things to come.

Wanting to communicate our interest in Iowa, James and I got into the car on a bright spring day and headed to Iowa City to see a practice. James was full of football talk on the way down. Hoping to play on both sides of the ball in his senior year, the conversation turned to defense. "Coach Whalen does not like to use guys both ways," he stated.

"Why not?" I asked. "You've got to go with the guys that can help you win. It's fine to try to play everyone, but that is not how the world works. People that deliver are the ones who get the opportunities."

"I don't know, he just doesn't like to do it," remarked James.

I wanted James to get a crack at "D," if only to demonstrate his prowess as an all-around player. This two-platoon approach had to have its genesis with Whalen, because James' brother Chris played at both wide receiver and defensive back during his days in the green and gold. We continued our discussion of defense, especially zone versus man-to-man pass coverage.

"I can understand why GBN plays man on defense," I chimed in. "They have very smart players that are fundamentally sound. But the level of athleticism in the secondary can move up and down from one year to another, so playing man-to-man can sometimes be risky. In the conference, and in the early rounds of the playoffs it should be OK, but as you get deeper into the playoffs, you'll meet teams that can really throw, and it will be tough to stop those teams going man-to-man." Zones have their risks as well, however, and you can't install them with a snap of the finger. GBN's defensive coordinator, Larry Heise, was a solid veteran of the gridiron both as a player and a coach, and had much to do with making the defensive squad as fundamentally competent as it had become in recent years. Moreover, he was thoroughly familiar with zone and man-to-man defenses, and had his reasons for why it was not in the best interests of GBN defense to go that way.

Such is the bane of any football parent. On one hand, you see things you may wonder about in the strategy of your son's coaches. On the other, you don't see the whole picture, and it is not your place to confront staff members presumptuously with your ideas. Hence, these father–son discussions.

"James, what would you have done to stop Zbikowski from getting that two-point conversion?" I asked, referring to perhaps the most memorable play of 2001.

"I would have rushed him hard. He had too much time to decide what to do."

It made sense to me. A blitz may have gotten to him before he had the opportunity to assess the situation and pick out his receiver. Of course, he might have ducked the onrushing cavalry of Spartans and glided into the end zone, but it would have been no worse for GBN than what had happened. Moreover, the Spartans had a bevy of sure-handed, wrap-'em-up tacklers that may well have sealed Tommy Z's doom. It didn't matter—it was after the fact—but I enjoyed swapping strategies with my son.

I had always been an adherent of the short-passing—California—offensive system. Chris, James, and I had talked about it often. "The strength of the short-passing game in high school is that by flooding the defense with receivers the other team becomes confused and somebody's got to be open. And you don't need a quarterback with a big arm to make it happen. He just tosses it to the open man.

"The best thing you can do to a defense in high school football is to force the players to think. Once they have to think rather than react in sequence, they start halting and becoming confused. Everything breaks down."

James agreed. "You can really score with a good passing team. Riverside-Brookfield high school passes almost all the time and they average about four to five hundred yards a game on offense. Teams can't stop them." James loved to talk football, and although the discussion was of little consequence in the larger scheme of things, this father–son banter had its own reward. It was always a high for me.

We arrived at the Iowa football office shortly after the practice had begun, and we were directed very graciously to the practice field. We left the football facility and walked about fifty yards, and then up a hill through an entrance to the field. We stood on the sidelines at midfield, watching the team scrimmage. It was a cool, clear day, and I was in shirtsleeves while James wore a jacket.

"We can take turns wearing the jacket," offered the ever-courteous James, noticing my rather warm-weather attire.

"I'm fine, but thanks," I replied appreciatively. Since I didn't even own a winter overcoat I certainly wasn't going to bundle up in the temperate spring breeze.

There were perhaps ten to twenty other recruits there along with parents and friends, in addition to some locals who simply wanted to get a preview of the 2002 Hawkeye team. Most of the position coaches were on the field exhorting the players, while Head Coach Kirk Ferentz stood rather impassively on the other side. Having seen myriad football scrimmages going back to high school days, and being unfamiliar with many of the ununiformed Iowa players, my interest waned and I looked around for someone to talk to. Soon Eric Johnson walked over.

"Thanks for coming," he said. "We're really glad you could make it. James is high on our list."

Given Johnson's twenty-something youth and open style, I decided to probe.

"Where do you have James?"

"Well, we begin with a national database, then we cut it down quite a bit as we do. He's made all the cuts so far, so he's still getting lots of mail from us. You know it would really be good if James could come down for our summer camp. That would give him a really good feel for what it's like to play here at Iowa. He could meet the coaches, and they could also get a close look at him."

There it was, the ubiquitous summer camp. We discussed the evaluation system further. "Right now we have James at a three-plus. Four is scholarship level, so James is as close as he can be to being offered at scholarship. A lot of three-plus guys become fours, and going to summer camp can really give a kid like James a chance to establish himself."

I was elated. A three-plus as a junior, and he was only going to get bigger and better. A scholarship was a lock. I asked about the summer dates, and the conversation flowed along smoothly. Johnson, who had spent some time at Vanderbilt, was impressed with James' demeanor as well as his academic status. "James is the kind of kid we want. He's not only a good athlete, but he's also a good student, and we put great emphasis on our kids graduating. Oh, yeah, could you do us a favor? Get a tape of James out to us as soon as possible. The only one we have is of him running in the rain (the Highland Park game), and that doesn't show what he can really do."

"We'll take care of it as soon as we get back."

"Give me a week or two after we get it," Johnson said. "I can give you a clearer idea of where James stands."

Johnson, a natural at selling the program, also put in a plug for the head coach. "Coach Ferentz is just great. Right from the start he had a plan, and even when we were losing in the early going he never deviated from it. Now that we are turning the corner and starting to win, we can see he knew what he was doing from the beginning." Ferentz, who had been a member of Hayden Fry's staff in the 1980s, had come back to Iowa by way of the NFL's Baltimore Ravens. He had taken on a Herculean task. After a marvelous decade-and-a-half run, the program had slipped badly in Fry's final years, less due to Hayden's advanced age I suspect,

than the beating the near seventy-year-old was taking on the recruiting trail. Schools will do virtually anything within the rules to
get an edge, and one of the most effective things you can do if you
are recruiting against a coach like Fry is to use his age against
him.

You could just hear a rival recruiter leaning on a blue-chip athlete considering Iowa. "Remember son, Hayden Fry is way up
there and it's highly unlikely he will be there all four or five years
you're at Iowa. And if he retires, where will that put you? You
don't know who the new coach will be, whether he will run the
same system, keep Fry's staff, or want his players. You could be
heading into your junior or senior year and be on the outside
looking in." This is the kind of attack Joe Paterno has been facing
for years at Penn State. And it is effective. There is so much un-
known territory a prospect encounters no matter where he goes to
school. To add to that the possibility that the coach that recruited
him will not even be there for his prime years is a daunting concern.

Ferentz, then, truly had to reconstruct the football program,
and make believers along the way, even while the losing continued
during his first two years. But he did make believers, receiving
high marks from nonfootball players as well. While waiting for
James before we made our way to the practice field I encountered
one of the school's female athletes, a native of the Hawkeye state
named Sarah.

"Are you visiting Iowa?" she asked.

"My son is a football recruit," I said proudly. I then used the
opening to gain an insight into her regard for Iowa football. I
would not have been surprised had she rendered a mixed review.
Often female students have less than positive experiences with the
entitlement attitudes of macho football players and the superior
airs coaches often have because of their status as members of the
always high-profile football staff.

Sarah harbored no such ill feelings, focusing particularly on
Ferentz. "The program is really picking up," she said proudly,
"and Coach Ferentz is just really wonderful." She went on to tell
me how Ferentz had voluntarily served on a committee that was
aimed at improving student life at Iowa.

As the sun began moving down, the temperatures did the same. I didn't want to acknowledge my discomfort and go back into the football building to warm up, but I was really cold. James, however, remained warmly attired in his jacket. The practice seemed to drag on interminably, despite Johnson's assurances each ten minutes or so that things were about to wind up for the day. Finally I said, "Is this practice ever going to be over? It's really getting chilly," looking at James in his coat.

"You got to tough it out," he said with a slight grin, no longer offering the jacket he was all too willing to share when the sun was high.

"Look at you, man," I said. "An hour and a half ago when it was sunny you were offering your jacket to me. Now that it's getting frosty, all you've got to say is 'You've got to tough it out.' Of course you're the guy wearing the jacket." We had a healthy laugh at that one.

Later, Lester Erb, the receivers and special teams coach, came by. Eric Johnson introduced him to us. "I'm really pleased to see you, James," said Lester. "You've had a great year at Glenbrook North—your team went into the playoffs, you had over 1,600 yards rushing and 22 touchdowns, and you've been an honor student with an over 3-point average." If Erb was trying to impress us with his research on James, he most certainly did. "Remember, James, this is a process," Erb went on. "There are ups and downs, be patient and let things work themselves out." Our conversation was brief. Lester's wife had just given birth at the university hospital and he was off to visit her.

The highlight came a few minutes later. Kirk Ferentz made his way over and greeted James personally. Ferentz, a tall, handsome, forty-five-year-old man dressed in fashionable tan slacks, exuded confidence and quiet presence. He has a smooth, relaxed, and polished mien. "Hi, I'm coach Ferentz; I'm glad you could make it," he said in his cool style, looking James in the eye. Even with the obligatory invitation to Iowa's summer camp, the conversation was brief. There was no need to extend it. The point was clear: the head coach thought enough of James to go out of his way to greet him personally.

We left filled with optimism. "You really like Iowa, don't

you?" I said as we headed back to the Windy City.

"Yeah, I do."

"All things being equal, would you say they are in first place right now?" I asked, probing James' feelings.

"Yes."

I put the "It's Great to be a Hawkeye" post-it sticker that I picked up at the football office on my car visor. Iowa City may have been receding in the rearview mirror as we drove home, but we knew we would most certainly be returning in June so James could strut his stuff at the Hawkeyes' summer camp.

13.

Badger Bravado

By the spring, James was on his share of lists. He had been contacted in one way or another by forty-one Division IA schools.

Air Force	Kansas State	Penn State
Arizona State	Kentucky	Pittsburgh
Army	Miami of Ohio	Purdue
Ball State	Michigan	San Diego State
Boston College	Michigan State	San Jose State
Bowling Green	Minnesota	Southern Mississippi
Central Michigan	Mississippi	Stanford
Cincinnati	Missouri	Toledo
Colorado	Nebraska	Tulane
Duke	Northern Illinois	UCLA
Eastern Michigan	Northwestern	Vanderbilt
Illinois	Notre Dame	Western Michigan
Iowa	Ohio	Wisconsin
Kansas	Oklahoma	

One that had been particularly consistent was Wisconsin. The Badgers were an intriguing possibility. They had a solid, winning Big Ten program, and—Heisman Trophy winner Ron Dayne notwithstanding—they did not shy away from small, quick running backs. Besides, Madison was close enough to Chicago for Rita and me to see James play. Getting to one of their spring practices, therefore, was a must.

Due to my travel schedule, this was one trip James took alone. I didn't feel all that comfortable sending him off on the three-hour Saturday journey to a Badger scrimmage, but James was OK with it. The trip did not start out too auspiciously, however, as he got lost finding the football practice field in Madison.

"The football offices are in the stadium," related James. "When I got there I parked my car. There were no 'Recruits' signs giving directions like the other schools I visited. I walked around and finally found a janitor or somebody like that, and he showed me how to get to the practice field."

The somewhat strange odyssey continued from there. "When I finally got to the field there was no one to greet me like some of the other schools. In fact, the guy who invited me was standing nearby talking to some people as if I weren't there. They were having a scrimmage, so I just stood there and watched for about two hours by myself.

"I did realize how good Big Ten players are when I saw a guy from Naperville who had been a huge star in high school playing third string on defense. It was kind of scary to see that."

Barry Alvarez, the head coach at Wisconsin since 1990, was front and center. Unlike Ferentz who stood off to the side, letting his assistants run the scrimmage, Alvarez was in the action. "He was right out there in the middle of the field. You could hear him cursing and swearing clearly. I was uncomfortable because there were a number of recruits, parents, and children standing on the sidelines hearing it. Even if you were in the stands you could hear him, because with Camp Randall stadium pretty empty his voice echoed."

Had it been an annual spring game it might have been different, but watching the scrimmage with no one to talk to was less than entertaining. In fairness, James is not proficient at small talk. In fact, his introverted manner is sometimes mistaken for his being arrogant or aloof. Were he more outgoing, James might have invited some discussion with members of the Wisconsin staff.

In any case, things improved little after the conclusion of the scrimmage. The recruits and their families were taken on a tour of the facilities, one conducted with Badger bravado, according to James. "They had very good facilities, but no better than the other top schools I visited. Yet they would describe them as the pride of the Big Ten, second to none, state of the art, as if they were superior to anyone else's," James related. "The tour ended in the locker room, where the team was still cleaning up after the scrimmage. Then we were told we could go home."

"Did you meet Alvarez?" I asked, given the other schools' prominent use of the head coach in settings such as this.

"No, he never said anything to us."

I was not surprised that James was put off by the arrogant Badger style. James had already scored thirty-nine touchdowns, but had yet to spike the ball even once in the end zone, do a rap dance in celebration, or engage in any other attention-getting conduct. And I was happy about it, having seen many athletes in many sports—high school, college, and pro—so full of themselves. I recall being in the Yankee clubhouse visiting a player I knew in Reggie Jackson's heyday. The wife of a friend of mine had asked me to get Jackson's autograph if I could. It was an uncomfortable request, but having been around Jackson a fair amount, I went up to him at his cubicle.

"My friend's wife will kill me if I don't ask you to autograph this, Reggie," I said, holding a ball and pen out to him.

"Let her kill you," Jackson said with a sneer. Chris Chambliss stood next to Jackson laughing. Later that evening I sat at a table next to Jackson while eating with a Yankee player at the hotel at which the team was staying. Seeing me with one of his teammates must have changed Reggie's outlook toward me. A now sheepish Jackson was only too willing to pass the condiments over from his table upon our request.

One night in Las Vegas I was defending Barry Bonds against the verbal "He's a jerk" onslaughts of a baseball fan. Given that the fan's experience with Bonds was only through the media, I suggested that Bonds may simply be a bit introverted and therefore ineffective in public situations. "He's no introvert, and he *is* a jerk!" exclaimed a businessman sitting a seat over. The man, an owner of a Bay area jewelry store, then went on to describe a disgusting incident at his business. "Bonds was in my store with a mutual acquaintance," the man related, "and he talked loudly and disruptively on his cell phone right in the store. He then started to label my jewelry as garbage. I had to ask him to be quiet or leave." This was not the man's only such experience with Bonds, just as the Jackson experience was not my only encounter with athletic arrogance.

In a word, James felt left out at Wisconsin. Although an admitted oversimplification, it seems that schools employ one of two general approaches to recruiting. Some use the Iowa style—doing everything possible to ingratiate themselves with the recruit and his family, always emphasizing how interested they are in the youngster and how valuable the school can be to him. In Iowa's case, the ingratiation extended to Rita and me receiving cards on Mother's Day and Father's Day. The other method—the Wisconsin style—is one in which the school and program are positioned as something to which the kid should aspire. If you can do x, y, and z, then you can become a Badger. It becomes a sort of play-hard-to-get style. It is possible that the styles are driven by the program's success. Iowa had been down for many years. They needed players and could afford to alienate no one. Wisconsin, however, had an established program. They could hold being a Badger out as a carrot for the anxious recruit.

Clearly, were James an absolute blue-chip prospect, one sought after intensely by myriad institutions, he may well have received the Iowa treatment from everyone. Tom Lemming, the Mel Kiper of high school football recruiting, has tabbed Alvarez as the nation's best recruiter, citing the Wisconsin mentor for his ability to project a warm, caring aura when meeting with a sought-after prospect and his parents. That skill may be why the Badgers have done as well as they have in the Big Ten recruiting wars, given that their native state does not produce many genuine Division IA prospects.

The fact does remain, however, that James was surprised at the less than welcoming approach of the Wisconsin method schools, given that they would send him invitations to their football recruiting events. To me, the Iowa School style is the only one worth using. A school is under absolutely no obligation to offer a youngster a scholarship just because they recruit him by showering him with letters. Provided they are honest with the young man, not leading him to believe their interest will lead to a certain scholarship offer, no harm is done. As for the teenage prospect, he is likely to be much more attracted to the school that appears to be interested in him—that wants him—than one that takes the "prove to us you are good enough" approach to the relationship. Beyond that, there is no way of knowing whether a prospect in his junior year will reach blue-chip status by the end of his senior year. Were James to put on twenty-five pounds, while retaining his speed and so bringing an additional element or two to his game, he could well move into the class Barry Alvarez aims at charming. As it is, Alvarez would have to be at his best to compensate for the less than rewarding experience James had in his Madison visit.

I didn't see James until the next morning in church. He came up to me and summarized his Wisconsin experience in a single, witty sentence: "It's great to be a Hawkeye," he said.

14.

Northwestern Wildcats

Northwestern, nestled just north of Chicago in Evanston, is the Big Ten's only private university. Academically elite and proud of it, Northwestern more often recruits against Stanford than it does the University of Illinois. James was invited to the school's junior day.

James got to the campus after the facilities tour, but having taken a number of them before, he missed little. The day began for him with the players broken up by position, with the respective position coaches addressing them. James was in the group led by Jeff Genyk, running backs coach. A slight man, with a matter-of-fact approach, Genyk explained the recruiting process. "I learned more about the recruiting process and the NCAA rules from his speech than in anything else I heard or read," said James. In addition, Genyk pulled no punches as to what the school was looking for in running backs. "Because we play a wide-open, spread offense, we put a premium on speed and agility at the running back position," he explained. "We will offer two scholarships at that position."

Two is not many, but that was for the 2002 season. In any case, James certainly fit the description. At the conclusion of the position meetings, the larger group was reassembled to hear an address from the school's academic support group. It focused on the institution's academic commitment and benefits, its expectations of the athletes, and the support and assistance available. Academics are truly first at this private institution, and this session underlined it. Current players joined in the segment, describing the nature of the academic experience at the school.

It was still not football time at NU. "We then got on coach buses and took a tour of the campus," said James. Highlighting the educational advantages of Northwestern University, the bus combed through the Evanston campus, with the driver pointing out buildings and sites of historical and academic interest. "It was impressive," said James, "and if were not so close to home I would have really been interested in going there. As it was, I found it very attractive."

When he returned he met his mother at a general session held in a press box–like room at the top of the football stadium, Ryan Field. There a large spread of food awaited the group of thirty-five or so. "It was clearly the best spread of any of the schools I visited," observed the omnivorous James, not surprisingly.

"It was really first-rate," chimed in Rita, "a step up from the hot dogs, hamburgers, and fries that are usually served to teenagers."

After a few preliminaries and a large spread of food it was time to hear from Head Coach Randy Walker. The setting was nicely staged. Walker stood in front of a window overlooking the football field, with the giant Jumbotron all but staring in the prospects' faces immediately to Walker's left. It was Northwestern's way of saying, "We're big league." Walker is a short, stocky man. "If you meet one-on-one with him," said one coach who interviewed for a position on the Northwestern staff, "those eyes will look right through you. He is straightforward, no nonsense."

Indeed he was straightforward in his presentation to the prospective student-athletes. He definitely was not selling Northwestern to those assembled. He did not use any "we're so glad you're here and considering Northwestern," as Iowa did.

"It was more 'if you do this and if you can do that . . . we may be interested in you,'" said James. "There was no unified theme to his speech." Walker spoke as if to say, "If you guys can measure up you could be at Northwestern." Whether intended or not, it radiated that air of superiority so typical of the elite schools. Given that James' sister, Christine, held a degree from NU, that his mother had done extensive academic work there as well, and that James himself had spent much time at the campus when he attended Evanston's Roycemore, a private school, it left James unimpressed. As for Walker, he actually contrasted stylistically with the more polished members of his staff. Nevertheless, he was the head coach.

James wasn't the only recruit put off by an air of superiority at the school north of Chicago. Later, he met another kid who had played at one of the elite Illinois football schools, a youngster who was being recruited by a number of topflight institutions. The young man had attended the Northwestern summer camp, finding it unpleasant. Upon receiving one of Walker's prove-that-you're-good-enough-for-Northwestern messages the kid's unspoken reply was, "C'mon coach, you guys can't even beat Air Force."

Nevertheless, Randy Walker is a well-regarded major college head coach. He was summoned from Miami of Ohio in January of 1999. Expectations were moderate at best upon his arrival. Here was another non-big-name immigrant, from a MAC school, stepping into the Big Ten furnace at Northwestern. The NU legacy has been, in a word, abominable. The program had employed six head coaches since the legendary Ara Parseghian had left after the 1964 season with an overall record that was but a single game over .500.

None of his six successors left with winning records. Their 34-year aggregate record had been 103–283–3. In fact, prior to Gary Barnett's scintillating two-year (1995–1996) run, the Wildcats had not had anything approaching a winning program since Alex Agase had recorded back-to-back winning seasons in 1970 and 1971. Despite those two years on the plus side, Agase's overall log was just 32–58–1, a set of numerics that got him fired at the end of the 1972 campaign.

From there, it was a bleak twenty-three-year trip into the football wilderness for the Wildcats. (Between 1973–1985, for example, the team played nearly a hundred games under .500— 23–119–1. The best season among those thirteen brownouts was 4–7, with the worst being a pair of 0–11 campaigns.) The 23-year drought began with John Pont, actually a proven mentor who had taken Indiana to the Rose Bowl in 1967. After winning but twelve of fifty-five games, he was replaced by a young, enthusiastic Rick Venturi. Venturi, who went on to carve out a solid gridiron coaching career as an NFL assistant, entered the Northwestern scene proclaiming that the school's high academic standards and stringent entrance requirements were positives, giving the program uniqueness. The most unique aspect of Venturi's reign was that he lost all but two of his games at the helm. His three-year mark was 1–31–1. Enter Dennis Green—the same Dennis Green who later assisted on Bill Walsh's Super Bowl 49er staff, then led Stanford to football success, and followed that with a successful decade as head coach of the NFL Minnesota Vikings. Green lasted five years. His record was 10–45.

In 1986 the school turned to former Green Bay Packer Francis Peay. Peay did manage to win thirteen games in his six years, but lost fifty-one and tied two. In 1992 Gary Barnett, a member of Bill McCartney's highly successful Colorado staff, took over. Little was expected and little achieved in his first several seasons. A 3–8 mark in 1992 was followed by a dismal 2–9 log the following year. Things appeared to moving backward. In 1994 the Wildcats posted a 3–7–1 record. Now 8–24–1 after three seasons, Barnett was firmly established as just another of the six unsuccessful coaches in the wake of Ara Parseghian's moderately successful reign. Then, in 1995 things suddenly changed. With no advance warning, the Wildcats sprouted gridiron teeth, going an undefeated 8–0 in the Big Ten and 10–2 overall. In 1996, the team took a share of the conference title with a 7–1 league mark and 9–3 season-long run. Barnett's two successive winning seasons equaled the program's accomplishments over the previous thirteen seasons. His two bowl bids represented two-thirds of the school's bowl invitations.

In the mid-1990s, Gary Barnett ruled the football world. He had done the seemingly impossible. He had turned water into wine. He had won at Northwestern. Not just won, but won the Big Ten, the conference housing Lloyd Carr's Wolverines, John Cooper's Buckeyes, and Joe Paterno's Nittany Lions. Not just won the Big Ten, but won it twice—back-to-back.

Any and every coaching opening invited speculation about Barnett. The Detroit Lions were interested, so was Notre Dame, and on and on. But Barnett wasn't the only powerbroker at the school. In January 1994, Northwestern hired Charles F. "Rick" Taylor as its athletic director. Taylor came from Cincinnati, where basketball was king, and he became a genuine presence at Northwestern.

By the time NU football was in its ascendancy Barnett and Taylor were butting heads. It was easy to understand. Neither Barnett nor Taylor have undersized egos. Taylor, officially the man in charge, had worked hard to raise money and establish the athletic program at the school. A glad-handing promoter, Taylor injected needed energy into the program. Nonetheless, the football tail often wags the athletics dog at major football schools, and Barnett was the master of a rather attractive canine pedigree by the close of 1996.

Power plays and pettiness typified much of Barnett and Taylor's relationship. "Big egos clash," as one coach put it. "Barnett wasn't completely innocent. He would go over Taylor's head on some issues, directly to the president of the university." After all, he was a much larger name than Rick Taylor. Taylor found his own way to make an impact. Prior to the gridiron breakthrough, Barnett had put together a modest local booster group to support the football program. "It was made up mainly of well-to-do, not superrich, businesspeople that would purchase computers and other items the team needed," said the coach.

The boosters, in a fit of elation after the Wildcats Rose Bowl season, anted up to send the football coaches on a cruise in appreciation for their achievement. Taylor quickly moved in, outlawing all future such perks if extended to the coaches of a particular sport. "Taylor claimed that such rewards undermine the morale of the rest of the [athletic] department," said the coach. It didn't end there. Barnett had negotiated a deal with Adidas, and Taylor nixed that as well.

One of the funnier bones of contention involved a bit of decoration. Coaches love to acquire any advantage in any game—often preferring a psychological edge. Hayden Fry, of Iowa loved to challenge the masculinity of his opponents. "When Fry was at Iowa he used to paint the visitor's locker room pink to humiliate them," a coach told me, laughing. When Barnett, on his own, did the same at Northwestern for visiting Iowa, Taylor was not amused and quickly returned the dwelling to its original look.

As for laughs, Taylor had the last one at Northwestern.

Barnett's ride at the top of the college football world ended after those two unforgettable seasons. In 1997, the Wildcats dropped to 5–7 overall (3–5 in the Big Ten). In addition, and despite his protestations to the contrary, there was plenty of evidence that Barnett was sniffing around for a new place to hang his football hat. Matters worsened, when it was reported after the

1996 campaign that one of his players had been betting on college games. Unfortunately, this is something that likely goes on far more than most fans or the NCAA even want to know about, and though there was no hard evidence indicating that he had tried to affect the point spread of any Wildcat contest, the issue was an embarrassing smudge on a program with the lofty NU label attached to it.

The 1998 season was even worse. The Wildcats finished 3–9—a mere 1–7 in the conference. Within forty-five days Barnett was gone. He returned to Colorado, taking over the Buffalo job when Rick Neuheisel exited for Washington. His departure was received with relief from many NU backers and media people who had grown weary of what they felt were less than candid admissions from Barnett that he would not be moving on. Curiously enough, Rick Neuheisel, the coach Barnett succeeded at Colorado, left under similar conditions.

The preppy Neuheisel got the head coaching position under dubious circumstances. After Bill McCartney had resigned after the 1994 season, Neuheisel reportedly charmed the university regents at his interview, edging out the logical successor, defensive coordinator Bob Simmons, an African American who was an eminently competent candidate with greater seniority. Simmons was subsequently hired as head coach at Oklahoma State. Once in place, however, the formerly celebrated UCLA quarterback indulged in some unorthodox methods. An amateur musician, he occasionally performed musically on his coach's TV show. In addition, he would take his players on outdoor ventures like rafting in the Colorado rapids. As long as Neuheisel was winning, all this may have been amusing to many Buffalo fans, but a 13–10 record during has last two seasons along with some backroom politicking were not.

While Neuheisel was settling in at Colorado, things were unraveling northwest at the University of Washington. The venerable Don James—winner of 153 games against just 57 losses and 2 ties—had left, angered by what he felt was an unjustified NCAA action against his program. His successor, loyal longtime assistant Jim Lambright, while enjoying some initial success with holdovers from the Don James regime, was presiding over a program in decline. Although 38–19–1 overall, Lambright was just 14–10 in his final two seasons, and 6–6 in his last. Barbara Hedges, the athletic director since 1991, feeling the pressure, began looking for a new coach, having plenty of money to hire one. Money talks, and her friend Rick Neuheisel, who knew her from his days at USC law school, where Hedges was an associate athletic director, listened on the sly. After some big dollars were agreed upon, Neuheisel up and left the Buffaloes after the 1998 season to take over the Huskies' football fortunes, leaving a host of angry, jilted, in-the-dark Buffalo fans in his wake. The unhappy episode was made even worse when allegations surfaced that "Slick Rick" (as Colorado fans called him) was trying to take a small herd of Buffaloes northwest with him

Back at Northwestern, with a bitter residue of distant scandal and recent acrimony in the air, Randy Walker entered the Evanston campus, his major credential being a 59–35–5 mark over an eleven-year period at Miami. His 3–8 1999 team suggested that the Wildcat football program was now safely nestled in its customary spot at the bottom of the Big Ten football heap. The glories of 1995 and 1996 appeared well in the rearview mirror for Wildcat adherents—mere aberrations from the norm of failure.

One year later, however, Walker's Wildcats were looking down at their league foes, grabbing a tri-championship with a 7–1 league mark, and going 8–4 overall.

Randy Walker had done in two years what it took Barnett four seasons to do, and he had done it with players he had not recruited. Maybe Northwestern Wildcat football had claws. Maybe it could be a Stanford rather than a Duke, a Brigham Young rather than a Baylor.

With running back Damien Anderson disdaining an early entrance into the NFL, and option quarterback Zak Kustok back for the 2001 campaign, Northwestern was pegged a certain league contender, if not the odds on favorite to take the league crown again. The future looked bright.

Then came August 3, the day the world came crashing down on Randy Walker and his Northwestern football program.

At about 6:00 p.m. strong safety Rashidi Wheeler was pronounced dead of bronchial asthma. It was not only that Wheeler died, but how he died. Earlier that day, with the temperatures in the eighties and the weather excellent, the team had engaged in a voluntary summer workout. At about 5:00 p.m. the 6-2, 212-pound Wheeler from Ontario, California, a town about 30 miles east of Los Angeles—who had been working out inhaler in hand—found breathing more and more difficult. He left the field and collapsed. CPR was administered without success, and he died about an hour later.

By the time the shock wore off the lawyers were hard at work. Wheeler's mother sued the school, claiming that no ambulance or oxygen had been present at the workout, the on-field telephone had not been in working order, there had been too few experienced trainers on duty, and that those present initially had thought her son was suffering from heatstroke or hyperventilation and provided Wheeler with a bag to breathe into. The most devastating charge, however, was that the voluntary summer workout had actually been mandatory and, worse, that the school had violated NCAA rules by conducting such a practice without an adequate emergency plan. In short, Wheeler's mother charged that Northwestern and Randy Walker had been negligent, resulting in the death of her son.

Walker, a celebrated coaching star less than a year ago, and renowned for his intense commitment to physical conditioning—an approach that had arguably served as the backbone of the under-talented Wildcats in its championship season—was now under brutal siege. Jay Marriotti, *Chicago Sun-Times* columnist, called for his scalp publicly. Others joined in the chorus, openly questioning Walker and his demanding conditioning regimen.

Complicating the tragedy was that Wheeler was African American. It was one of the worst situations possible. A young, black man attending an academically elite university, one with a seemingly unlimited future, dies on the football field after enduring the grueling physical regimen designed by the white head coach. And with Johnnie Cochran as one of his mother's lawyers, the racial reverberations could not have rung more loudly.

The program has yet to recover from the death of Rashidi Wheeler. The 2001 team started auspiciously—4–1—but lost its last six in a row to finish a meek 4–7. Moreover, the losses were not all cliffhangers. The Wildcats were all but declawed at powerful Ohio State (38–20) and at home by a 6–5 Iowa bunch, 59–16.

It is hard to imagine that recruiting black athletes can be easy, especially now at Northwestern. First, the lofty academic standards favor students from exclusive college prep schools. They all but systematically obviate the admission of the vast majority of African Americans who have attended an inner-city high school. In addition, it is very unlikely that the Wheeler incident is not familiar among the remaining pool of eligibles—youngsters from well-informed middle-class homes. Moreover, with the case not yet settled, little can be said about it by any of the parties, most notably Randy Walker.

James and I returned to the Evanston campus on April 18 for a spring practice. Perhaps Northwestern was not interested in James; I don't know. But if they were, the staff used the Wisconsin method and badly flunked the hospitality test.

When we arrived at the football office no one was there to greet us. Instead, we were told how to make our way to the practice field. Once arriving there, we were "greeted" by a less than enthusiastic, forgettable young man who was in charge of squiring the recruits around. Practice had already begun, and James and I positioned ourselves just beyond the south end zone. Eventually the team scrimmaged.

Walker stood not more than twenty yards in front of us for much of the practice, constantly yelling, "Let's go, let's go," to his hurry-up offense virtually the instant a play ended. Walker's focus on the football equivalent of a fast-break offense was interesting to watch. Again, the key to it was a quick return to the line of scrimmage after each completed play, a tactic aimed at wearing down a less fit opponent's defense. Although these were quality, scholarship Big Ten athletes, none of the players seemed all that remarkable to James and me. Seeing the quality level of the players, particularly at his particular position, is one of the advantages for a junior who attends a spring practice. He can etch a performance standard in his mind.

Despite the lengthy, repetitive nature of the practice there was one non-Northwestern highlight for James and me.

"Hi, I'm Ed Zbikowski," said a barrel-chested, vital man with his hand extended.

"I'm David Claerbaut, James Velissaris' dad."

Zbikowski then greeted James warmly and said, "Let me tell you, you were by far the best player Tommy played against last season."

Spartan nemesis Tom Zbikowski may well be the most celebrated player with 2002 eligibility in the sate. His father's compliment was much appreciated.

The conversation turned to recruiting. "Say, I know Urban Meyer over at Bowling Green," Ed offered. "They run that spread offense and Jimmy would be just perfect there. In fact, I'm taking the whole [Buffalo Grove] team down there this summer; you guys should come."

I didn't know how to take Ed Zbikowski, what with his over-familiar style. He seemed genuine. The conversation continued and then he broke in, "Hey, here's my phone number. Give me a call and get Jimmy out to our place to work out with Tommy this summer. Tommy needs someone to push him and Jimmy can do it."

The practice ended without Walker making the twenty-yard trek over even to say hello. Amazing. Kirk Ferentz came from across the field to greet James personally at Iowa. Mike Dunbar, the offensive coordinator, did stop to introduce himself. A pleasant man, Dunbar said he would be in touch in the spring when coaches could visit the schools and call the kids. We talked briefly about the mind-numbing tide of letters and options for prospects like James.

"Believe me, it will be a relief when it's all over. It becomes a pain in the butt," said Dunbar with a chuckle.

15.

A Big MAC

James was getting antsy. Word was out about players, most particularly Tom Zbikowski, getting "early offers." An early offer is a nonbinding scholarship offer from a school, granted before the beginning of the youngster's senior year. It is nonbinding in that a student cannot sign a scholarship letter of intent until February of his senior year. For James, this was more than half a year, and a full football season away. Schools can rescind these early offers any time they choose. Sometimes they have to, having offered more kids than they are able to take. Some schools will "over-offer" as a policy, knowing that (a) every player offered is not going to accept, and (b) that such an offer can always be pulled off the table. The value of the early offer, however, is to communicate strong interest to a prospect such that he is favorably disposed toward the institution making the move.

"Why do you think I'm not getting any early offers?" James wanted to know. Players whose high school careers had been far less gaudy were receiving them.

I felt badly for him. He had worked hard, very hard, physically and mentally. It didn't seem fair that he, having truly paid the price, was being ignored while others were proclaiming to the local news media their good fortune. I was almost certain it was a matter of size. Although James was now pushing 175, the colleges didn't know it. All that most of them had was a tape of his sophomore and junior highlights, a tape that highlighted his diminutive physique as much as it did his gridiron exploits.

"Son, they don't know how much bigger you are," I explained. "Don't worry about it. Just dig in and have as much fun as you can in your senior year and the offers will come. You're the best back in the state as far as I'm concerned."

I was echoing Steve Helminiak's advice. "Doc, early offers

mean nothing," he said. "They're not official. Kids make way too much of them. Sure, most schools honor them if a kid verbally commits, because they don't want to get the reputation of not keeping their word. But most of those offers go to the absolute top guys, and the schools know they won't get all of them anyway. Tell James to have fun and have a big senior year."

But it nagged at James. He does not seek attention, but he appreciates what recognition he receives. He was noticing that although the talk about him was most flattering, it did not include scholarship offers. I could see getting an early offer would cement in his mind that he had made it—that if everyone else passed him over he would be playing football on a scholarship at some Division IA school.

I decided I would do what I could to get him one.

Central Michigan's Butch Jones had been very high on James and had urged him to come to a spring practice on Saturday, April 20. That date had originally been set aside for a Nike Camp at Michigan State to which James had been invited. Nike Camps are wonderful venues for an athlete to showcase his speed and strength. These camps are available by invitation only and are for "elite high school players with college potential" according to the Nike promotional piece. James, taking it seriously as he does virtually everything, trained in earnest, particularly on the forty and in his bench pressing. Several weeks before the camp, however, James pulled his right hamstring and decided not to go. It was silly for him to go with such an injury. Either his usual 4.4 forty time would be out of reach, or he might injure himself more seriously trying to burn up the track. Or both. As for weight training, however, he could now bench-press 255 pounds.

Central, then, was on the itinerary. Central Michigan University (CMU) is inconveniently located in Mount Pleasant, tucked away in an otherwise rural locale, more than an hour from Grand Rapids, which is more than three hours from Chicago. In short, going to Central entailed a considerable commitment. Western Michigan, located in Kalamazoo, had also been in regular contact. I suggested that we do a MAC twin bill, stopping at Western en route to Central.

I called Coach Bruce Tall, of Western, and told him we would like to stop by on our way to Central. "It won't be necessary," he said. "We are in the very early stages of our recruiting, but I would be happy to meet you."

The drive to Kalamazoo took a little more than two hours. When we got within about twenty miles of Western we stopped at a pizza restaurant for lunch. I was busy thinking about Western, Kalamazoo, the MAC, and Central as James devoured his pizza. He looked up and asked, "Do you think the country would have reacted differently to the Vietnam War had FDR been president?"

This was vintage James. He would be quiet and involved in some mundane activity, all the while digging deeper mentally. It was great fun to explore his question. I was a child of the 1960s, and I remember well the reverberating effects of Vietnam, civil rights, and the student revolts. I used to tell my daughter regularly, "Nothing has happened since the sixties." James had been taking a class at GBN that focused on recent American history, and despite his penchant for mathematics, he had found the class fascinating.

The pizza gone and the discussion suspended, we arrived at Western about an hour later. The football office, lodged in Waldo Stadium, was modern and extremely attractive. A young assistant, Brad Beerwinkle, then took us on a tour of the school's football facilities, ones that paralleled those of the Big Ten. Everything was shiny and new, or under construction. Waldo Stadium, already impressive, was being turned into an entirely closed facility, with stands wrapping around it completely. The coaches' offices were on the top level of the stadium, and they converted into luxury suites on game day. The weight room was cutting edge and designed for football use only. In the locker room, players' names were fastened on their lockers with gold plates. The training room was spacious and modern.

Bronco football was big league.

George Allen once said something to the effect that "there are a thousand clichés, and I believe every one of them." Head Coach Gary Darnell was a clone of Hall-of-Famer Allen when it came to gridiron proverbs. In every room there were myriad banners in gold and black trumpeting the virtues of hard work. "Having fun doing hard things," was the one I best remembered. Darnell was an established presence in college football, having done stints at places like Florida State and Notre Dame over his thirty-plus year coaching career. He had been at Western for five years and had won more games in that span than any other MAC coach. In 2000, faced with the prospect of losing him to a bigger-name school, Western signed the then fifty-one-year-old to a five-year contract.

Trying to ease my way to the subject, I asked Beerwinkle about early offers. "Although James is getting a lot of attention from some Big Ten schools, he is very serious about playing in the MAC. I know some MAC schools do offer early to get a jump on some of the bigger schools. Where does Western stand?"

"Coach Darnell is old school. Unless a kid is an absolute game-breaker he doesn't believe in early offers. I've talked with him about it, but he feels strongly on the issue. We evaluate each kid carefully and usually don't make any offers until the senior season is under way."

We met Coach Tall. A pleasant, African American man, Tall had been the defensive coordinator for an undefeated Harvard team in 2000, and was only now situating his family in Kalamazoo. "We're just getting organized now with our recruiting," he explained. "Things will gear up quickly. It would be a good idea to get James to our summer camp in June, though."

In two hours, I had already fallen in love with Western Michigan. It had everything—a beautiful campus, first-rate football facilities, and a location close enough to Chicago for Rita and me to visit. And it exuded success.

It was now on to Mount Pleasant. We stopped to eat the Friday night fish fry at a local restaurant off the highway, between Grand Rapids and Mount Pleasant. The food had been good, and I was enjoying our conversation when James asked, "Are you ready to go?"

"Why?"

"I don't know, I'm ready though," said James.

When we got in the car he told me, "I was feeling uncomfortable; there were people really staring at me."

Such is the luxury of being white in a white country, even with people of color in my company. I was completely oblivious to the reactions of those around me, feeling at home in this white, rural establishment. James, however, is not hypersensitive to race. He is accustomed to being in largely white environments. One of his birth parents is white. But he is alert to unfriendly surroundings, and this he felt was one of them.

We had a terrible time finding a place to stay because an amateur basketball tournament was being held in the town. By the time we settled in it was late, so we would have to find the university in the morning.

On Saturday morning we headed to the home of the Chippewas. The team gets its nickname from the Native American tribe associated with the locale. In fact, a rather gaudy Chippewa casino draws thousands to this little city. We, however, were not interested in slots unless someone was referring to an offensive set. CMU is spread over a wide expanse, so I asked at a service station for directions to the football stadium.

When we got there for our 11:00 meeting with Coach Jones, he was not there. We waited for about a half hour and Jones did not show. "Another coach took us down to the field reluctantly," as James puts it. "Our initial impression was somewhat tarnished." Indeed it was. "When you're coming off a three and eight season and trying to turn it around," said James later, "you better make sure you are impressing your recruits." CMU was impressing us, but not favorably. When we met Jones on the field, he did greet us enthusiastically: "Great to see you; I'm so glad you came; how're you doing?"

"Better now," I said tersely. "We waited a half hour outside your office before someone finally brought us down here."

"I'm sorry, I had some things I had to do," was his limp reply.

"I was glad you were forceful with him," James later said, "because I was upset about his being late." James also noted that Jones did not make eye contact with me when he talked, something on which James puts high value. "I really try my best and work extra hard at looking people in the eye when I talk," James explained on an earlier recruiting junket. "I know if I can do it, as hard as I try, I can expect them to do it. If they can't, how can they be honest? Lester Erb (of Iowa) did not look me in the eye when he gave me the spin."

As for Jones, James felt he was not being truthful: "He just didn't have any good excuse for why he wasn't where he said he'd be." Jones' style is, in a word, disarming. He speaks slowly and softly, his voice if not his eyes oozing sincerity and care. "We're really happy you came; I know it was a long drive," he said, smoothing the waters.

Soon we were off on a tour of the facilities. It was conducted by a polite and likable young man from Florida who had been re-habbing a knee injury. The athletic facilities, like that of Western, were new and "top of the line" by James' now experienced stan-dards. Interestingly, the student, a much-recruited fullback with whom James felt very comfortable, had had a similar experience to that of James with Wisconsin. "He told me he had been re-cruited by Illinois, Northwestern, and at least one other Big Ten school," related James, "but the guy really was interested in Wis-consin. He sent his tape there, and they sent it back saying that their recruiting was complete and they were not the least bit inter-ested. No thanks. Nothing. They just sent his tape back."

After the tour we went out to the field to watch the spring game. James was very impressed with what he saw. "The running backs didn't have a great deal of acceleration through the hole, al-though the defense was pretty strong. If anything, I was confident that I could play at this level."

Throughout the game, James and I stood on the sidelines or at around the fifty-yard line back from the action. Jones occasionally spoke with me in a friendly, familiar fashion. When the game ended, Jones invited James and me inside the dressing room, say-ing Coach DeBord wanted to meet James. We were taken past the players into the coaches' section, where DeBord was waiting to meet with James.

Mike DeBord, a pleasant-faced, balding man in his middle for-ties, was entering his third year at the Chippewa helm. After a 2–9 and 3–8 season, DeBord was anxious to move the program for-ward. He entered the Mount Pleasant campus with an excellent coaching pedigree, having served on Lloyd Carr's Michigan staff from 1995 through 1999, and holding the post of offensive coor-dinator on the Wolverines' national championship squad of 1997.

DeBord greeted us and after making a bit of small talk turned to James and said, "We're very interested in you, James. We would like you to spend a day with us at summer camp in late

June. It's very important. There our coaches can get a look at you more closely. A lot of decisions are made that first week after camp."

"I liked Coach DeBord a lot; he was one of the more genuine head coaches," James said later. "He was not arrogant, very likable, and straightforward."

We also talked again with Butch Jones. He was a key figure. Now offensive coordinator at CMU, Jones had spent three years associated with the NFL Tampa Bay Buccaneers and began his college coaching at Rutgers. Given his expressed interest in James through the mail and on the phone, I decided to make my early offer play. Sounding encouraging, Jones beat the drums for the summer camp. "James is high on our list. We really are big on him. It would really be good for him to get here in June, even for a day. The coaches meet as a group right after camp, and a lot of recruiting decisions are made then. If he impresses us there, he might hear from us very soon after."

Despite the early snag, I liked Jones. He took his time and answered our questions. Mainly, however, I really felt he was excited about James. That he got James and me in to see Coach DeBord reinforced that belief. I knew head coaches do not waste their time with marginal prospects, and I saw no other prospects brought that far into the inner circle.

We penciled CMU in for the last week of June. Central Michigan, however, had some huge barriers to negotiate should they want James to become a Chippewa. "I didn't feel very comfortable in Mount Pleasant," said James. "Something didn't feel right." He also had doubts about Jones. Tardiness, excuse-making, and an avoidance of eye contact put his credibility in question, something that is not good if you want to impress James.

16.

Valleys and Peaks

In the spring I e-mailed Edgy Tim about James. The advantage of having a different surname from my son was that I could get information about him anonymously, posing as a fan. The general skinny on James was that he had big-time speed, topflight moves, and excellent quickness, but lacking size (155 pounds) he did not figure to be able to carry the ball in major college competition. Knowing of his familiarity with James, I wanted to get Edgy Tim's slant. After updating Edgy on James' recruiting status, I asked him for an appraisal. Here is what he wrote.

> *Again, thanks for the heads up on Jimmy V! I feel that his overall size will be looked at closely by bigger D-1 schools, but that his overall speed and skills will most likely win them over . . . he won't be a full-time RB in the Big Ten but I can see him as a third-down type who will also return kicks and punts.*

Several months had gone by and we had not heard anything from Eastern Michigan, nor had anyone from EMU visited or contacted Glenbrook North. This really made no sense. Diaco had fawned all over James when we visited in February, my visit with Woodruff confirmed that James had all the correct fundamentals, and the Eagles did not employ heavyweight running backs; James was being sought after by far better teams than EMU while still showing strong interest in Eastern, and above everything else, here was a school that most definitely needed good players.

It was a mystery. James asked periodically what was going on. I decided to find out.

I tried to get through to Diaco several times, but with no success. After I identified myself as the father of a recruit, the receptionist would try to be as helpful as possible, but the answer was usually, "I'm sorry; he's in a coaches' meeting. Would you like to leave him a message?" or "I'm sorry; he's in Florida recruiting. Would you like to leave a message?" There was no point in leaving a voice mail. Diaco was not allowed by NCAA rule to call me during his blackout period, so I continued to try to catch him in the office. Finally, I did.

"Coach Diaco, this is David Claerbaut, James Velissaris' dad," I said cheerily.

"Oh, who is it again?"

"James Velissaris' dad, the running back from Glenbrook North. We haven't heard anything from you and so I wanted to see what was happening."

"I don't have that area anymore," Diaco said rather tersely. "I'm not certain who does; I'll have to find out and pass his name on to him."

The call gave me a pretty good idea of why Eastern Michigan was not winning, and why they probably would never win under Woodruff. Here was a virtual Marx brothers handling of a kid that could certainly help them. Most likely Jeff Woodruff would not have approved of this embarrassing snafu, but it was happening on his watch, and Woodruff would most certainly be the fall guy if the program didn't turn soon.

I did not pursue the name of the Chicago area recruiter for Eastern. I had had it with EMU. In retrospect, it was possible Eastern just wasn't interested in James. Perhaps he was too small or they didn't need running backs. That, however, didn't add up. Diaco seemed to know who James was when he visited in February, and he left no doubt that he would be at GBN in the spring to see Coach Whalen. Furthermore, James is an athlete—able to play in the slot, run back kicks, or play in the secondary if he isn't at tailback. We had given EMU no reason to believe he wouldn't play wherever they may need him, and judging from the condition of their program that could be a number of places.

I had called Eric Johnson several weeks before but he had nothing yet on James' tape. I decided to try again. "Iowa football, how may I help you?" the receptionist said.

I identified myself as James' dad and asked for Eric.

"He is here somewhere; let me see if I can locate him."

"Hello." It was Johnson sounding sleepy and grumpy.

"I'm getting back to you on James' tape," I said enthusiastically.

"We looked at it, and he's really too small for us," was the rather abrupt, less than friendly reply.

All that Iowa excitement dismissed so matter-of-factly. The solicitous treatment was no more sincere than the electronic "Thank you" one hears at a checkout counter.

"Are you all right?" I asked, hoping to elicit some warmth and an extension of the conversation.

"I just didn't get enough sleep, that's all."

"Well, thanks for the feedback," I said, groping for something to close things out on.

"OK, feel free to call if you need anything," replied Johnson, trying to sound a bit more cordial as our relationship was about to end.

I also spoke with Mark Hagen of Purdue. "Coach, this is David Claerbaut. I'm calling about where you have James. You did see his tape, I think."

"James is really not big enough to play for us on offense. We have him in the middle of the list as a possible d-back, but that's about it."

Here was another school that had pressed us to get to its summer camp "even if it's just for one day," just a few months ago. Now they couldn't care less.

"How big do you want your running backs?"

"Have to be at least 190 or better."

"Well, I thought James would be a good fit, what with his speed and your spread offense. Vinny Sutherland is in the NFL and he's about 170 I believe."

"We're going for big backs now," said Hagen, sounding as if he were hoping to get off the phone quickly.

"Well, thanks anyway," I said weakly.

Just like that. Two Big Ten schools that had appeared so promising were off the board. Not interested. Didn't want to be bothered. James was just a name to be deleted from their database. Worse, while James was being unceremoniously removed from consideration, there was more and more scuttle about kids getting early offers from Division IA schools.

The football world seemed to be passing James by.

I didn't know how to tell him. How do you tell a kid who is working out every day, downing carbs and protein by the gallon, and lifting weights every spare minute that he's not big enough? It's about as cruel as telling a teenage girl, after she has spent hours on her hair and makeup, that she is not pretty. I didn't want to break his spirit. No parent wants to do that. I flirted briefly with not telling him but decided that would be even more harmful. When he eventually did find out, it would take little deductive reasoning for him to realize I had not been candid with him, and his trust in me would be irreparably damaged.

"James, I talked with several coaches," I began, "and unfortunately the news is not good. Iowa and Purdue looked at your tape and feel you aren't big enough to run the ball in the Big Ten."

I don't remember what James' reply was, but he handled it with equanimity.

"You've got to remember, son, you were probably under 150 when that tape was made, and you're gaining weight. Look, you're probably 165 now and you may hit 180 by doubles. Then ten more after your senior year and you're Big Ten material. So stay with it."

"Well, I guess we can forget about Iowa and Purdue this summer," said James casually.

"I think so too. We need to get to Western Michigan and Central. You should have a good shot at the MAC schools."

Just as things looked the most bleak, James received a call from Jeff Monken of the Naval Academy. He was very interested in James and wanted him to consider going to Annapolis and playing football there.

I also talked with Monken. Navy had gone into almost complete football hibernation over the past years, and I was concerned about that. The Naval Academy is demanding enough without being a certified loser week after week. In a joking way, I alluded to this concern.

Monken was ready. "We're going to win," he said with his southern Illinois drawl. "We are going to win. Our coaching staff is almost completely new. It is from Georgia Southern, where we went sixty-two and ten over the past five years, including two Division IAA championships."

He had more to say—again very calmly. "Our head coach, Paul Johnson, was the offensive coordinator here at Navy the last time Navy went to a bowl. Then he left to take over Georgia Southern. Before that he was the offensive coordinator at Hawaii, where his teams were at the top of the nation in offense. It's just a matter of time, but as we get the players we will win here at Navy."

After talking to Monken, I felt, in a word, differently. I was impressed with the calm, confident, measured way with which Monken asserted his surety that all would soon be well for the midshipmen. Indeed, the coaching staff had quite a résumé, and I firmly believed that in the world of athletics, winners win and losers lose. Vince Lombardi is one of the first people to observe that winning (and losing) is a habit. People who win will simply not accept not winning. They may not win immediately, but they will eventually win. It coheres with their very identity. Conversely, a losing coach may win occasionally or in the years immediately following his taking over a winning program, but eventually he will be back to losing.

Paul Johnson is a winner. He was successful at Hawaii. The last time Navy went to a bowl, he had made them an offensive dynamo. Then he went south and won a pair of Division IAA national championships at Georgia Southern. If he left a plum job like that, he must have believed he could win at Navy. A guy like Johnson could have continued to play .800-plus ball and contend for NCAA championships at Georgia Southern until he got the offer he wanted if Navy were a guaranteed coaches' graveyard. But he didn't, and now he and the core of his staff were ready to turn it around in Annapolis. How exciting is that?

I was euphoric. The U.S. Naval Academy is one of the most prestigious and difficult institutions to get into. One of my best friends, Jeff Cummings, had graduated from Annapolis. I called him and told him about the contact from Navy. I told another Naval graduate, Walter Morris, one of the salespeople I work with in New York. I also told Steve Helminiak.

"That's great, doc!" he said. "If James graduates from the Navy he will have it made. It's really a great opportunity."

James was not as excited. Neither was his mother. After a week or so, James turned to me in the kitchen and said, "I don't think it's a very good idea for me to consider Navy. I know there's a lot of yelling and barking orders, and because I was exposed to so much of that in my family, I think it would be damaging to me emotionally."

When a seventeen-year-old uses terms like "damaged emotionally," you know three things. He is bright. He is self-aware. And he probably is correct.

I was disappointed. Navy was such an incredible opportunity, and if the program turned it would be ragingly excellent for someone like James who could cut it academically. But no healthy father wants to see his son damaged emotionally. No academic or career opportunity is worth that. "Then remove it from consideration, son," I said softly. "If you know the Navy would be harmful for you, we have to take if off the board. Nothing is worth that."

I suspect James was surprised, anticipating that I would try to talk him into considering Navy. But I would not. I had too long been trying to give friends and loved ones well-meaning advice and direction, and it had often been unwise. It would be arrogant for me to believe I knew better than James what was good for him. So, I took him at his word and resigned myself to looking at other options.

Then, just as the football sky was getting dark, the academic sky brightened. "Hi, how're you doing?" It was James, uncharacteristically calling on a Saturday morning from Northbrook. He was excited and halting. "I got my ACT score back. It's a thirty-two."

Thirty-two! A thirty-two will get you into any school in the country. The average Harvard football player enters with a twenty-nine. This changed everything. It had to open new doors. Although I never doubted that he would get an athletic scholarship, I was all but convinced he would now. James had now gone from being one of many outstanding college football prospects to being one of a very few student-athletes—African American or otherwise—capable of performing academically at any school anywhere.

But there was more.

In early June, James received a letter for CBS-Sportsline's *Prep Star* magazine. It read in part:

Dear Preseason All-America Nominee,

__Congratulations!__ You have been nominated by __PrepStar__ magazine as one of the nation's most outstanding football prospects for the upcoming season.

__PrepStar__ is the official college football recruiting source for __CBS-Sportsline__ and is the nation's #1 College Football Recruiting Magazine subscribed to by thousands of fans, sportswriters and college coaches across the country.

James was requested to fill out a questionnaire and send in a photo of himself for possible inclusion in the magazine.

There are a number of recruiting and rating services. It has become a virtual industry. For example, Coach Whalen told Rita and me that the Forbes Rating Service—based on an evaluation of a game tape—uses a four-tier approach running from "Now" (meaning the prospect was clearly a IA talent presently), down to marginal. Forbes had James at a two-plus. (A two placed a prospect in the "keep a close eye on" category.)

These bits of recognition paled, however, in comparison to a letter James received, dated June 10. Written on Falcon Football stationery, and signed "Sincerely, Urban Meyer, Head Football Coach," from Bowling Green State University, it read:

Dear James,

This letter is to officially offer you an athletic scholarship to Bowling Green State University. We felt you would be a great asset to our Bowling Green Football Program both as an athlete and as a student. When offering scholarships we will perform a thorough check on you athletically and academically throughout your senior year.

We are looking for players who can excel on the playing field as well as in the classroom. Our records indicated that we have that type of student-athlete in our program. Since the 1950's, Bowling Green is one of two football programs in the Mid American Conference that has won 60% of its games. Bowling Green has also won 10 MAC Conference Titles on the playing field. The tradition here far exceeds any of our competition.

*Our academic standings can be matched by no other oppo-
nent. In the last 10 years, our Bowling Green Falcon Football
team's graduation rate has either been first or second in the
Mid American Conference. Also, in 1998 our graduation rate
of 93% ranked first among all state supported schools in the
nation.*

*These statistics prove that you will be involved with a qual-
ity Division I program. Only twenty players will be offered
what you have been offered today. Remember, first and foremost your obligation as senior high school athlete and leader.
We hope you will become a future Falcon.*

Meyer added in handwritten script, "James—I enjoyed our
phone conversation in May. I look forward to meeting you. Come
see us—Give us a call—Coach Meyer."

There it was. An early offer, and from a MAC contender. The
Falcons had gone 8–3 in Meyer's very first season at the school after leaving Notre Dame, a campaign that included wins over Missouri, Temple, and Northwestern. For us, the offer came out of
cyberspace. James had heard little from the school before Meyer
called Coach Whalen, informing him of the impending early offer
letter. The hand of Ed Zbikowski was almost certainly behind it
("Say, I know Urban Meyer over at Bowling Green. They run that
spread offense and Jimmy would be just perfect there"), and I
could not have been more appreciative.

17.

The First Camp

Summer football camps, customarily held in June, are promoted as teaching enterprises. The football staffs of the schools offer fundamental and positional instruction largely to local youngsters that pay to attend. Most of the camps run for a week and are moneymakers for the institutions that sponsor them. They also serve a secondary purpose: They are thinly disguised tryout camps for college prospects willing to spend a day displaying their football wares to a coaching staff poised to evaluate them.

Virtually every school had invited James to its summer camp. The strategic challenge was to select which camps he should attend. Initially, Iowa and Purdue were high on our "must-attend" list, but they were eliminated once they decided James was too small. James was not interested in either Wisconsin or Northwestern, so both of them were dropped. Northern Illinois was beginning to make a lot of contact, but DeKalb was too close to Chicago for James, so we eliminated Northern. We also ruled out all schools that had not shown heavy interest, either by phone or mail.

As the winnowing-out process accelerated, we agreed to go to CMU first. There were several reasons. First, Central was not high on James' wish list, so he may as well acclimate himself to these tryouts where there was not much at stake. Second, it was a school open to making an early offer. Another such offer, once it became public, could open the gates for other IA schools to become serious.

With one offer in hand, and Rita joining us, we began our jaunt south out of Chicago, into Indiana, and into Michigan. I couldn't get Western Michigan out of my mind so I suggested we go through Kalamazoo on our way to Central. Because it was a weekend and we did not have an appointment with the people there, I was hoping at least to drive through the campus with Rita and perhaps see Waldo Stadium.

When we got to the stadium and parked in the lot, we noticed the gates were open. I hurried around the edifice to the side on which the athletic offices were located. Just as I climbed the steps to see if the door was open, a car suddenly pulled up. A large fiftyish gentleman, in construction clothes, got out.

"Can I help you? Who are you looking for?"

"My son is a Western Michigan recruit and we stopped by with his mother to see the campus. I was hoping someone might be able to show her around. Who are you?" I responded quickly and politely.

"I'm Gary Darnell, head coach. Our team is on a work project for Habitat for Humanity and I needed to run back here for a minute. I'm in a bit of a hurry, but I can show your family around for a few minutes if you like."

I was euphoric. Darnell, the renowned head coach would be able to meet James as well as present Western to his mother. "That would be just wonderful," I said. I raced back to Rita and James to tell them of my good fortune, and we hurried back to meet Darnell.

Gary Darnell, with his Texas twang, could not have been more charming or impressive. A powerful man with presence, he was gracious to Rita and James and gave them essentially the same complete tour as the one Brad Beerwinkle had conducted for us just a few weeks previous. I was really excited for Rita to see the interior of a major college football program.

Darnell did not try to sell the Western Michigan program. He simply showed it to Rita, James, and me. We spent a considerable amount of time walking along the second level of an addition to the end of the stadium, still under construction. "This will be our indoor practice field," explained Darnell. He was enthused about the facilities and his commitment to the Bronco program. "I have a revolving (self-renewing) contract," he said in passing, "so I will be here for awhile."

Darnell had been hot stuff after the 2000 season, when he posted his second consecutive West Division championship in the MAC. In his first four years—1997 to 2000—he had posted 8–3,

7–4, 7–5, and 9–3 overall marks, to go with a 24–8 MAC log.
When, fearing his defection to another, larger program, the university offered Darnell the five-year pact, I suspect it was sweetened with additional control and upgraded facilities. The past season, however, had not been a good one—5–6 overall and 4–4 in the conference—but with facilities and security like this, Darnell had to be confident that happier times lay ahead.

When we finished the tour, he took us upstairs and spoke with us in the hallway next to the coaches' offices. He was relaxed and unhurried.

"Coach, James is an honor student with a thirty-two ACT score, so we were wondering about a possible honors program," I inserted.

"Thirty-two!" Darnell exclaimed happily. "We have an excellent honors track here called the Leeds honors program. In fact, if he applies to that program, even though he would count as one of our scholarship athletes, the money would not come out of our budget."

Coach Tall was also there, and he told James he would get the honors packet out to him in a day or two.

"Your people have been staying in touch with James and we are really interested in Western," I said, setting up my punch line. "He does have an early offer or two. Do you know when you will be deciding on him?" I had already manipulatively inserted James' 4.4 speed into an earlier conversation during the tour.

Darnell didn't take the bait, and confirmed Beerwinkle's statement of a month ago. "We don't usually offer until a youngster is into his senior year. We are very thorough," he explained. "But keep us informed as to what's going on with other schools. I really hope you can get to our summer camp in June. There you can meet the coaches and get a better sense of what we do here."

The ubiquitous summer camp offer. This, however, was one I wanted James to attend.

"Let me see if Coach Cordelli is here," said Darnell. "I would like you to meet him. He's our running backs coach.

Cordelli, who had been the top man at Kent State in the early 1990s after serving on Lou Holtz's Notre Dame staff, is a sturdy, vigorous-looking man with dark hair, a ready smile, and a pleasantly firm approach. He greeted us and took James aside, handing him a ball. "How do you hold the ball?" he asked in a terse, yet friendly fashion.

James cradled the leather carefully. "That's it, that way no one can strip it," Cordelli said approvingly.

James was gaining weight but worried about its impact on his speed. "It won't make any difference," Cordelli said reassuringly. "You're putting on muscle, not fat, so if anything you'll be faster."

Thanking Darnell and his coaches profusely for being as gracious with us as they were, we left for Mount Pleasant.

Rita was impressed, particularly with Darnell. "I really like that Southern gentleman," said James' discerning mother. "I feel comfortable having James with him." She was no more impressed than I was. Western Michigan was now my first choice.

James was not very talkative. Tomorrow was his first camp, his first opportunity to perform under the evaluative eyes of a college coaching staff. He did not want to fall short of his best.

It was a warm June morning when we drove to CMU. Once again we were to meet Coach Jones at his office, and once again he was not there. Once again we had to find him on the field, and once again he was charming and affirmative when we caught up with him.

Summer camps vary in routine, but this one began with an issuing of workout clothes and a weigh-in. Rita and I watched through the glass as James stood in line with the one hundred or so other boys waiting to be weighed in. After the weigh-in there would be a bench press test as well as a timing on the forty. Not being able to see much of this, Rita and I left for a while. We ate and toured the town of Mount Pleasant. The city is a college town with a sizable enough resident population to provide all the basic amenities of urban or at least suburban life. You had to find those amenities in Mount Pleasant, however, because the city is isolated in the core of the Wolverine state.

When we returned in the afternoon it was hot. I repeatedly went down to the sidelines and filled Rita's water bottle using the drinking hose provided there. In the stands with us were the likable Paul Saad and his son, Nick, whom we had run into at Eastern Michigan in February. I introduced Paul to Rita, and soon the discussion turned to football and recruiting. Nick was unable to participate in the drills due to an undiagnosed injury.

Asked about James' recruiting status, I sailed right in. "Things are moving along. He's got one early offer already—from Bowling Green—and we are getting a lot of interest here and from Western."

"Nick is getting some attention from Purdue, Indiana, and a number of MAC schools, but he hasn't got anything yet," Paul related.

I felt like a heel, shooting off about James' early offer with Nick right there feeling the way James had felt just a month ago. It was unintentionally insensitive, but Paul was classy enough to overlook it.

I could sense Nick's pain—unable to perform and filled with teenage uncertainty.

"Nick, early offers don't mean anything. They're not really binding," I said gently. "James wanted one in the worst way, too, but the colleges told him he was just not big enough. He is blessed to get one, but it just came in. Besides, it's early and things will happen. Try to have fun and keep going hard."

I could guess why Nick had not yet been offered. He was a 'tweener. He was well over six feet, really too tall to be a running back in college. Yet, he was not heavy enough for tight end or linebacker. I didn't know if he had the speed to play d-back. In a word, Nick was the perfect high school player who may or may not be able to fit physically into a college role. We talked about that.

"Where do the colleges have you playing?"

The answer was what I thought, everywhere and nowhere. It was hard for me to believe, however, that he would not be offered eventually. Schools like Purdue and Indiana do not linger over kids with no future. This was a big, bright, and polite young man, willing to do what it takes to play in college.

"You have a lot of options, Nick, and you're going to get bigger. Once they decide where they want you, you should be getting some attention," I said sincerely.

I lowered my tone the rest of the time as the conversation continued with Paul, Nick, and Rita. All the while I kept my eyes on the field, noticing everything James did. He was easy to spot—faster and darker than most of the boys. Drills included both pass catching and pass defense. There was no contact, as the kids were not insured against injury.

When the drills ended I went down to the sidelines to greet James briefly. He was sweating intensely in the blazing heat. One Detroit area college coach came up to me and said, "If they don't take this kid here, we have a place for him." James looked satisfied with the day and headed into the indoor facility with the rest of the participants for Coach DeBord's closing remarks.

With the youngsters sitting on the Astroturf surface, and their parents and friends standing farther back, DeBord was at his best. "If there is a word I want you guys to remember, it's the word 'finish.' That's right 'finish.' A lot of guys can start, keep going for a while, and play well. The question is: Can they finish? Bill Parcells has said that he looks for guys who can finish—guys who play through the adversity, through the last down of the fourth quarter. To do that, you have to have mental toughness. You have to be resilient, able to get up when you're knocked down, and able to keep going. You can't quit. You have to be tough enough to persevere and stay with it. You also have to be physically tough. Football is a tough game. You have to pay the price, be in shape, ready to go long and hard."

DeBord was impressive, intense, and inspiring. It was the perfect address to give to a group of sweaty, winded youngsters after a long, hot day of practice.

When the group was dismissed, Coach Jones rounded up Rita, James, and me. Hoping for some assurance of an early offer, I listened to Jones carefully. "James had a very good day," he said in his slow, soothing tone. "He has a lot of ability and he did well."

"You know he's got an early offer from Bowling Green, and he scored a thirty-two on the ACT," I said matter-of-factly in as low-pressure a tone as I could muster. "I know everyone does things differently. When will you know something, coach?"

"We're going to be meeting as a staff over the next week or so to discuss the kids we are recruiting. I'll know more then. Feel free to call me anytime. I'll help you any way I can."

It was encouraging but noncommittal.

Rita and I waited enthusiastically for James in the car, while he showered and cleaned up. When he got to the car he jumped in, slammed the door, and crossed his arms across his chest. He was enraged.

"How did it go, honey?" Rita asked sweetly.

"Let's go!" he said in an uncharacteristically demanding tone.

"James, we're interested. It looked like you had a good time. How did it go?"

"I said, 'Let's go!'" James repeated, jerking his folded arms abruptly and angrily. He had a furious expression on his face.

"You seemed to be enjoying yourself," I said.

"I was terrible."

"But James, Coach Jones said you showed well," I countered.

"He's a liar."

"That other coach even came up to us on the sideline and said if Central didn't want you, you could play for him."

"Yeah, at Division II!"

James was angry, hungry, and inconsolable. He didn't want to go to any other summer camps ever. He softened a bit once he ate, but he persisted in the belief that he had had a terrible camp.

"The guy who did the d-back drills was a jerk; he kept getting on me," James stated. "I told him I hadn't played defense before, but he made fun of me." Some players respond with healthy anger to a demeaning coach. James does not. He will give it everything he has in any sporting activity, and he assumes the coach involved will see how deadly serious he is as he goes about his business.

There was more. He had gotten off to a bad start on his forty-yard dash time. He had turned in a 4.7, three-tenths slower than his usual 4.4. That is a huge spread—the difference between speed and blazing speed, between major college speed and wanna-be speed. He had also fallen well short of his usual bench press numbers.

James had allowed a diminution in performance, particularly in his speed number, to play with his head. From there he pressed all the harder, enjoying nothing, and beating himself up internally over everything. The sprint issue is an interesting one. Tom Zbikowski's forty times have ranged from 4.3 to 4.9. Ed, his father, spoke to me about it.

"Those times are almost never the same," he explained. "So

many factors—the weather, how a kid feels, if he has an injury—
have an impact." Add how quick the timekeeper is with the gun,
whether the players begin standing or are in a three-point stance,
the condition of the surface, and a host of other things, and time
variances become the norm. Nonetheless, a slower than expected
forty time can be distracting to kids like Tom and James.

"I don't let anyone time Tommy on the forty anymore," Ed
later told me. "If they want to time Tommy I say, 'Get your fastest
player out here and let Tommy race him.' There's no way a coach
will take that challenge. He's not going to risk his fastest kid losing to a recruit."

By the time we got home, James had settled down.

"This is a good experience, son," I said calmly. "You're probably not going to go here anyway, and now you know what to expect when you go to Western and Bowling Green."

"Maybe I overreacted a little. There was only one kid, a running back from Detroit, who could compete with me."

I did wonder if we would be hearing from Coach Jones any
time soon.

18.

Broncos in Heat

James and I left Sunday afternoon after church for what would be a summer camp twin bill. On Monday he would be in Kalamazoo at Western. We would then drive through the night to Bowling Green, Ohio, for a Tuesday session there. I loved the commutes because they gave us uninterrupted time to talk and the ambience seemed to stimulate James verbally.

We began discussing the importance of making the right college choice from a football standpoint. "I talked with my cousin, Nick, from the University of Michigan," James related. "He has a friend who got a scholarship but never played. I don't want to go to a school like that and not get a chance."

I knew all about the impact of talent differences. There is a huge talent jump from high school to college, and from college to the NFL. At each level, the athletes get bigger, faster, and stronger. Northwestern, in 1970 and 1971, posted winning seasons being led by an All–Big Ten quarterback, Maurie Daigneau. I remember a conversation I had with a friend of mine several years later. He had played with Daigneau. "Daigneau was really good. He was all-conference and could really throw," said Dennis Boothe. "I hadn't seen many guys throw the ball with any more zip than he could. Then the following summer I went to a Dallas Cowboys practice here at Northwestern. They were getting ready for the annual College All-Star game held in Soldier Field back then. I saw Roger Staubach get up from the bench and start warming up. That ball came out of his hands tighter and faster just loosening up than I saw it come out of Daigneau's in game conditions."

Boothe wasn't the only person I had met who had eye-popping experiences watching the finest athletes perform. In 1994 I was sitting next to Calvin Jones on a cross-country flight. Jones, an impressive 6-3, 185-pound African American, was on his way to a tryout with a major league team. He had spent part of two years as a relief pitcher with the Seattle Mariners. Jones had been a teammate of Michael Jordan's on the Birmingham Barons, during Jordan's ill-fated attempt to make it as a Major League outfielder. Jones raved about Jordan's generosity and willingness to be one of the guys. That, however, is not what I remembered best about our discussion. It was a story he clearly enjoyed telling, about a first-hand experience with His Airness' athletic greatness.

"One off-day, my buddy and I decided to take Jordan on in a two-on-one game of hoops. We were going to bet a hundred bucks each against him. When we told Jordan, the first thing he said was, 'You're going to need a third.' We didn't believe that. Both of us were professional athletes. We figured if we spread the court out he couldn't cover us. We were going to play to ten.

"'I want to be able to dunk on you guys,' Jordan said. 'So let's play to seventeen. I have to get seventeen before you guys get ten. I'll bet you two-to-one—four hundred to your two hundred.'

"We took the bet and had the ball first. We spread way out. My buddy led me perfectly on a long pass, and I got a wide open break to the basket. Then, just as I laid the ball up, I see this hand snapping the ball out of the air.

"He beat us 17–4. Once he really got going he started trash talking. 'I hate to take food out of your families' mouths,' 'how're you going to eat with me taking your money?' that sort of thing.

"When it was over we each gave him our money. He took it, looked at the money slowly, and then threw it on the ground. 'You peons,' he said laughing, 'you need this worse than I do.'

"We scooped up our cash and never challenged him again."

James was not trying out for the NFL, but in his case even a small talent difference could have powerful implications. Big-time college football is just that, big time. For coaches, it's a Darwinian enterprise. They either win or go. Therefore, no matter what a kid may have been told when he was recruited, they will play the players they believe give them the best chance to win. You may be an All–Big Ten talent, but if the guy in front of you is a sliver better, he will play and you won't. How often do you see a star running back get injured, only to be replaced by the number two man who, himself, turns in hundred-yard rushing performances?

Where was that kid before the starter was injured? On the bench. Not playing.

And sometimes they stay on the bench. "Some years ago Michigan had a kid who had been the state sprint champion," Paul Saad told us at Central. "I doubt that kid had fifty carries in his career."

This, then, is the argument for the MAC. Our door to the Big Ten and the other power conference schools is wide open. I was convinced James could play d-back at that level now, provided he improved his vertical leap. But we can only make one choice, and James' primary criterion is to play—preferably running back. He has the best chance of doing that in a MAC school.

Once settled in our room in Kalamazoo, James turned to me and said, "Do you want to get something to eat and go bowling?" Because James is always hungry—for food and activity—the question hardly took me by surprise. I was hungry for neither, but I knew it would be selfish not to go out with him.

I asked if the Olive Garden would be satisfactory.

"Very satisfactory," was James' verdict. After eating the endless salad items and watching James plow through a heavy plate of pasta, we took off for a nearby bowling alley. Not once did I break a hundred, but I did manage to split the four games we played. It was most amusing trash-talking James and watching him burn with rage in the games in which he bowled poorly.

The next morning when we arrived at Waldo Stadium it was already blazingly hot. Temperatures were ninety-plus with the humidity high. We were greeted by Coach Tall, who took James with him. I went back to the air-conditioned room until noon, and then spent the rest of the day at the university library doing some research. The library, also named after its first president, Dwight B. Waldo, was as spectacular as the rest of the campus was impressive on this sultry summer day.

At 5:00 I went back to the stadium, where I ran into Recruiting Coordinator Mike Cummings. I wondered if he had moved over from EMU or simply had the same name. "If you want to relax here you can use my office," he said invitingly. The office was new, modular (to make it adaptable as a luxury suite), and spacious. There were chairs, a couch, a computer, video equipment, and snacks. "If you take a nap, you're going to be waked up," he said, warning me of occasional drop-ins.

One such visitor was a young man named Mark Ottney. "Is Coach Cummings here?" he asked.

"He's hiding under the desk," I said in an attempt at harmless sarcasm.

After explaining who I was, I probed Ottney to get a sense of his feeling about life as a Bronco. He was a lineman from Troy, a suburb of Detroit. A redshirt, he had gone from 265 to 287 over the past year. He proudly pointed to his name, prominently situated on the depth chart written on a metallic board. I asked why he had chosen Western, despite getting early offers from other schools.

"They were no-nonsense. They were honest with me. They said they would look at my tape and see me play and get back to me," he explained. "And they did. Not all of them follow through. You'll see that as you go on. Got any early offers?"

"Yes, Bowling Green offered him."

"I won't lie to you; Bowling Green has a good program," the big lineman replied, "but I like it here."

With the camp day over, I went outside where James was with Coaches Tall, Cordelli, and Cummings. "There were sixteen beers in that fridge; how many are left?" Cummings asked with a laugh.

"Sixteen, but a few waters are gone and some food." I was intensely curious about how well James had shown, confident that he had done much better than he had at CMU. I probed Tall, his recruiter, but I couldn't get anything out of him. He said he hadn't been with James.

"James did really well," said Coach Cordelli in typical coach speak. "We're very interested in him." The most encouraging sign was nonverbal. All the coaches were together lingering with James and me, rather than dashing off for home or other duties on this boiling night. They were talking with James, when I made a quick exit in the direction of the stadium men's room.

I felt very optimistic, upbeat, and ready to go. With Western behind us—and maybe better yet, in front of us—we were off to Bowling Green. At least I thought so.

"I don't know if I should go to Bowling Green," James blurted out. "It was really hot today. I'm really tired. My legs are dead."

I was stunned. How could he be that impulsive? I less than kindly told him he had better go to Bowling Green, that this was not the last tough day he would have, and that the kids down there were probably pretty exhausted from their day in the Ohio sun.

"If you think it's mandatory, I'll go," James replied politely.

I lightened up. "Just get something to eat, lay back; we'll be in Bowling Green by midnight. Just eat and stretch out."

James is partial to Jimmy Johns submarines, and there was one such establishment coming up as we drove. James ordered the ham submarine. After devouring it in the car he recovered his energy and spirit.

I asked him how it went, thirsting for some substantive information. Now more talkative, James came through. "Coach Darnell talked to me a lot. He said I was on top of the list. I don't know if I'm number one, but there was only one running back there who could play at that level. Coach Cordelli, the running backs coach, talked to me a lot and said how happy he was I was there."

"OK, son," I said. "I have a question. Based on your experience at Western today do you (a) like it less than you did, (b) like it the same, or (c) like it more." I hoped he was leaning toward the Broncos.

Ever brief, James managed to answer in a single letter. "C."

But now he had a question. "What if I like Bowling Green? Should I commit?"

"I want you to be happy wherever you go, and have a good experience," I answered. "There's plenty of time."

We talked on and listened to the Cubs–Reds seesaw baseball game. With the runners on base and the game in the balance, I looked at James. He was asleep.

We traveled east on I-94, then south on I-69 (to Ft. Wayne, Indiana) on the way to I-80 east and on to the Ohio turnpike. We got to Maumee, Ohio, between Toledo and Bowling Green, at 11:30. I ran the bath for James, as he got ready to stretch out and send his aches into the warm water.

19.

BGSU

James was not talkative when he got up on Tuesday, June 25. I could feel the heaviness in him and asked him what was wrong.

"My stomach hurts."

We drove through Amish country, down state highway 25 to Bowling Green State University. It was very rural, flat land, with no evidence that a major university lay anywhere ahead. Then suddenly there was a sign. We were entering Bowling Green, population: 29,000.

"This is the first time I've been to Ohio," James said. "Five-sixths of the town's population is the university."

We couldn't find a place to eat until we went all the way through the town. There was Godfrey's, a local restaurant. A kindly, wrinkled old woman waited on us. James, however, was quiet, in another zone. He was not friendly to the waitress or me. After returning from the bathroom he was a bit more cordial.

"My stomach hurts."

"How?" I asked.

"Upset."

"Why so quiet?" I wanted to know.

"Thinking." James had, by his standards, done poorly at CMU. Although he had fun playing at Western, I found out later he was not really comfortable there. Now it was down to Bowling Green. He didn't want a negative experience there. We left the restaurant and headed north on the main street. We then turned on Wooster and passed some of the campus. There were a series of 1950s-constructed buildings, not new like WMU. We proceeded off into the edge of a rural area on to Doyt Perry Stadium, an older-looking brick structure surrounded by acres of flat land and not many pathways to it.

From there it was up the stairs to the athletic office to meet Gregg Brandon. Brandon, a tall, instantly likable, athletic man

with glasses, delivered a welcoming handshake. James was happy
to see him. The early offer, backed by Brandon's warm style, was
assuring.

"You're his dad. Come along with me," Brandon offered.

We went down the hallway. The building was old and long
with small offices on the side, giving one the feel of walking
through a large mobile home. It was very un-WMU. Brandon's office was small, consisting of two chairs, a desk, and a metallic
board with the usual assortment of sayings displayed. One involved some seven keys to success, beginning with having a burning desire and ending with the value of reading the Bible.

"Really glad you're here. Are you staying till the end?"

"We'll be here the whole day," I answered.

"James, do you want to play some defense? We have seven-on-
seven drills at night till dark."

The defense question was a dreaded one. Although James was
hoping to play running back, and said so, the question raised an
important issue. Often schools will recruit a player at one position
and then move him to another once he gets on campus. The concern is not whether the school moves him, but rather whether the
coaches intended to move him all along—in a sense deceiving him
by having an unverbalized agenda. James and I wanted to know
where each school intended to play him. It would enter into any
final decision.

"Well, they're going to play till about eight or nine, until it gets
dark. We'll get you on a team."

James nodded eagerly. I guess his stomach didn't hurt too
much.

"Excuse me," said the informal, extroverted Brandon. "I'll call
Coach Mullen [all coaches are called 'Coach']. 'Hey, I got a top
draft choice for you. You'll whip up in seven on seven. Come in
and meet him.'"

The younger Dan Mullen was similarly extroverted. "Where
you from, Chicago?" remarked the hyper Mullen asking an empty
question and giving us no time to answer. "Hey, we've got a lot of
guys here from Buffalo Grove. Tommy Zbikowski is here."

In walked Urban Meyer, the head coach. Very poised and professional, Meyer is under forty, and like Brandon and Mullen,
looked like one of those guys you see running the health club or

the beach volleyball tournament. He turned to face me, "You're his dad," he said, looking for confirmation.

Meyer's style was more official. (I only had to say my name once to Brandon and he was already calling me "David.") We entered Meyer's office. He shut the door, an immediate indication that he was going to dig in. Though also old and small, Meyer's domain was a bit larger and sported a "2001 MAC Coach of the Year" plaque right behind him.

"How long a drive is it from Chicago?" he asked as a warm up question.

I told him we had come from Kalamazoo, but that was also a good trek.

"Well, we're really happy you came. I understand your staying into the evening."

After a bit more small talk, Meyer was ready to sell. Whether because it is politically correct or not, he opened with academics and how pleased he was with the performance of his Falcon players in the classroom. Then it was on to football.

"We finished twenty-ninth in the country last year—twenty-ninth," he repeated for impact. "We've been moved to the Western Division of the MAC, because Central Florida has joined the conference."

"Central Florida?"

"It was between Central Florida and Navy," he explained. "The conference wanted to hit that southern bowl market. This addition gives us a tremendous boost. There is big TV in that Orlando market, and now possibly as many as five bowl opportunities."

I mentioned my academic and athletic director career experience, and how I was happy about the annexing of Central Florida, what with the MAC getting but one bowl bid the previous season.

"Two. In addition to Toledo, Marshall played East Carolina in the GMAC," he corrected.

"Anyway, this is good because the MAC never gets the proper credit. You guys have proven you can play belly-to-belly in the Big Ten."

"We beat the purple (Northwestern) last year," he chimed in. "We pounded Toledo." He then went on to list other MAC triumphs over Big Ten teams along with near misses. "Look at Marshall. Everyone knows who they are. They have a Heisman Trophy candidate there (quarterback Byron Leftwich)," he stated proudly.

Quickly the subject moved to academics. "James, what are you interested in studying?"

"Economics. What are the college's specialties?" James inquired.

"The business school and school of education are big here. We have the highest graduation rate in the conference," Meyer responded. "I can tell by talking to both of you, you'll graduate."

"James has an ACT of thirty-two. He's interested in an honors program," I said.

"My goodness! Thirty-two! I can't count to thirty," Meyer exclaimed. "My sister is an economist. She did a dissertation—isn't that what it's called?" I told him I had done one too, and that indeed is what it's called.

"It was book length—on the Russian economy," he said, sounding impressed. "What was yours in?" he asked. I told him briefly and we went on.

"Be back here this afternoon and we'll set you up with some of the academic people right away. With an ACT of thirty-two, man, I imagine you have some goals," said Meyer, raising his tanned left arm. I noticed that a wedding ring was his only piece of jewelry. He had a picture of a strikingly attractive wife and youngster on his desk. Then he started to sell. "You know, James, successful people like to be with other successful people. Out here you will be with college kids. You know in some of the larger places— places like Cincinnati and Ohio State—you get kids off the street in those schools, mixing with the real students. You get this (he banged his fists together to indicate a clash). Here you hang out downtown with college students."

He went on. "You probably noticed. You really get evaluated at this level. I coached at Notre Dame (his last stop), and at schools like that it isn't that way. They go off Tom Lemming's national master list, circle the top three names in an area, and that's how they recruit. If you're one of the top three in Phoenix, a school like Notre Dame will recruit you. Here we look at the names, check into a kid, look at the tape, and decide—working an area from Cincinnati to Chicago. We looked at your tape—great speed, excellent moves, strong ball possession, and we really liked you."

"I always felt the MAC should rival Conference USA for publicity," I said. "They're up in hoops and down in football compared to the MAC.

"I can tell you are up on things. We are above the WAC and right there (arm parallel) with the Conference USA. Our league played in two bowls last year and won both—Toledo over Cincinnati, and Marshall over East Carolina."

We left and went down the stairs and outside to register and pay for James' participation. Soon he went running to the car, stomach obviously OK, in search of his helmet.

I walked over to Urban Meyer and Gregg Brandon, standing among throngs of youngsters, who were in the shadows outside the walls of the stadium warming up. I asked what time I should return.

About noon was the agreement. Urban Meyer lingered for a moment giving me a sense he wanted to talk. "We got five hundred kids here," he said, impressed.

"You're a young guy," I offered, "the kind I would have been looking for in my days at North Park. What was the draw here?"

"You can win here. Come along with me." We walked inside the stadium—a typically majestic structure. A high scoreboard adorned the south end with Kroger a prominent advertiser. "See that," he said, pointing to the press box with a list of the years Bowling Green had been MAC champions. "Second-most championships in the MAC.

"I coached with Lou Holtz, Earl Bruce, Bob Davie, and Sonny Lubick," he said, rattling off his coaching résumé, "and they all told me the same thing. Go somewhere where you can win. I could have gone three or four other places, but I didn't want to get buried and lose."

I told him of Ron Ellett's unhappy experience at North Park.

"It takes a commitment," he said firmly. "I wanted to be sure I had an AD who wanted to win. All I want to do is win and graduate kids."

I could feel the ambition radiating out of him, despite his controlled demeanor. Later I talked with an insider about Meyer. "Urban is a straight-shooting in-your-face coach. 'Here's what it takes to win a championship. If you pay the price you'll win.' If not, then (the man raised his thumb) the term in the business is 'running 'em off.' He probably ran fourteen, fifteen guys off of last year's team." It was what I expected. I had no reason to dislike Meyer. He was courteous, professional, and accessible. Yet there was a distant quality about him, the sense that he was not a guy who might be easy to get close to. That under that polished, controlled exterior was a hard-nosed competitive man, did not surprise me.

"It's tough in South Bend now," he volunteered. "High academics, a tough schedule, and demanding alums." Indeed it was, particularly for Bob Davie. The word was that Davie had back-doored Lou Holtz, reporting on the looseness of the program. There was much to the charge. Celebrated author John Feinstein described Holtz as "an intense, paranoid little man who tried to hide the intensity and paranoia behind a self-deprecating sense of humor that was amusing for a while, though it soon wore thin."[*] Bill Parcells has described coaching as a narcotic—an addiction to the highs and lows of competition. In his book, *The Final Season*, he says that it makes no difference how much a coach may have won; if he is not winning now the question arises: Will I ever win again? Holtz won early—a national championship in his third year, 1988. In the six years from 1988 to 1993 Holtz's teams finished the season in the Top Ten five times, four times in the Top Five.

Holtz may have been a tortured soul, but he enjoyed his celebrity, appearing on late-night television shows and regaling audiences with quips, witticisms, and magic tricks. All of this was rather cute as long as he was continually contending for national championships. But when in his last three years Notre Dame's highest ranking was eleventh, with one of his teams failing to finish in the Top 25, his act became old. Beyond that, his wife had become seriously ill. Worse, however, he had pushed hard to get talented players into Notre Dame, some of whom were hardly em-

[*] *Civil War*, p. 179.

blematic academically or socially of the values of the nation's
foremost Catholic institution. This was chronicled in a bitter, one-
sided 1993 book entitled *Under the Tarnished Dome*. Holtz eventually became vulnerable, his lack of victories the target of angry
and often unreasonable subway alumni, and his lack of control of
the program the legitimate concern of defenders of the tradition of
the institution.

Enter Bob Davie, who had gotten the job without much trac-
tion. He had no previous major college head coaching experience,
nor did he have Notre Dame ties. He had joined Holtz's staff from
Texas A&M. But it was worse. "You can't lose at Notre Dame,"
a man well connected there told me. "If you win inside the rules
they'll stay with you. If not, you're in trouble.

"Davie, however, did not do the politically correct things.
Never even had dinner with the admissions director—you've got
to stay close to that guy. Tyrone Willingham did that his first
week. Besides that, Davie didn't believe in Midwest players. It was
all Florida and Texas. Then Midwest kids proved they can play at
the highest level. He lost and was out."

It's hard to assess Davie's tenure. He entered with the cupboard
less than full, and he did seem to tighten up on the type of young
men Notre Dame recruited. But he made some terrible coaching
gaffes, particularly in game situations, leaving him open to the ire
of disgruntled Irish fans longing for a return to annual national
prominence.

The Notre Dame job is often described as the toughest job in
coaching. The man sitting in Rockne's chair is at the vortex of national attention. There are promos to do, speaking engagements
to make—enough to fill every day on the calendar—charities to
support, and interviews to grant. And then you have to win football games in your spare time. Ara Parseghian left after the 1974
season and ,though still in his prime, never coached again. Neither
did his able though often vilified successor, Dan Devine. Gerry
Faust was ground down by the job, and Holtz spent several seasons recovering in the CBS broadcasting booth before resurfacing
in South Carolina.

Meyer and I walked out of the stadium and I half picked his

brain, "You've got to figure Eastern Michigan is struggling," I said hoping he would deliver an insight.

"They haven't been winning," said Meyer, returning to the theme. "I don't know the guys well up there."

I told him of junior day at EMU, my meeting with Woodruff, and that we "never heard from them again," hoping to draw him out.

"Hey, how are we doing with recruiting? How do we compare?" he asked, not taking the bait.

"You came a little late but the mail is really coming now," I said. "And with personal notes."

"You got to mail things," he said authoritatively, "make it visual on the envelope, show pictures of teams, and add those notes."

"Only Iowa really keeps up," I said, remembering the Hawkeye persistence. "But it's a lot of clichés and they get old. Others will send stuff with the gummed label."

"Can't have that. Need to be personal," said Meyer, although James had received some gum from Bowling Green.

With that we parted.

In the afternoon, I returned to Brandon's office, where James was watching tape intensely and with great enjoyment. "We are waiting for a business prof who doesn't show up," said a welcoming Brandon.

Soon James was off with a pretty coed for a tour of the facilities, and Brandon invited me to ride around the campus on his golf cart. I asked him what condition the program had been in when he and Meyer arrived.

"Terrible. The last coach won with his predecessor's guys and then didn't win since 1995."

I asked him if he was surprised at the turnaround. "Nothing surprises me since Northwestern," he answered.

The tour of the larger campus was actually rather impressive. Being with the gregarious Brandon was especially enjoyable. We stopped in the student union at a Wendy's for lunch. "How does your wife like it here?" I asked.

"My wife is OK with it, but she liked Chicago a lot," he

replied. Brandon had done stints at Wyoming and Northwestern, and his wife was from a Chicago suburb. "My youngster at home is happy anywhere. My older one is at Purdue."

I talked about the size of the Bowling Green running backs. "Our running back this past year took a real beating, wore down by the end of the season," the offensive coordinator related. "He was about 190."

Later that day, as he marveled about James' athletic skills, he told me, "Keep helping him get bigger."

"How much?" I asked.

"We want him about 185." Later his number dropped to 180.

After lunch we got back on the golf cart and headed back to the stadium. "How have kids changed since when you started in 1981?" I asked.

"They've changed," Brandon quickly replied. "It's become 'what can you do for me?' Quick outcomes, a weaker work ethic. It's part of the computer age. You punch in the keys and get the answer. It undermines the learning process."

"Do you want to be a head coach?"

"I still think about it," said the forty-six-year-old. "But I see what Urban goes through and I wonder if it's worth it. He's had so little time to coach. You have to fight so many battles. Then there's always the NFL, but it's so hard to break in."

With the afternoon drills about to begin, Brandon graciously told me to make myself at home in his office if I chose.

"Hey, you know Eddie Zbikowski's here and he's looking for you," someone informed me. Soon Ed entered Brandon's office for a chat.

Tom Zbikowski already had thirteen early offers. "Now he's leaning toward Nebraska for quarterback, Notre Dame, and Iowa, in that order. He likes it here as well. It's just too early," said the expressive, robust Ed.

We talked about how surprisingly clean the recruiting had been up to now for both James and Tom. "You wonder how it will get when you start saying no," Ed mused.

Neither of us liked Illinois or Wisconsin. Reemphasizing how early we were in the process Ed said, "You know there have been guys offered in June after their senior year! Some guy gets an offer, accepts it, and then gets involved with the cops over some gang-banging incident, and, bingo he's gone. Now the coach is short one player and says, 'Whose good out there and will graduate? Hey, Jimmy Velissaris is a thirty-two ACT; offer him.'"

I told Ed of our strategy: Go to the MAC schools so they know we're interested, and if James lights it up in his senior year there will be plenty of Big Ten interest anyway.

"That's the way to do it," Ed affirmed. "If Jimmy has the kind of year he had last year, man, if he gets that kind of yardage, boy he'll be OK! No hurry at all. Listen, James may start number three on somebody's depth chart—and that's not bad—then number one goes to Michigan, and number two to Penn State, and bingo your number one.

"It's an industry," said Ed with a laugh.

"I know Edgy Tim," Ed offered. "I'll have him call you and get it on the wire that James had a strong camp at Bowling Green and got an early offer from them, and you'll see more action," said the ever-helpful Zbikowski. "But getting those offers is a blessing and a curse [he moved his hand in an up and down motion]. They're not so nice when you say no."

"Why doesn't James get interest from Notre Dame?" I asked.

"Tommy got an early offer because he's Polish and Catholic and has good connections. They had him offered before Tyrone Willingham got there, and you have to wonder if Willingham is saying, 'I don't know if I want this guy.' You've got to figure they're going to the West Coast to get kids. That's where the staff is from." Later in the recruiting process, Willingham visited the home of the Zbikowskis. With his honest, articulate, and warm manner, he made a superb impression.

Ed and I then left Brandon's office. He invited me to get in his car to ride around on the perimeter of the field and watch the kids play. The conversation turned to the MAC and how it stacked up with the Big Ten. "The difference between the MAC and Big Ten is depth," Ed opined. "They can stay with those guys and beat 'em in the opener, but by the third or fourth game they would wear down."

Soon Darren Hamilton, an assistant athletic director, came in. Hamilton's story was inspirational. Born in the Bronx, Hamilton had gotten into trouble and was sent to a military academy. He lived with his grandmother for a while and then was adopted by a family in North Carolina. A marvelously gifted athlete, his unstable background figured to doom him. "I entered Penn State with the equivalent of a thirteen ACT," he stated. "At Penn State, from 1982 to 1985 I played in three bowls, twice for the national championship. Won one, lost one. I went on to play in the USFL, which folded." Then things crashed again.

"I blew out my knee and had little money left," he related. "When I looked around, I saw four things: Guys in the army, on drugs, in jail, or dead. I made a decision to change my life. I started associating with successful people and left that behind. Then Joe Paterno called and asked me if I wanted to be an academic adviser. Watching my money run out I jumped on it. I spent a few years there, got a master's, and became an assistant athletic director at Cheyney State. I worked for the state in education, got a Ph.D., and came here where I'm now over all the student athletes."

Then he turned to James and asked about his grades and interest in learning. "The importance of learning was inculcated at an early age," he answered. "My mother's in real estate, and my dad in consulting." I was flattered to hear him refer to me as his dad.

Hamilton was impressed. "James is so well spoken," he observed. "I never ever heard a seventeen-year-old use the word *inculcate*."

During the afternoon session, I rode the golf cart with Gregg Brandon while a series of seven-on-seven games was played. In seven on seven, each team gets the ball forty yards from the end zone and has four downs to score. James labored anonymously among the players that had already been at camp for several days. Then, on a single play, he was all the rage. The quarterback faded and threw the daylights out of the ball. It sailed hopelessly over James' head, or so it seemed. Sensing the moment, James flashed on his burning speed, stretched out his hands, and grabbed the ball coming not over his shoulder, but over his head.

"He made the play of the camp!" exploded Brandon. Brandon looked around, hoping Meyer had seen the circus catch. "Urban is jacking around back there and didn't see it," said Brandon, "but Coach Bowers [the recruiting coordinator] did."

At dinner time, Ed Zbikowski gave me the key to his room so I could take a nap to rest. The drive to Chicago would take the better part of five hours. In the early evening it was more seven on seven until it became too dark to play. Brandon and Meyer could not have treated James better. They walked us to our car together, leaving the other five hundred campers for the moment. Each gave James "the Bowling Green handshake."

"Be careful," said the ever-expressive Brandon. "That can mean you're going to be a Falcon." Both coaches hugged James. Then Urban Meyer looked him in the eye and said, "You got the offer; how do you feel now?"

James felt very good. "E-mail us and we will be in touch," said Meyer. He then added, "Dr. Claerbaut, good to meet you and please drive safely." With that it was one more hug for James and a handshake for me.

20.

Ready to Blow the Doors Off

I was not enamored of Bowling Green. While the staff was sprightly, charming, and loaded with energy—an extremely attractive group—the facilities were substandard and the school's distance from Chicago was almost intolerable.

It was a long trip home, but in this case I looked forward to it. The car was our best venue for conversation. I had mentioned earlier to James that there were three reasons why I was not favorably disposed to Bowling Green. "So what are the three reasons?" James asked almost the minute he shut the car door.

"The staff is young. I don't like their backgrounds, and Urban Meyer won't be there." What I meant was that I sensed a lack of long-term stability at Bowling Green. The youthful staff had scarcely gotten there, they had come from high-pressure you've-got-to-win backgrounds, and their leader, I felt, might jump ship the minute a larger, more prestigious program beckoned.

James, however, loved it. I asked him why.

"This was, by far, the most fun I had. This camp was the best run, had good instruction, and I didn't feel as if I was trying out, that I was being evaluated. I could just have fun. The coaches seemed to enjoy coaching rather than just evaluating you."

"So you're glad you went. You seemed pretty uneasy this morning."

"I guess that experience at Central really messed with my mind," he admitted.

I then addressed the issue of belongingness. "If that feeling of not being evaluated, being part of the team, is the major issue, then you will definitely be deciding for Bowling Green," I replied, "because they're the only offer so far. But it's so early. You may hear from another school—Western, a Big Ten school—and once they offer, you may feel exactly the same when you hear how certain they are about you.

"Son, these guys are young—ambitious—there's some selling going on. I would take Western's word to the bank. Their campus is much better, but Bowling Green is nice once you get on the inside of the campus."

I talked about their setting James up with a "flirty" girl for the tour. She wasn't obvious, but James confirmed her flirtatious quality.

I went over Ed Zbikowski's point about depth charts, and so on, and the discussion moved to styles. "I like Bowling Green's offense better than Western's. But I really need to know how Western would see using me."

How suggested position, and Urban Meyer had talked with Ed about James' potential as a defensive back. James had a quick response when I passed that tidbit along to him. "If I'm going to play defensive back, I can do that in the Big Ten."

"There's no doubt in my mind that you can play d-back in the Big Ten," I said. "You're just as fast, can recover as well, are much smarter, and are just as athletic as guys there right now. All you lack is height."

"I would have to work on my vertical leap. But do you think they lied to me at Bowling Green?"

"No, I think they are buying some wiggle room to put you where they need you in case they're set at running back but weak at d-back," I said.

We talked about the importance of football. "For a long time football was all I had. When I came to the realization that so much of what I had been living in emotionally was unreal," he said, referring to his life after his parents split, "football was what kept me from going crazy."

The conversation moved to the issue of size, a subject about which James was very sensitive. He got up in his seat and talked energetically about it.

"Taking a beating is a mental, not a physical, thing. Let's be serious; what is weight anyway? I ran at 140 as a sophomore and I just decided to put the pounding out of my mind."

Nevertheless, caloric intake and working out had been the focus since the end of his junior season. "I want you to eat any and every time you are hungry," I would tell him. "But there's more. You have got to get enough sleep. You are not going to get bigger if you don't get enough sleep. You will be counteracting the effects of the food supplements and the lifting and running. It is in sleep that your body repairs itself and growth is stimulated."

It was a hard sell that off-season, especially for a young man who now had a teenager's social life and talked on the phone late into the night.

There were discouragements along the way. James would weigh himself and be found a bit wanting. The eating, lifting, and sprinting weren't loading him up sufficiently by his standards. I veered back and forth in my conversations with him. Usually I was upbeat. "Look, son," I would say, "next season is a long way off. You put on about fifteen pounds between your sophomore and junior year. If you can put on just 20 before kickoff next season, you will be at 175, pushing 180. There are Big Ten guys running at 175. Then you have a year after that to get bigger yet, not to mention possibly being redshirted as a freshman."

Occasionally, however, I took a lower road, once again focusing on getting in early and sleeping adequately. "I don't need that much sleep," James would retort, thinking perhaps I was trying to excise all social dimensions from his life. Although I succeeded in assuring him I had his well-being foremost in my thinking, getting home early and sleeping more were tough items to promote to the high-energy teenager.

With the summer camps in the history book, James' primary focus was now on his senior year. He had made it to 175 and I felt he would be OK on the weight front by the following spring. Just ten more pounds in a year and he would be within five pounds of what many major college running backs played at.

He was also much, much stronger. Driven by a desire to break tackles and run with power, his body now rippled with definition. "Don't worry about the colleges, son." I kept telling him. "You've got one early offer and a number of other schools on the edge. Besides I think you'll blow the doors off this season."

Returning from Bowling Green I asked him about the lack of early offers and our not employing a recruiting service to promote him around the country. "I think this will turn out for the best. If

I had gotten all that attention that Zbikowski got as a junior, I might not have worked as hard. Now every time someone says I'm too small or not as good as someone else, I use that for motivation to drive me."

"Why did it mean a lot to you when I told you that you would always be my son?" I asked, moving to the personal.

Again, a thoughtful response: "It meant that it wasn't just because of my mother that you spent time with me."

"Did you have trouble trusting me?"

"Actually not, because you were with my mother and I trust her," said James calmly.

"Any particular thing that helped you trust me more?"

"Just time and getting to know you," he replied.

I talked with him of how hard being a stepson or stepparent can be. "It's not like being a birth parent. All authority and respect has to be earned. If you don't like something you can always say. 'You're not my father.'"

Shortly after our return from Bowling Green, James got another surprise. This one was from the Bearcats of the University of Cincinnati. The letter, which came later, was dated July 8 and sent over the signature of Head Coach Rick Minter. It tells it all.

Dear James,

Congratulations on your outstanding accomplishments as a student-athlete and a major college football prospect. We have reached a very important step in our evaluation process of you as a potential University of Cincinnati Bearcat Football player. We have determined that you are a young man that represents the successful qualities from which our football program has been built.

I would like to offer you the opportunity to receive a full football scholarship to the University of Cincinnati. The offer includes room, board, tuition, fees, and books. This is the same full scholarship that any Division I school can offer you. Our future success will be enhanced by your commitment to the University of Cincinnati. This is an outstanding opportunity for you to further your academic and athletic careers at one of the top nationally recognized academic and athletic uni-

*versities in the country. We will be informing your Head Foot-
ball Coach of our interest and intentions.*

*Once again, we encourage you to take advantage of this im-
portant opportunity at the University of Cincinnati.*

This one came totally without warning. Cincinnati, a Conference USA school, had made little if any contact with James before
we received word, through Coach Whalen, that they were offering
him. Though caught by happy surprise, we knew that once the
word got out, this could only help to prompt some other schools
to step forward.

It was July, and with doubles starting in a month, training continued in earnest for James. High school football is now a year-
round sport for athletes in large schools with successful programs.
In fact, one of the distinguishing characteristics of a successful
program is that its athletes engage in off-season, unofficial practices. Four summers ago, with GBN coming off a winless campaign, football began essentially with the opening of doubles in
August. James has not had a summer job in the two years he has
lived with us, but has worked harder than most teenagers with
paid employment. His daily summer regimen included unofficial
practices with teammates, followed by lifting and other workout
activities, and then more football practice of some sort.

Although I would love to see an IHSA (state) rule, outlawing
virtually any semblance of off-season practices, moving prep football out of the category of an industry back to a sport, his mother
and I supported his efforts. We viewed James' football prowess as
a gift, if you will, not unlike that of a highly skilled musician. We
felt we owed him the opportunity to develop that gift if he had the
discipline to do so.

James was most assuredly not spoiled. In a high school heavily
populated with students from society's upper economic stratum—
teenagers owning or driving new cars and having the latest tech-
nological toys—he drove a thirteen-year-old car and did not own
a cell phone. The reason for such frugal treatment was that we
knew his peers were wholly atypical socioeconomically of the nation's high school student population at large, and we wanted him
to prepare for a life in reality.

"Are you looking forward to this season as much as the last
two?" I asked him as the season drew nearer.

"More, because I'm now a leader and have responsibility for the other players," said the conscientious cocaptain.

He had indeed paid the price. He had faithfully taken the food supplements, the power protein/carbohydrate mix. He had lifted the weights and now had genuine, muscular upper-body definition. He had practiced throughout the spring and summer, leading his teammates in unofficial practice sessions, and had led the team in seven-on-seven park district league tournament play.

Glenbrook North was also ready. GBN, as it is referred to, is no longer a school with a football team. It is one with a successful football program. A few short years ago there was not enough interest in off-season weight training, let alone unofficial spring and summer practices. Three successive Central Suburban North (CSN) championships and three straight trips to the IHSA playoffs changed all that. GBN was riding a fifteen-game conference winning streak and had posted a 27–5 overall record over those seasons, 25–2 in the regular season.

The coaching staff was intact. Frank Whalen was in his second year at the throttle, while Bob Pieper, who had begun the GBN football turnaround, was now assisting with the offense.

"I asked you this last year, son, so I'll ask you again. How do you see the team compared to last year?"

"We should be stronger on offense," said James. "We have three starting linemen back as well as Kevin [Kaspers, an all-conference quarterback with solid pocket throwing skills]. We lost a lot of guys on defense, but about five of us are going both ways." In brief, the games figured to be shootouts. The veteran offense, which averaged nearly thirty-five points a game in his junior season may well post bigger numbers in 2002 while the defense may take a while to jell.

All that sounded just fine to me. A veteran line meant big holes for the tailback. Big holes meant big rushing numbers and big recognition. Should the defense struggle a tad, well that wouldn't be altogether bad either, because it meant closer games and more time on the field for the starting offense.

With two early offers in hand, and a passel of schools from the Big Ten, Big Twelve, Big East, and Southeast Conference showing interest, an explosive season could dial up James' opportunities.

21.

The Opener

At last, the daily unofficial summer practices were over. The college camps were over. Doubles were over. Preseason hype was over.

It was time for Illinois high school football.

With the opener scheduled for a Saturday, James and I headed for River Park near our home in Chicago, at 10:00 p.m. on the Friday night before. He wanted to test his shoes. I stood in the light of the street lamp on Foster Avenue and watched while James ran and jogged back and forth, back and forth on the sod. He was so much bigger than two years ago. No longer a boy, he had become a young man. After about ten minutes he said, "OK, I'm ready." We got in the car and returned home, and James went to bed.

"I'm leaving," said James hurriedly and excitedly as he stepped into our bedroom and let his mother and me know he was on his way to school on the summery Saturday that followed. The team would open at Vernon Hills, a school about fifteen miles north of Glenbrook North High School. I expected big things. James had been mentally and physically ready for this day for weeks.

The Vernon Hills Cougars, their initial opponent, had a solid 8–4 season in 2001. They were coached by Tony Monken. Monken was a cousin of the Navy coach, Jeff Monken, who had unsuccessfully recruited James. A playoff team in the season previous, the Cougars figured to provide the Spartans with some decent competition in the opener. Nonetheless, they did not come into the game with as strong a recent history as GBN, they had no player as renowned as James, and they are a 6A school, one level down from GBN. A careful look at the schedule indicated that a victory here could put the Spartans on the way to another undefeated regular season. Game two was at home against a hapless Taft team from Chicago, and this was followed with a game at

Evanston—a team the Spartans beat a year ago—and then Niles West, another beatable squad. That did it for the nonconference schedule. The rest of the games involved CSN opponents, none of which had defeated a GBN team for the past three years.

I had mixed feelings about the 2002 season. I simply lacked the same enthusiasm of the previous years. I knew what James could do. I fully expected him to blow the doors off this season, anyway. In many respects I just wanted the year over with James healthy and settled in at the right college. But there was a season ahead, and one toward which he was really looking forward—his senior year—his and his senior teammates' last hurrah.

Let the games begin.

James would not have the opportunity to duplicate his sophomore achievement of turning the opening kickoff into a touchdown. He would have to wait this time, because Vernon Hills would receive the opening kickoff. Nonetheless, the season got off with a bang. For Vernon Hills. Two fumbles by James—one of which was turned into a touchdown—and no holes through which to run had us down 14–0 by the second quarter. "We need to get a score here and go in at the half with some steam," I said to Rita as the clock ticked down toward the half. "We get the ball to open the second half, and if we can score then, we will be back in business."

We didn't, and it was 14–0 at the half.

I felt terrible for James. The first half had been an absolute disaster for him. Two fumbles. I remember him "putting the ball on the ground," as he put it, perhaps three times all last season and he lost only one. I knew he would beat himself up emotionally over those turnovers. He always did. In 1997, when he was in seventh grade and playing junior Spartan football, he fumbled late in a game, contributing to a tight loss. He was so distraught his mother put me on the phone with him that evening, and I reminded him that even one of his then heroes, Barry Sanders, fumbled on occasion. Only time and success seemed to heal those hurts for James. Now, however, there was little time and little obvious portent of impending success on the horizon as I drained my beverage and waited for the second half.

Playing at defensive back on third down and other obvious passing situations, he did get a big pick in the first quarter, the in-

terception halting a key Cougar drive. His rushing numbers, however, were lilliputian as the Vernon Hills defense keyed on him
and the line produced little daylight. In addition, with GBN
putting two men in the deep receiving position on kickoff returns,
Vernon Hill prudently kicked away from James, taking away a
major part of his game.

My mind was spinning back and forth. After losing but one
regular-season game in two consecutive dominating seasons, and
that loss nearly two years old, staring defeat in the face in the
opener was very hard to come to grips with. Constant winning
hides both the difficulty involved in winning but also the pain of
defeat. You just don't factor in the possibility of losing. But now
we had to. GBN was not just down, they were down two scores
and showing no signs of football life.

The Spartans would open with the ball in the second half. If
they could put their stamp on the game right out of the second-
half gate, they might be able to reverse the tide and restore order.
That seemed the only hope. Two touchdowns were really not that
much for an offensive juggernaut like that of GBN, but up to now
there had been no points at all.

With my mind generating happy scenarios of hope, the second-
half kickoff approached. GBN took the kick and marched down
the field resolutely. The Spartans looked very different. They were
disciplined and efficient as they drove toward the south end zone.
James powered in from the four to make the score 14–7. Vernon
Hills did not answer with a score, but GBN did push over another
touchdown, tying it up at fourteen. Now we had them on the
ropes. "If we score again," I said to the knowledgeable fan standing next to me in the back row of the visiting stands, "this could
still be a blowout."

My optimism was fed by the emotional nature of the game. For
Vernon Hills, this was a chance to spring an upset, and they had
set the stage well in the first twenty-four minutes. But the ferocity
of the Spartan response, I thought, might sew the necessary seeds
of doubt in the home team's mind and open the door to a comfortable GBN win.

But the Cougars had the stuff. Ace running back Matt Leffler
busted the ensuing kickoff registering a ninety-five-yard touchdown. Twenty-one to fourteen. Then another fumble by James on

a last-second attempt to return a punt, with the Cougars cashing another seven-point ticket, and the game was an out-of-reach 28–14. The debacle ended 28–21.

The whole thing was—to use a popular word—surreal. It was one thing for James to play on the losing side of a football game. He had done that but three times in two high school campaigns, only once in the regular season. It was quite another for him to be a factor in a defeat. That, quite simply, did not fit into my scope of reality. In other losses, the opponents simply took him out of the game, ganging him every time he touched the ball. The Cougars most certainly did plenty of that, as the statistics indicated. They held James to seventy-one yards on twenty-one carries, and one short yardage tally. In addition, James had only one run for double-digit yardage. "We wanted to pile as many blue shirts on him as possible," Coach Monken was reported to have said. Nonetheless, this loss owed to more than stopping James. It involved turnovers. I was having a difficult time getting my psychological arms around the event.

Enough of that. I wanted to see if I could make some connection with James before he left the field.

I stood by the end zone gate through which the visiting players would pass as they left the field. There were very few other parents there. I hoped to greet James as he went by and stared closely at the field looking for number 22. As he approached, our eyes met. "It's only the first game, not the last," I said, as we touched hands on his way by.

So this is how it feels to be the parent of a member of the losing team. All the clichés come to mind. You feel worse for your kid than for yourself. How can it not be so? Though only a game, it's such a huge event in a life not even two decades long as compared to all the events in the life of an adult well into the middle years. For the youth, it is one of nine days for which he has prepared intensely and about which he has had perhaps the most grandiose of dreams.

I hoped James would handle the loss maturely. There were reasons to worry, given his intense personality. So intense is James that early in his junior year he told me he didn't like to talk about an upcoming game after Wednesday of game week. I recalled the day of his very first game as a varsity regular two years previous when his mother called me at a consulting assignment over the problem with his shoes. He had hid his discomfort with my joking well, as he immersed himself in his inner teenage world.

In any case, with a lot of free time on a Saturday night to brood, a high school peer group located many municipalities away from our home in Chicago, and a likely stay-over with his father, calamitous opportunities were everywhere. The less than serene thoughts of fast cars and the ever-present allure of under-age drinking rippled through my mind.

The drive home was awkward. There was not the usual victory to celebrate. Even worse, Rita and I were both thinking the same thoughts. I wanted to say something if only to break the tension. "They weren't ready; I didn't see much emotion out there, " I said to Rita as we drove home. "The wins have come so easily, so reg-ularly. They thought they could toss their helmets out on the field and win."

"I hope James is OK," she said, stating the only thing on either of our minds.

22.

A Surprising Turn

The phone rang about 8:00 p.m..

"Hi, how 'ya doing?" said the monotone voice. It was James.

"How are you, son?"

"I'm OK," he said, not sounding OK. "What's going on?"

"I'm just sitting here watching the Notre Dame game. Look, you're welcome to come over and watch it with me, or just be by yourself if you would like," I said, wanting him to know there would be no unwelcome rehashing of the game in the offing. He remained noncommittal, and the conversation ended moments later.

Nevertheless, I was relieved. It was James' way of telling us he was handling things well. About 11:30 the front door opened. It was a quiet James. He went to bed almost immediately without a word said about the game.

The next morning I saw him sitting forlornly on the couch, ready to go to church. Knowing he was feeling responsible for the abrupt end to the hopes of an undefeated season, I walked over, put my arm around him, and said, "This is the worst game you will ever have, and again it's only the first game of the season."

He broke into an anxiety-expelling laugh. "I played scared," he said quietly. "I put pressure on myself. I wanted to break every run for a touchdown. I wanted to do everything perfectly."

James had played "tight." There is a difference between being tight and choking. Choking refers to a fear of failure, often a desire to flee, not to compete. James wanted to play, wanted to do battle. He had simply wound himself up way too tightly with an eye toward reaching perfection. He tried to avoid making a single mistake only to make a bundle of them. Nonetheless, there would have been no shame had he choked. Often you will hear a professional athlete say, "We don't choke; we're professionals." What rubbish. Presidents choke. Surgeons choke. Lawyers choke. Ministers choke. Unemployed people at an interview choke. Choking goes on at all levels.

I learned this firsthand working in sports psychology with professional athletes. I once worked with a highly renowned, American League lefthander from a divisional championship team. In between one of our sessions he started against a powerhouse team from another division. I listened on my car radio with dismay as he loaded the bases in the first inning, only to throw the home run ball to the opponents' premier hitter, all but putting the game out of reach. When I saw him several days later I asked him what happened. "When I saw him up there with the bases loaded, I had a brain cramp," he said.

One utility player wanted to see me because he couldn't handle the pressure of going into games as a late-inning middle infield replacement. "I can't win," he said. "If nothing happens no one notices, but if I make one error I've failed because all I'm out there to do is field the ball perfectly." In another case, I had a series of long, wrenching conversations with a one-time 100-rbi hitter who, after years of physical recovery, was getting one more chance. He was terrified of failing, wondering if his mind would release his body to hit.

Sports are about pressure. Vince Lombardi said that the more you've got to lose, the greater the pressure. This is why free throws are missed at critical moments, why hitters develop hitches in their swings when the game is on the line, and why football players fail to make routine plays at game-deciding moments.

As for James, the whole experience was ugly. "The team wasn't ready," he went on. "Then right before the game, a coach turned to me and said, 'I only want one statistic from you, James, no fumbles.' That really messed me up."

The no-fumble directive was an innocent remark. It's the kind of thing coaches regularly say to ball carriers. In fact, he may have said it to get James to relax and focus on fundamentals rather than try to ring up a touchdown every time he touched the ball. Given how focused James is on perfection, however, it was the wrong thing to say. It was a negative, distracting thought. Its negativity is important in a subtle way. Psychologists have determined that the use of a negative term like *turnover* or *fumble* only focuses the mind on the negative item, thereby increasing the likelihood of its occurrence even if the word *don't* precedes it. Hence, some coaches use positive phrases like *take care of the ball* or *possess the ball*, to keep the focus entirely positive. Nonetheless, no responsible player would be so defensive as to attribute James' fumbles to a single ill-phrased remark.

I asked about the fumbles. There just had to be a reason other than carelessness, given James' obsession about taking care of the ball. "On the first two, I was trying to pick up an extra yard and they tore the ball out as I went down. On the last one, the punt, I was going to fair catch it, but then at the last second Coach Pieper yelled, 'Return it!' and I dropped it." It made sense. Certainly the two rushing ones. James is obsessive. Obviously, this was a year in which he had purposed to break tackles, grudgingly gaining every last yard, and going down only when the defenders could pull him to the turf.

I didn't want him to carry the mental effects of this catastrophe into the next game. I wanted him to put it behind him. "You need to get a big win Thursday [against Taft] to get this out of your mind," I said.

"I will be over it if we win the afternoon road game at Evanston," said James.

"Is James there?" said the man on the other end of the phone Sunday night.

"No, he's out with his friends."

"This is Coach Brandon from Bowling Green. Did you guys play this weekend?"

"Yeah, they played the opener Saturday afternoon," I replied, hoping to duck the "Did you win?" question.

"How did you do?" There it was.

"It was a tough one, coach. The other team hit us with early scores, and we just ran out of time trying to catch them. It ended 28–21 with us having the ball. They were really prepared and maybe the toughest team we will face this season."

"How did James do?" There it was, the inevitable question.

"He broke a few, coach," I said, spinning like a politician and realizing that "not well" would have been more honest. "But by the time we really got it going the guys just ran out of time."

"Well, tell James hello and tell him the scholarship offer is still good and we're very interested in him. Sunday and Wednesdays are the best nights for me to call, so I'll call again Wednesday."

Not long later the phone rang again. It was Bowling Green Head Coach Urban Meyer. It was a near repeat of the call with Brandon, but very reassuring.

"James is taking it hard," I said at the close of the call, once again spinning intensely. "This is just his fourth loss in three seasons counting the playoffs."

After still another coach called with a similar perfunctory conversation, Jeff Monken of Navy weighed in. Curious as to the impact of the new coaching staff at Navy, I asked Monken how Navy did in its opener against favored SMU in Texas. "We won 38–7," he said matter-of-factly. "There were over a thousand students waiting for us at the airport when we got back from Texas."

I was greatly relieved. Although James would never state it openly, I knew he would be wondering if the Vernon Hills debacle had hurt his standing with the colleges.

James was groggy from an early-evening nap on the couch when I handed him the phone from a college coach on Tuesday night. The conversation went on for some period of time, and when he put the receiver on the cradle he turned to Rita and me with a somewhat befuddled look on his face and said, "I don't know for sure, but I think I've just been offered a full ride from Navy." (The fact is that anyone accepted to the U.S. Naval Academy in Annapolis gets a full ride. The Academy sifts through some 11,000 applications yearly and grants entrance to 1,100 new members of what it calls the brigade. Those 1,100 get what amounts to a quarter-million-dollar education when one divides the federal allotment by 4,400, the total enrollment at the Academy.)

The excitement in the living room was discernible. This changed everything. We knew of the Navy's interest in James, but this was different. It was a commitment to one of the most exclusive institutions in the country. And it had come just after James had turned in his worst career effort in front of the Navy coach's cousin from Vernon Hills.

"I guess the Vernon Hills coach said some good things about me," said James. "Navy invited me for a visit whenever we can come. He would like us to come this Saturday for their home game."

Despite the ambivalence on both James' and his mother's part, we quickly agreed he needed to get to Annapolis to see the Academy for himself. Fortunately, because the next GBN game would be played on Thursday night owing to a Jewish holiday that weekend, Friday and Saturday were open for a visit. It also meant possibly connecting James and me with my daughter, Rochelle, attending law school at George Washington University in nearby D.C.

First, however, there was a game to play on Thursday night.

I felt sorry for Taft. I didn't count even twenty players on their sideline, symbolizing what has happened to football in so many city schools. Football is a tough, physical game. The season is long, running from mid-August till at least the end of October—November if your team makes the playoffs. It starts in the heat of summer and ends in chilly, late autumn when the leaves are brown and the nights are cold. And the season seems a lot longer if you are on a losing team. I played two years in high school, often serving as hamburger for the varsity in practice. Our coach, Pat Baggott, used to say after a bad varsity outing, "It's a long season if you lose." Fortunately, we had no losing seasons under Baggott, but the season did seem long to me. Day after day, there were tough physical practices, and often intense scrimmages against guys much bigger than I. Getting into varsity games, even during mop-up moments as a freshman or sophomore, was for me an ambivalent experience. On one hand, the thrill of being on the main stage of my high school football team was pulsating. On the other, I was trying to perform well against much larger varsity players, already angry about losing to us and anxious to lay it on the guys off the bench.

The experience at schools like Taft had to be even more trying than my own. Even as a varsity player, there was no status in being a member of a dead-end football team. On the contrary, it meant being humiliated week after week by more talented, better equipped, and more acutely trained teams. As such, I admired the small band of youngsters on the Taft squad. Their very presence was a statement of character and courage, given the violent hits and almost certain series of embarrassing drubbings they would be sentenced to. Furthermore, they would have few fans to support them. Only a sprinkling of parents showed up to watch the city team face off with the vengeful Spartans. Secretly, I rooted for Taft at least to make a showing.

They didn't.

It would be a 60–0 rout. James scored four touchdowns, playing less than ten minutes in the demolition. It could have been 100–0. The game was so one-sided that as the team closed out the first half, Whalen—who admirably tries not to run up the score—mercifully had Kaspers take a knee while in Taft territory rather than score yet again in the closing minutes of a half that ended with GBN forty-seven points ahead.

Rita and I left early in the second half, realizing James was not going to play anymore in the massacre. It was just as well. Taft may have been on the field, but I had Annapolis on my mind.

23.

Anchors Aweigh

James and I were on the first plane out to Baltimore-Washington International (BWI) on Friday morning. While waiting at the gate for our seat assignments I told James to keep his identification handy.

Referring to our different skin hues and last names, I coaxed a laugh out of James, saying, "Let's face it, son, you and I have credibility problems even being seen together."

James is a wizard at directions, so rather than turning back after making an incorrect exit with the rental car I had him guide me back in the direction of Annapolis. The ride was pleasant and pretty. The Maryland countryside is nothing less than beautiful, with the interstate expressways sandwiched between a green stream of trees and forests.

Annapolis, a thirty-minute drive from BWI, is a quaint little town. It has a New England, historical landmark character to it. Perhaps the biggest structure in the municipality is the Navy Marine Corps Memorial Stadium, an edifice one passes on the way into the downtown area. Not surprisingly, James was hungry upon our arrival, and so we looked for a suitable place to eat. This is always an adventure in a college town. Unless you want to eat at a national chain establishment, assuming one is in the vicinity, you really have no idea which places are good and which are not.

After driving around somewhat aimlessly, we flagged down a couple of pedestrians and asked (a) where the downtown center was, and (b) where we should eat. They gave us directions to The Roost, telling us it was a nondescript restaurant, though immensely popular with excellent food. We were not disappointed. It most certainly was plain, replete with Formica-topped tables crammed together to seat the maximum number of patrons. It was also famous, the walls adorned with pictures and inscriptions from well-known entertainers and politicians. The food was good, served quickly and well.

Given the dense crowding of the patrons, while waiting for our food, I began a conversation with a sixty-five-ish local gentleman sitting at the table to my left.

"You here to see the Academy?" he asked, noticing my pairing with James, a teenager.

"My son is a Navy football recruit," I eagerly replied.

"That's terrific," he said, looking at James. "Remember this, young man: once you get a degree from the Naval Academy you will never need a résumé."

The location of the Academy is impressive, particularly on this bright, sunny September day, as the sun shimmered off the waters of the Chesapeake Bay bordering the Academy. Casual entrance to the Academy was no longer permitted since the incidents of September 11, so we parked on the street just off Academy property, and showed our identification to the guard at the gate. Once cleared, we began about a quarter-mile walk down a long, rather narrow street toward the bay and the academy itself. We were looking for Ricketts Hall, which housed the football office.

I wanted to be certain that James had enough time to meet with Jeff Monken, the slotbacks coach who was recruiting him, so we got there early. We told the receptionist we were there to see Coach Monken. Monken, a tall, lean man who looked younger than his thirty-five years, was in his office and greeted us with delight.

He told us he would not be available until early afternoon, when he had anticipated our arrival. He suggested we might want to walk around, then go over to the gift shop and take the Academy tour, beginning around 12:30. We took the tour, conducted by a pleasant, middle-aged woman. Though generally interesting, James and I tired of some of the historical trivia and made our getaway before the tour was over, heading toward what would be called the student union at a civilian university. James got a snack and soon it was time to see Monken.

Monken's style all but defines the term *laid back*. Making excellent eye contact, he spoke slowly about the Academy. Eleven thousand people apply annually. Eleven hundred are admitted. The faculty consists of a near even split between military officers and civilian professors.

"The Princeton Review ranks Navy number 1 in professorial accessibility," he added. "The graduation rate is 87 percent. Everything is done to help a student graduate. Math, physics, and engineering professors accompany the team on road trips, providing tutoring as necessary."

The subject moved to football and James' desire to play on the offensive side of the line of scrimmage. "James, you are a Division I player. Face it, no school is going to talk with you unless they feel you can help them. You wouldn't be sitting here if you couldn't haul butt, and you should feel free to tell a coach where you want to play."

He talked about Head Coach Paul Johnson, who left the offensive coordinator post at Navy after the 1996 season to coach Division IAA Georgia Southern. In his five years there, he went 62–10 and won two consecutive Division IAA championships (in 1999 and 2000).

"Coach Johnson is just great. His offense is just incredible. He was the offensive coordinator here the last time Navy made it to a bowl. At Georgia Southern his teams averaged forty points and 470 yards a game on offense. We have a great staff here. Most of the Georgia Southern staff is here, and Buddy Green came over from North Carolina State, where he was defensive coordinator, to coach the defense."

The Navy program needed to be turned around. After a very auspicious start, things turned sour for the previous coach, Charlie Weatherbie. Weatherbie was fired seven games into the 2001 season, having lost seventeen of his last eighteen contests. Monken spoke to that.

"It's not X's and O's, it's Jimmys and Joes," said Monken, "and that's why we're interested in you, James." With Johnson's staff at the throttle and a 38–7 victory at SMU in the opener, spirits were high. "There were a thousand students waiting for the team at the airport," Monken reported with enthusiasm.

He pointed to the metallic board and the offensive set displayed on it. "Here is where you'll play," he said, pointing to a slotback position. And size was not an issue for the coach. "If I lined up the last ten slotbacks we had at Georgia Southern, you would be bigger than seven of them. We don't care about how big you are. In our offense, all you have to do is haul butt."

Later Monken took us on a tour of the Academy. Though there was some overlap with the earlier tour, Monken pointed out a number of distinctive features. Perhaps the most impressive was the Navy chapel. The main floor worship area was simply spectacular. He then took us into the basement. It was filled with historical items, much of which was devoted to the memory of John Paul Jones. Jones' tomb was in the center of the room. The football facilities were Division I level, first-rate. Navy greats were prominently featured, including Napoleon McCallum and Heisman Trophy winners Joe Bellino and Roger Staubach. The locker room is named after Staubach.

We left late in the afternoon and headed for Silver Spring, where we would connect with my daughter, Rochelle. For me, being with Rochelle and James was a highlight. After dinner and a driving tour of Washington, D.C., we headed over to the George Washington Law School, where Rochelle is a student and the student newspaper is named *By George*. Once outside, the ever-exuberant Rochelle ran into one of her classmates. Eagerly she introduced us to him. "This is my brother, James, and this is my dad," she said happily. That Rochelle, an only child, would refer so naturally to James as her brother—not stepbrother—was both significant and a matter of delight to me.

The evening was not over. This being James' first visit to the nation's capital, Rochelle then directed a more extensive auto tour, pointing out the historical sights—from the White House to the Washington Monument to the memorials for Lincoln and Jefferson. Despite the lateness of the hour, and with many of the historical sites closed to visitors, we were able to park and visit the majestic Jefferson Memorial.

After dropping Rochelle off at her apartment, a tired James and I headed to our hotel in Laurel, Maryland.

James insisted we take Rochelle with us to the game the next day. With his geographic wizardry James directed me back through Silver Spring to pick up Rochelle and then over to Annapolis for the game. We got there several hours before game time, encountering legions of happy tailgaters as we made our way into the stadium.

Once inside, we were taken down onto the field, where just beyond the end zone a huge tent was pitched. Its sole purpose was to serve as a reception center for recruits. A huge spread of food was tastefully set out buffet style, and Navy media guides adorned the tables. There, with players warming up but a few yards away and the stands filling, we ate comfortably. Coach Monken came over and took James and me to the sidelines just before the kick-off. With exquisite timing, Coach Johnson came over and shook hands with us, welcoming us to the game.

We were still on the field when suddenly a startling, all-encompassing, voluminous sound thundered throughout the stadium. It was the Navy jets roaring through the sky just above the structure. We hurried to our seats high in the upper tier of the stadium. Expecting the midshipmen to vie effectively with the powerful visitors from North Carolina State, the three of us focused our eyes on the action. A close contest it was not. Navy was soon out of the game, drowning in a self-defeating sea of turnovers and defensive breakdowns. Wanting to leave us enough time to get to the airport, we left what would eventuate into a 65–17 blowout in the third quarter.

The game, however, was anticlimactic. There were plenty of high points to compensate for the disappointing performance of the Navy gridders. James and I had experienced Annapolis, seen the Academy, toured Washington, D.C., and been honored guests at a major college football game. And best of all, we had been able to do most of it with James' new sister, Rochelle.

24.

Bittersweet

Navy was now on the recruiting map, and the Spartan football team was on the march. At Evanston, GBN defeated the Wildkits 16–8, with James rolling up 184 yards on 27 totes, including an 87-yard touchdown jaunt that sealed the victory with less than two minutes left.

An unbeaten Niles West squad was next, as was a visit from two of Rita and my dearest friends, Ivan and Ann Eernisse from Wisconsin. Ivan, adopted as am I, is my first cousin and someone who had followed James' odyssey from afar over the past year. They were treated to James' finest 2002 effort to date. The Spartans put away their visitors by a 21–7 margin, as James exploded for 260 yards and 3 touchdowns. Among his twenty-six carries was a ninety-five-yard touchdown sprint to open the fourth quarter. His rushing exploits pushed his career total well past Sean Brandt's 3,206 yardage mark. James now had 541 ground yards in four games, 444 of which had come in the past two contests.

Ivan and Ann joined Rita and me down on the field to congratulate James after the game, something we had done regularly during the previous two years. It was good for James to have two new rooters, after losing perhaps his greatest fan, Barry Capaul, one of our church friends, who had lost his battle with Lou Gehrig's disease back in February. A dying Capaul, formerly a topflight musician, had summoned every unit of his waning energy to attend a number of James' games during his junior year. James had taken special delight in hugging Barry after wins during the 2001 season.

Rita and I spent an enjoyable, celebratory weekend with Ivan and Ann at our place in South Haven, Michigan. On Saturday morning, Ivan and I picked up the *Chicago Tribune* and saw James at the head of the seven-player "Friday's Heroes" list. Earlier, Taylor Bell, the *Chicago Sun-Times* legendary high school sports expert, had done a column on James. Using the size issue as his slant, Bell opened the article stating that James sometimes dreamed "of being 6-1 and 210 pounds with 4.4 speed." James had reported no such dream to Bell, but the lead-in was clever. Bell did quote James rather believably on the size matter. "I think when people say I am too small to be a running back in college, that drives me to work harder and become a better player. Maybe I wouldn't be the same player if I was as big as they want me to be. They say I'll have to play cornerback or wide receiver in college. I want to prove I can be a running back. After playing the position for eight years, it's hard to listen to someone who says you can't."

Bell noted that "recruiting analyst Tom Lemming insists Velissaris is a Division I prospect, probably at wide receiver or cornerback, where 4.4 athletes are in desperate need." The article, entitled, "Velissaris plays big for Glenbrook N.," went on to recite some of James' rushing statistics, in addition to his thirty-two ACT score.

After one game I listened to an interview with Tom Lemming on the radio. Lemming, in response to the question of why players with super high school statistics are often passed over by colleges for lesser-publicized athletes, emphasized what colleges look for. Colleges are not interested in how good a player is while he is in high school. They are concerned about how that player *projects* as a college player. As a result, it's about size and speed, not statistics.

Having righted the ship after their comeuppance at Vernon Hills, the 3–1 GBN squad was ready to make a charge into the major dailies' area football rankings. Not having tasted a league defeat since 1998, they would now take their three-year fifteen-game CSN winning streak into the conference opener against visiting Deerfield the following Friday night.

With his dad, Steve, another victim of Lou Gehrig's disease, watching from a wheelchair, Deerfield's Billy Nardini shredded the Spartan defense for 4 touchdowns, amassing 211 yards on just 10 carries in a 33–19 trouncing of Glenbrook North. Nardini and his mates also put a blanket over James. He rushed for just seventy-seven yards on twenty-six attempts.

The loss was crushing. Not only was it the team's second loss of the season—they had not lost more than one regular-season game in any of the three previous campaigns—it was a conference defeat, endangering GBN's stranglehold on the CSN. Worse, however, this second loss all but pushed Glenbrook North out of the prep media spotlight for good. This latter point was critical for James. The best way for James' efforts to gain attention was for him to be playing on a highly ranked team. With legions of Chicago-area teams vying for limited space in the major newspapers, media attention is focused on the big winners. For three years, GBN had been one of those winners, and James justifiably profited from the attention the team received. He now would play in comparative metropolitan anonymity, something that would do nothing to attract more scholarship offers. By contrast, Tom Zbikowski's Buffalo Grove team was 6–0, with the celebrated quarterback publishing a recruiting diary on the Internet.

For James the season was no fun. He was taking a beating running into a wall of defenders as the holes of seasons past were not there in 2002. The next game was easy, a 38–7 trampling of Niles North. Though a disappointing 4–2, the team had bounced back well from the Deerfield disillusionment and could still close the regular season books at 7–2. A trip to Maine West was next. The good news for James was that he added another 226 yards to his rushing total. The bad news was that he strained a hamstring, an injury that would dog him the duration of the season.

Rita and I did not go home after the game. With James in the backseat, we made the long commute to Bowling Green. Coach Brandon was among James' most faithful callers. Head Coach Urban Meyer also dialed our phone upon occasion. Understandably proud of their 3–0 Falcons, they had consistently invited us to the campus to see a game. This was the week. Though I dreaded the drive, I had agreed to take James to Bowling Green to see the team in action, and so it was time to make good on the pledge.

We reached our hotel well after midnight, had a brief night's sleep, and headed to Bowling Green. Outside the stadium a tent was pitched for recruits and their families. Coaches Brandon and Meyer stopped by and greeted Rita and me, but because there were a number of other prospects and their families present we had little time with them. With pizza the sole item on the menu, Rita left in search of more healthy fare. Brandon found time to pull James aside to reiterate his recruiting pitch. It was clear how Bowling Green had ramped up their program so quickly. They did it by persistent and personable recruiting and almost nothing else. The physical plant was old, the paint on the stadium peeling, and facility space limited. Yet, no one recruited more energetically and relationally than the Bowling Green staff. The entire group exuded energy and optimism.

Although the visit did not include a complete tour of the football facilities, we did stop in the weight room, where the group was addressed by one of the strength coaches. The coach dismissed there being any real distinction in terms of effect between working with stationary or free weights. "That's not correct," said James. James then explained briefly how different the impact can be among the various weight training methods. As game time approached, the recruits and company were walked inside Perry Stadium into the north end zone. Coach Meyer addressed the group.

"This is an easy place to recruit," stated Meyer firmly, "because there is tremendous support for a successful program here. You will be sitting in our student section during the game and see the enthusiasm. We want you to keep that in mind when you consider your college choice." Meyer tried to strike a balance between supply and demand. On one hand, he made clear that the school valued the attendance of the recruits. On the other, he was not going to plead with them to come to Bowling Green. Above all, he wanted to communicate that football success enveloped the environment and any kid who chose Bowling Green was choosing an exciting college football career.

We took our seats about twenty rows up at midfield. Indeed, the student section was vocal and enthusiastic. The problem was that Doyt Perry Stadium was sparsely populated on this homecoming weekend. Sitting among a group of postadolescents in an old and not very well-filled stadium just did not give one the feel of big-time college football. In fact, the experience felt more like what I had experienced in early-season games each year at North Park before the weather turned cold and enthusiastic students would become jaded as the defeats piled up.

From the opening kickoff, the Falcons absolutely pounded the visiting Bobcats from Ohio University. At the half, with the score

37–14, we left. Later that night I checked the final score on ESPN. It was 72–21. Faithful to his mission, Brandon called the next night. I ribbed him about running up the score. "We didn't try to do that," said Brandon, a humane guy, "but Ohio just seemed to become dispirited and let up a bit, making it hard to keep the score reasonable." Brandon had a point. Bowling Green was an offensively geared team. They ran a wide-open, let-'er-rip spread offense—one that rolled up points and yardage with abandon—often deploying as many as five wide receivers. In fact, Brandon would often include the team's yardage totals and national rank when leaving voice mail messages for James when he was not present to receive the call. Certainly a team like the Falcons could hardly help but pepper the scoreboard with points against a dispirited opponent.

Navy, Harvard, and Bowling Green were now separating themselves from the recruiting pack by placing weekly calls to James. Northern Illinois was also pushing, regularly inviting James to a home game, but their proximity to Chicago placed them low on James' list. Conspicuous by its absence was Western Michigan, still one of my favorites. I decided to stir the Kalamazoo coals with a phone call to Bruce Tall, who recruited the Chicago area.

"Coach Tall, this is David Claerbaut, James Velissaris' dad," I said, reaching Tall's voice mail. "You may not be interested in James and of course we understand that. But we are still very interested in Western Michigan, and if James is still on top of the board, it would be good to hear from you, perhaps with an offer or something. He has several already and is hearing from a number of schools. Anyway, take care and hope things are well with you."

I felt good when I hung up the phone. Sure, it was pretty direct, even presumptuous. But Western had constantly stated that James was among their key prospects, but they just didn't offer early as a matter of policy. The season was now half over and I felt it was reasonable to ask them for a reading on James.

And we got one. The next evening the phone rang. It was Tall. Yes, indeed, Western was still very interested in James. "He's still on top of the board for us," he said. "I may fly out Friday to see him."

He did and saw James carry the ball 29 times for 198 yards

and 3 touchdowns. James might have hung even bigger numbers had his hamstring not been tender. Later he asked me if I had noticed his decreased speed in the game. "Remember that one run that looked as if I was going to score, when they caught up with me?" he asked. I hadn't noticed because, typical of James, he had not told me about the injury. Unfortunately, James also made a contribution to a 29–22 defeat, by fumbling at the Maine West nine-yard line midway through the fourth quarter of what was then a 22–22 game. With 7.6 seconds left in the contest, and facing seemingly certain overtime, West's Victor Gomez raced sixty-one yards down the sideline for the win. Gomez's 263 yards on 26 carries trumped James' otherwise banner evening.

Tall had left before James' miscue, but that was little consolation. GBN was now just 4–3 and 1–2 in the CSN, and any thoughts of a conference title had given way to concern about making the playoffs. GBN had to win at least one of the remaining two games to see postseason action. The next one was against Highland Park.

The game started nicely, as the Spartans poured it on in the first half to the tune of 24–0. Apparently, however, the team decided to take the rest of the night off against a never-say-die Highland Park squad. The visitors put up twenty unanswered points in the second half to come within four of GBN. The Spartans sealed the win by recovering an onside kick attempt with 1:33 left. James scored twice and contributed 134 yards to the team's rushing total. He was now over 1,150 yards for the season, not bad considering his hamstring was sore and the line was not as successful in creating openings as it had been in the previous two campaigns. It was, however, a bittersweet season—not the blowing-the-doors-off campaign we had expected.

25.

Playoff Time

There had to be a very good reason why Rita and I would miss the last regular-season game of James' career. There was. We were in Las Vegas celebrating our anniversary. As special as the event was, we would have skipped it for James' game were there much likelihood that Glenbrook North would lose and so miss the playoffs.

A few nights before we left, James and I got on the Internet and looked at the IHSA playoff picture. We tried to handicap the games on this final week of the regular season in order to project against whom GBN would open the post-season. In 2002 there would eight classes (as always, based on school enrollment) with the usual thirty-two entrants in each class. There was little doubt that a 5–4 record would get a team in. GBN was now 5–3 and pointing toward a likely win that Friday, one that would remove all doubt as to their playoff status. Nonetheless, a win was important, because a 5–4 log would both send the Spartans into the postseason on the downtick, and would most certainly result in drawing a killer first-round opponent, owing to the seeding arrangement. The opponent that Friday would be Maine East, a squad entering the fray with a 1–7 mark, one that meant they most definitely would be playing this season's final game. Moreover, Main East had already lost to every league opponent other than Niles North, so little appeared to be at risk. Should the team lose, GBN would still likley get a postseason berth, albeit a tough seed. But a win seemed almost certain.

Worry-free I headed to Las Vegas, after directing James to leave a message on my 800 business number as to how the game with Maine East turned out and what the playoff prospects were.

The news was good. GBN smoked East 45–0 and was safely in the playoff picture. That was the good news. The bad news was that the Spartans would open on the road at St. Charles North.

On the face of it, one might think that the North Stars would not be a very tough draw given their 6–3 campaign, but records are deceiving in high school football. North had closed the season with six straight wins and was a member of the Upstate Eight conference, a loop located west of Chicago in DuPage County where football is king. The western suburbs of Chicago continued to turn out the strongest gridiron squads. Kids are big, superbly conditioned, carefully coached, and highly motivated. There simply is no comparing the strength of that area to the quality of play in the CSN.

"Just five games left," I said to James somewhat jokingly as we turned our attention to the postseason.

In reality, this figured to be the final game of the season for the Spartans. The team had shown little fiber when facing a tough opponent during the season. Two of the three losses were by a single score, and there had been an inability to summon the mental toughness to bounce back from mistakes to come from behind and reclaim the contests. James, however, was upbeat. "We've got a whole new offense for St. Charles North," he said enthusiastically early in the week. "We're going to spread the field, and throw. I'm going to line up in the slot quite often and be used as a pass receiver.

"And guess what, if we win, we get Buffalo Grove at home in the second round."

Now that was a thought to savor. All season long, the pub had gone to Tom Zbikowski with unrelenting intensity. He deserved it. Zbikowski was having a dream senior season. Not only was Tommy Z exhibiting his brilliance week after week, the Bison were undefeated in 2002. I liked the Zbikowskis. How could I not? Ed had nothing but good things to say about "Jimmy," as he called him. More than that, he had proven to be a good friend. Ed regularly recommended James as an offensive dynamo to colleges recruiting his son.

The value of such recommendations is not to be underestimated. So much of recruiting is caught up with networking. Coaching staffs—given their size and time limitations—simply cannot remain abreast of every prospect in the United States. Watching tape on every conceivable Division 1 prospect would be more than a full-time job. Hence, coaches talk to other coaches, to parents, and to media people about prospects. This had happened in my own experience. Early in the recruiting process, before his senior year, I called a coach from a school that had shown interest in James. Before I could identify myself as James' parent, but having already made clear the call pertained to recruiting, the coach interrupted, "Great, do you know of any good prospects?"

Coaches' ears are always open to a find, especially one outside their immediate territory. Recruits can be roughly subdivided into regional and national recruits. There is a layer of kids that can play Division 1 ball and are recruited largely by schools in their region. A Chicagoland player, for example, will likely get special attention from Midwestern universities. Other kids are simply studs. Tom Lemming and everyone else in the nation are trumpeting their skills and so the powerful football schools coast-to-coast enter the chase. Without doubt, Zbikowski was such a prospect. He may very well have been the number 1 prep prospect in Illinois this year and, therefore, was drawing interest from all over the continent. James was somewhere in between a national and regional prospect. The majority of activity was coming from schools within 250 miles, although at least in the early going, feelers flowed in from all directions.

In retrospect, perhaps I could have stretched the interest in James had I been a bit more of a promoter. Lots of parents make the promotion of their football-playing son all but their day job. And there is a near cottage industry out there that will assist in that process, as in the case of a man I met in James' junior season who discussed the "packaging" of James. But I didn't want to do that. I was skeptical of the value of "selling" James to a school, and it was expensive. I wanted schools to be sold on James by doing their own investigations. Perhaps if James had been a marginal Division 1 prospect, or a youngster attending a 1, 2, or 3A high school, and in need of exposure, I might have taken to the hustings in an effort to get him a scholarship. But with everyone from Tom Lemming to Edgy Tim declaring him a certifiable Division 1 performer, I did not think it was necessary.

In any case, Ed Zbikowski was always willing to encourage a school to look closely at James. And I appreciated it. Coaches listened to him, because Ed has a good grip on high school football and, of course, has a son who is a can't-miss prospect at the highest levels. When Ed would tell colleges that James Velissaris was clearly the best player his son had played against, they were inclined to listen. His recent touting of James to Boston College was typical of Ed. "You should be hearing from Boston College," he told me in a telephone conversation. "I told them Jimmy was the guy they needed to throw the ball to out of the backfield."

Nonetheless, the attention Tommy was getting was simply eye-popping. Zbikowski's stardom was so celebrated, his recruiting diary was an ongoing enterprise on the Internet. Indeed, if any young man was to enjoy such celebrity I would be hard-pressed to choose anyone over Tom. The problem was that publicity is a discrete rather than continuous variable. There are only so many newspaper column inches, so much Internet space, and so much radio and television airtime available for area high school football. This is particularly true in the Chicago metro area, given the hundreds of high schools and the presence of major college and professional athletic teams. Because Zbikowski was dominating the area high school football scene to a degree reminiscent of Michael Jordan's domination of professional basketball, James' achievements were all but driven off the radar screen.

James never complained about it, and he never would. Although we never talked about it, it had to bother him a little. There was certainly no reason to blame the Zbikowskis for their good fortune. On the contrary, they had done more to spread the word for James than anyone, including James' coaches. Nonetheless, I didn't like to see James pushed so far to the perimeter. No parent would.

A 2002 playoff matchup with Buffalo Grove, then, was almost too much to wish for. Beyond giving James another chance to shine on the same field with Zbikowski, it would give GBN an opportunity to avenge as bitter a defeat as the team had experienced in James' tenure with the Spartans. Unseating the mighty Bison, with James displaying his wares, would be the ultimate vindication—football's version of poetic justice.

I was particularly delighted about the decision to diversify the offense for the St. Charles North game. In my subjective opinion, the 2002 GBN offense was too predictable. Game after game, the under-sized Spartans ran out of the power I, with James the workhorse tailback. This fundamentally sound, grind-'em-out style worked well against most CSN opponents, but now things might have to be more diversified.

I took a friend of mine from the church, Roger Falk, to the late-season game against Highland Park. Falk, a scholarly history teacher and former football player at Chicago's legendary Lane Tech High School, is a very football-literate guy. Ever courteous, he spent nearly the entire game bantering back and forth with me about why GBN lined up this or that way on both offense and defense.

"They might want to wing James out and create some space for him to run; he's a speed back," was one of his observations. When I saw Roger several days later, he returned to the subject by bringing up a recent Notre Dame success.

"I think Tyrone Willingham is an absolutely great coach when it comes to preparation," he said. "He studies his opponent and puts together his game plan accordingly. Look at what he did against undefeated Air Force. He knew his team would not be accustomed to the high elevation, so to keep them from getting tired he just ran the ball down their throats. He knew his guys had a size advantage so he played time-of-possession ball and just wore down Air Force."

Then, after referring to another well-conceived game plan in which Willingham took a much different, yet equally successful approach, he delivered the punch line. "Willingham did against Air Force exactly the opposite of what Glenbrook North does with James. They need to run him outside and throw short to him to give him some space to maneuver in."

I had heard it before. The previous season several coaches—college and high school—attended a GBN game. They remarked about the tight, conservative nature of the offense. "Man if I had a kid like Velissaris I would never run a two tight-end set," said one of the area's more renown high school mentors. The college coach agreed. "You've got to spread the field and take advantage of that speed."

This style was not necessary for most of the games. The team needed a bread-and-butter runner and James, like Sean Brandt before him, was it. Now it was playoff time, and with James being keyed upon in every single game the value of opening up the offense seemed even more apparent. The whole value of a player with James' speed resides in what he can do once he gets past the line of scrimmage into the secondary. Short throws would do exactly that. In fact, that is what the colleges that were recruiting him openly had in mind for him on offense. Furthermore, short passes to an over-the-middle tight end could open some deep routes for James and ace wide receiver, Kyle Miller.

There was another concern for me. Not only did the team employ a two-man deep set when receiving kickoffs, James and his teammate Marc Neuman assumed their positions on opposite sides of the field well before the kick, all but assuring that the opposition would be able to kick away from James. And that is exactly what they did. For the 2002 season, James was almost extinct as a kickoff return man. I didn't understand the reason for this. Veteran Chicago Bears' fans could remember how the team deployed the elusive Gale Sayers. He would stand shoulder to shoulder with another returner as the kicker approached the ball. Then, an instant before the kicker got his foot into the leather, the two would suddenly break to their respective sides allotting the Bears an even money shot that the ball would go to Sayers' side. Still other teams simply used a single safety on kickoffs.

In any case, it is human nature for a football father to wonder about coaching strategy. Besides, these coaches were not gridiron illiterates. They were veteran high school coaches—guys with quality football résumés. Almost all of them had played college ball, several at major programs. Some even spent time in the NFL. Not only did they have sound gridiron credentials, they tried to help the more able kids get to the next level. Pieper, in his coaching days, regularly put together videotapes and sent them to colleges in hopes of boosting the chances of his players being able to continue their careers in college. Coach Whalen continued that tradition. A lot of coaches are far less helpful.

In the end I attributed this white bread approach to what coaches call "philosophy." Apparently, these were conservative, meat-and-potato football guys. The straight-stick, power I offense is what they evidently believed in, were comfortable with, and that is what they ran. And they had won with it—four straight runs into the playoffs and three conference crowns along the way. Strategies always look worse in defeat.

Now, however, there was reason for postseason hope. If indeed, they could present St. Charles North with a different look in the postseason two things may happen. First, St. Charles North's preparation on one side of the ball would be useless, but second, perhaps this new approach might reinvigorate an up to now less than sprightly GBN team, helping them flush the toilet mentally on what had been an underachieving season and ready them for a playoff run. At least it was good to see some enthusiasm in James for the playoffs.

I was afraid to hope. The smart money was on St. Charles North. I didn't want to see James' less than fulfilling senior season end with a frustrating defeat. But who was I kidding? It was playoff time and all thirty-two entrants were starting this second season undefeated, with visions of state championships dancing in their heads.

26.

Round One

The weather in the Midwest turns cold by late October. I remember how much I looked forward to the end of the football season in my own freshman year so many decades ago in Wisconsin. I dreaded the contact in practice. Every hit hurt even more in the chilly weather. The new millennium was no different. The season may have begun in the August heat, but James' last few games had been played in winterlike temperatures.

The first day of November was cold. I put a turtleneck on under a bulky running suit as I prepared for the jaunt to St. Charles. There was plenty of interest in the game. The *SunTimes* featured the contest among the top Chicagoland confrontations of the weekend. The recruiters were also alert. Western Michigan's Bruce Tall called one evening when James was out. "I see you've got St. Charles North in the opener," he said. "I'll be on the Internet checking to see how you do."

I was pleasantly surprised at how much he knew about the Chicago area playoff scene as we talked on. Although Chicago was Tall's territory, he had spent the past few seasons at Harvard, well out of the region. I wondered about Western Michigan. Tall continued to hang in there, showing interest, and wishing James well, but he offered nothing. Meanwhile, the Broncos were going nowhere. The program had everything but wins. Western Michigan had decidedly the best facilities in the MAC—truly major college in quality. In Gary Darnell they had a proven head coach at the controls, and the rest of the staff was dotted with quality football people from first-rate institutions. But they were just 2–6, a puny 1–3 in the conference.

"It's been a tough season for you guys," I said, liking Tall and so trying to sound encouraging. The Broncos were coming off back-to-back killer losses to the best two teams in the Western division. They had lost in overtime to Bowling Green on the road, and then took a 24–20 verdict on the chin at home. They were facing a 3–5 (1–3 in the MAC) Ball State squad in Indiana Saturday.

"We really need a win," Tall said somberly. "It would restore a lot of confidence." We talked briefly about the losses to Bowling Green and Northern Illinois. "We actually had the ball at the end of regulation with a shot at a field goal against Bowling Green. We win that one and the season is totally different," he lamented. The team had also led most of the way against Northern. Earlier in the season, the Broncos fell 28–24 at Purdue and 31–27 to Central Florida.

Western Michigan was experiencing the dark side of big-time college football. With but 12 games on the schedule, you just can't afford to let any winnable game get away. Lose a couple like that and the season is irreparably disfigured. With every game representing nearly 10 percent of the season, the "it might have been" acid of a blown opportunity has to burn in the stomach of any coach. Here was a team that could play belly-to-belly with a Top 25 team like Bowling Green, and a Northern Illinois squad that had beaten Wake Forest in the opener and lost at Wisconsin amid some extremely questionable officiating several weeks later. The Broncos were that close. Just fifteen points separated Western Michigan from a 6–2 mark—one in which the team's only losses would have been to Michigan and Virginia Tech.

But it doesn't work that way. No points are awarded for valiant efforts and nice tries. Close only counts in horseshoes and hand grenades, as the late Al McGuire would so frequently say. I recall Bill Parcells putting it more bluntly. "What I like about football is that whatever your record is, that is what you are," was one of his favorite points. "If your record is four and twelve, you are a four and twelve team. Don't tell me that you were ten points away from being eight and eight. All you're telling me is that you can't win the close ones. You are a four and twelve team." Well, Western Michigan was a two and six team and now Tall seemed concerned that their spirit might be broken. His fears were well founded, as the Broncos went on to drop a 17–7 encounter to Ball State.

Life was very different these days at Bowling Green. Coach Brandon called and gently turned up the heat on James. "It's still very early," he said to James, "but it's not hard to recruit here." Recalling Meyer's reference to Bowling Green no longer being one of the nation's best kept-secrets during James' visit there a month ago, this subtle use of the law of supply and demand seemed to be part of the Falcons' recruiting strategy. In any case, the message for James was inescapable. Bowling Green thirsted for a commitment, and understandably so. Schools can only focus on a given number of players. Of course, they rank these players. The last thing a school wants to do is to chase a high-priority prospect, only to lose him at the last minute, leaving them little time to court successfully the next kid on the list before he commits elsewhere. Besides, Bowling Green had to be feeling its oats. They were now a glittering 7–0 and firmly ensconced in the nation's Top 25. In just two short seasons, Urban Meyer, Gregg Brandon, and the rest of the staff had put together a topflight major college program and getting commitments from prospects like James is what they needed to remain that way.

Jeff Monken of Navy never missed a week. "Hello, is James there?" That was a question I had become used to hearing since September 1.

I knew it was Monken and greeted him pleasantly. Navy had the Western Michigan disease. Too many losses were eating away at the confidence of their players. Things had looked so promising after the team's rousing 38–7 opening season triumph at SMU. Six straight losses had taken their toll. Paul Johnson's offense was showing promise—the Midshipmen were averaging better than 21 points a game—but the defense was porous. The 46–21 loss at Boston College the previous Saturday typified their campaign. Monken was one of my favorites, and I had talked with him a number of times during the season.

I commiserated with Monken over what had to be a viciously disappointing season for a staff that had been so ragingly successful over its previous five campaigns at national champion Division I-AA Georgia Southern. "We really need a win," was a typical comment. "We should have beaten Northwestern. (Navy had fallen 49–40 to the Wildcats at home in the third game of the season.) We get that one and we probably would have beaten Duke and the atmosphere is totally different."

But they hadn't and it wasn't.

"We need more athletes," Monken said to me in an earlier conversation. "James is the kind of kid we want, and he can play early."

Monken seemed a class act, never missing an opportunity to connect with James. He sent a personal note to James congratulating him and wishing him well in the playoffs.

The recruiting calls had an energizing and comforting effect on me. The Spartan season had been less than sterling and the end seemed in sight. Hence, looking toward college brightened my emotional horizons. At least James' status as a Division 1 prospect was secure, so there was every reason to take comfort in the hope of better days ahead at a higher level of competition. Still, I couldn't help but hope GBN would somehow be the 2002 version of the *Hoosiers*, and make a miracle run at the state crown, with James finally getting the recognition I felt he was due.

We left from Rita's downtown Chicago office, where James' cousin Archie Weston joined us. The drive was not a pleasure. No area of metro Chicago has grown more than the western suburbs. Owing to the heavy, rush-hour traffic crawling along the corridor of interstates and roads in those now densely populated suburbs, we simply could not get to the game by kickoff. We arrived midway through the first quarter. Given the size of the crowd we had to park the car in the nether regions of the parking lot adjacent to St. Charles North High School, leaving us with a long walk to the field. The sound of the crowd erupting over what were for me unseen events created palpable anxiety for me. I tried to interpret the meaning of each roar, hoping that these sounds were not evidences of good things happening for the hometown heroes.

With the $3 tickets purchased, we hurried on our way to the top of the bleachers on the near—visiting—side of the field. I looked at the scoreboard as soon as I could. I was relieved when I saw the game was scoreless. The bad guys had not gotten off to the early lead. At least not yet. The roars, however, were because North had the ball and were on a drive. By the time we settled in to our frosty abode at the top of the bleachers next to the GBN vocal student section, however, the North drive had stalled and we had the ball deep in our own territory.

James had been correct. Although he was carrying, occasionally the offense had some real variation and Kaspers was throwing. The first quarter ended in a scoreless deadlock. Early in the second canto, the Spartans marched down the field and into the red zone. Then Whalen's staff pulled a brilliant surprise. From thirteen yards out they sent Kaspers around left end on a keeper, a play I had scarcely seen run in the two years he had been taking the snaps. Kaspers scored. With the PAT, it was GBN 7, North 0. GBN had the lead. Rita called Chris and Sean Brandt on her cell phone—those two faithful backers of James and the team had been unable to get an early enough start in the heavy traffic to get to St. Charles. She gave them the update. The score really fired up the defense, and they shut down the ground game on North's next series. Even better, GBN struck again. Kaspers did it again. This time the call was equally astute—right up the middle on a quarterback draw from seven yards out, another Spartan rarity. It was now 14–0.

It didn't stop there. With GBN now having the "big mo (momentum)," the Spartans simply took over what was clearly becoming a bitter game. The North Stars, not expecting this turn of events, appeared to be grabbing facemasks and delivering other skulduggery under the piles. "They were the dirtiest team we played all year," James told me later. "They didn't expect to lose. In fact, they were laughing at us before the game. One guy even said, 'Look, they brought a black guy to help them.'"

I was really into the game, feeling an unbounded joy as GBN ripped into North. I kibitzed backed and forth with GBN students, even unofficially leading them in cheers as the Spartans continued to have their way.

Clearly, St. Charles North could not pass. They threw the ball in only the most obvious of passing situations and then exhibited a rather primitive air game. The teams filed out right below us as they left the field at the half. Something about St. Charles North had elicited my ire during the first half. Perhaps it was what seemed to be less than honorable play. Anyway, nasty emotion had me yelling, "Hey, bring your offense," at North as they went past us en route to the field to begin the second half. Several students echoed my insult, leaving me somewhat less than proud about my rather unsportsmanlike conduct.

In any case, the second half was more of the same. Kaspers, having a career night, hit Kyle Miller on a big seventy-one-yard aerial putting the Spartans up by three scores. GBN was turning in its best game at the most opportune of times. The offense rolled and the defense was stifling as the Spartans repeatedly gang-tackled the North ballcarriers. It would take a very, very good team to defeat them. The score was 35–0 when James and the other offensive starters were pulled early in the fourth quarter, and we made an early exit in the arctic temperatures. The final was 35–6.

Even though we had to make a stop well south of the city to drop Archie off at college, the commute didn't seem as long as the drive out to St. Charles. With the car heater blowing warm air and an unexpected victory to savor, life was good.

Now if Buffalo Grove could defeat Maine West tomorrow at home, James and his teammates would have a chance to erase the pain of a year ago. It was the perfect script.

27.

The Afterglow

James was jubilant on Saturday morning, and I was delighted for him. I gave him a hug and told him what a terrific job he and the team had done. We talked a little football and he headed out the door to scout Buffalo Grove's game with Maine West—a game the Bison won handily, 35–12. It seemed as if this one victory could well reclaim the season for James and the rest of the team. For the first time all year there was an afterglow following a strong outing.

It had been a hard season, one with many injuries and not many holes to run through. Yet James had toughed it out quietly, without complaint. He had turned his third straight one thousand–plus yard rushing season, and now had scored sixty-one touchdowns and gained over four thousand yards on the ground —all in just thirty games. I wanted to do everything I could to get James some pub, so I e-mailed Edgy Tim and included our home phone number. Here was my message.

> *Edgy,*
> *Congrats on what continues to be an excellent website and service. By the way, I am James Velissaris' dad and appreciate your good words about him. Hope you can make it to the Jimmy V/Tommy Z matchup Friday. (Ed Z is a friend and we have been at camps together with our boys so we have our own rivalry.)*
> *If you want an update on James' recruiting status give me a call at home. Maybe we can say hello at the game.*
> *Again, excellent work!*
> *DC*

Within hours, Edgy e-mailed back one of his typically prompt, but terse responses.

I've been DYING to get a good number for Jimmy V. . . .
I'll call you tonight.

EDGY

He didn't call that night, but came through on Wednesday. We exchanged greetings and I referred to him lovingly "as a football junkie" and kidded him about how he once "cruised the high school scene in a rusted van and now has a website taking paid subscriptions." With that, I handed the phone over to James.

James was his usually polite, noncontroversial self, telling Edgy about the offers in hand and some of the other ancillary recruiting stuff. Edgy is a class act. He immediately included an article on James in his website and sent me a copy.

Glenbrook North RB James Velissaris Recruiting update!
James Velissaris, a 5'10" 175lb senior RB from Glenbrook North High School gets EDGY caught up on his recruiting.

"I still have offers from Bowling Green, Navy and Cincinnati. I have also gotten steady calls from Wisconsin, Western Michigan, Northern Illinois and a ton of Ivy League schools as well."

"I'm going to wait a few weeks before I set any official visits. We're in the 2nd round of the playoffs and I've been focusing on getting our team downstate. I would say that my Top 5 schools right now are Bowling Green, Navy, Harvard, Cincinnati and Northern Illinois."

James Velissaris has rushed for over 1,400 yards this season for Glenbrook North and has also scored 25 touchdowns in 10 games. The Spartans will face Buffalo Grove this Friday night in Northbrook in an IHSA Class 7A Round 2 playoff showdown!

James was clearly learning media-speak. In reality, the primary choices now were Bowling Green and Navy, with Harvard creeping up because they were showing consistent interest and offered a lofty academic experience. Cincinnati had all but dropped out, and Northern was just too close to home. Nonetheless, we needed to keep our options open. What happens if suddenly Bowling Green dropped out and Navy just isn't attractive? What if, God forbid, everyone but Northern or Cincinnati was to go away? James most assuredly would shut the door on no one at this early stage.

As James concluded his side of the call with Edgy, I asked him for the phone. I wanted to pump Edgy a tad. "If I may ask, what is going on at Northwestern?" Steve Helminiak did not understand why Northwestern was not all over James like a cheap paint job, saying, "They run the same offense as Bowling Green who is better than they are and James is faster than anyone they have right now. Besides, he's in their backyard with a thirty-two ACT." Helminiak's incredulity was exceeded only by my own.

Edgy Tim was as confused as Steve and I. "I don't know if anyone knows what's going on over there. They do try to recruit nationally, but still not one of the top recruits in the state I have talked to has heard a peep from them."

Like Eastern Michigan, Northwestern was another recruiting anomaly. Here was a program moving at top speed in reverse, and not at all pursuing a local kid better right now than some of the guys they were currently playing, and faster than probably all of them. There was simply no way they could not have heard about James, starring as he had for three years within fifteen minutes of Evanston. My conversations with Steve and Edgy strengthened my own suspicion that all may not be well in the Randy Walker football regime.

Although later I heard NU had but ten scholarships to offer, Walker seemed to be doing all the wrong things with his team psychologically. A month before, after two tough losses to Michigan State and Ohio State, the then 2–4 Wildcats headed to Minnesota to take on the Gophers on a Thursday night. Minnesota, a robust 6-1 at the time, is just murder at home in the Humpdome. They had beaten Illinois by three touchdowns there a week earlier. For the record they had won all four of their home tilts, and had done so by an average of better than twenty-four points. Translated, this means any football fan with even a few neurons firing in his or her brain expected a blowout.

Well, it started that way as Northwestern fell back early. Then, the Wildcats exhibited some competitive character and came roaring back, ultimately falling short by a meager 45–42 margin. Ten more minutes, maybe even five, and Northwestern pulls the stunner. A textbook case of too little, too late. Or maybe just too late. In any case, to the outside observer, the comeback seemed to provide Walker and his staff something to build on. Unlike basketball, football, as my high school coach Pat Baggott—one I really liked—put it, is a "rough game." A loss, particularly a cruel wire job on the road, is agonizing both physically and mentally. I've been in the locker room of college teams after such painful events, and watched those squads recover neither their confidence nor their mental edge for the rest of the season. As such, how a coach handles the delicate psyche of his team on the heels of a cruel defeat is often critical.

I was interested in how Walker would handle his physically and emotionally bruised squad. According to the Chicago papers Walker saw nothing to build on. He was angry and made clear there was little solace in coming close. He reportedly lit into his team, excoriating them for their poor play. My sense was that such a red meat approach would backfire. It did. Northwestern went on to lose the next two games by a combined seventy-eight points. It looked as if they had quit.

Perhaps his discouraged charges have also lost confidence in Walker and his staff. I had been told that one player claimed members of the team wondered if the coaching staff could get it done. Once that happens, it's over. It's one thing for a team to lose confidence in itself. It's another when they lose confidence in their coach. Maybe it was only one player, venting his spleen. Who is to say? But the way the team flattened out after the Minnesota game had me wondering, particularly since the team rolled over in the last half of 2001 as well, losing it's last six outings.

One coach who is out is Bobby Williams of Michigan State. He was waxed the day after Michigan administered a 49-3 whipping to the Spartans in the Big House in Ann Arbor. The first year athletic director, no-nonsense Hockey Coach Ron Mason, conducted a somewhat convoluted press conference in which he on one hand claimed no single on- or off-the-field incident resulted in the dismissal, while on the other said a postgame remark by Williams "was the most defining moment."

Michigan State has had the year of the locust. They were now 3-6. Worse, their quarterback, Jeff Smoker, has gone into drub rehab and their tailback, Dawan Moss, had been arrested over an altercation with a police officer. In any case, Williams, when asked after the Michigan brownout whether he had lost control of his team, answered, "I don't know."

What would you expect a man to say after his team has taken a pounding like that at the hands of an archrival? "Definitely, my man, we've got everything cooking"? But for Mason, this remark was a *defining moment*. As for the off-the-field shenanigans, Illinois Coach Ron Turner (quoted in the November 5, *Chicago Sun-Times*) put it well. "When you deal with 100 colleges kids, especially 100 aggressive college kids, things are going to happen. Sometimes it's their fault. Sometimes they're at the wrong place at the wrong time." Williams was in the wrong place. He was on the losing side of the ledger. That's why he was fired. This season one Wisconsin player was stabbed in a dispute and another busted on a marijuana charge; a Purdue player broke his hand in a fraternity party fight. Barry Alvarez and Joe Tiller, however, are still employed. They differ from Williams in that each has a winning career record, been to the Rose Bowl, and have hopes for a postseason game in 2002.

The Williams story does, however, show what happens to a team when players do quit. Jason Randall, a sophomore tight end, explained the mental devastation associated with a rout. "After a team starts scoring on us, people give up," he said after the Michigan humiliation. "That's what Coach Williams is searching for right now, people that will stick with it. We have people giving up on the field."

There's more to the Williams story. His ousting leaves NCAA I-A football with a grand total of three African American head coaches among its 117 schools. I have a strong sense that race played into this during the season firing, at least subliminally. On the face of it, such a precipitous firing makes little sense. It's not as though Williams was on a twenty-one-game losing streak. He was 3–6 (just one game under .500 for his career at 16–17) and coming off a 7–5 season with a bowl win, after which he had signed a five-year pact. Now he's gone, and in a very humiliating fashion, something black people are understandably very sensitive to.

No one is going to go public on this one, but I've been an athletic director, and I've just got to believe that Mason got some pretty hostile phone calls about this losing *black* head coach—a guy Mason did not hire and so did not have to protect. For Mason, the cure was easy. Wax Williams and finish out the season with a veteran member of the staff, Morris Watts, a guy who has been an assistant for about a thousand years, putting him past the point of consideration for the top spot. Then once things cool off and the program is out of the headlines after the season, you can find your own guy—a guy like, maybe, Urban Meyer.

"Hello, is James there?" It was Urban Meyer.

"No, he isn't. He should be in a bit later."

"Is this David?" he asked.

"Yes."

"How you doing; this is Coach Meyer."

Meyer exudes seriousness and is not big on small talk, so I pushed ahead, trying to put him to a little test. "You guys really got it going. You're all over the sports talk shows for every available coaching opening." An ESPN commentator had him first in line at Michigan State.

He slipped out of my trap like Houdini.

"Nobody's talking to me and I don't see any sure-win jobs out there. We can win here."

Then he delivered the punch line. "Do we have a chance at James?"

I was unprepared for the direct, yet appropriate, question, so I answered it honestly.

"You're right there. You and Navy are at the top of the list."

"Tell him I called."

Trying to regain my equilibrium, I commended him on the season Bowling Green was having and asked about how the postseason arrangements in the MAC played out.

"We've got a big one at Northern Illinois Saturday. I hope James can get there. If we win there we can take the Western Division. Then there's a playoff with the Eastern champion and a bowl after that."

"Wow, you really have a shot at a big year; you guys are really having a great season," I said sincerely, realizing that the now number 16 Bowling Green could well close the books 14–0 and solidly in the Top Ten.

You had to be impressed with Meyer. This was a head coach of a now undefeated, sixteenth ranked team in the country, obviously overloaded with things to do, and here he was spending part of his weeknights calling recruits personally. No other I-A coach had done that with James, and Meyer had done it often—in addition to Brandon, the assistant head coach, calling James weekly. Contrast that with Western Michigan and their every-other-week approach; or with Central Michigan and Butch Jones, who seemed to think he had a shot at James contacting him little more than once a month.

Northern Illinois had really dialed up their recruiting. After leaving James alone in the early going, Mike Sabock was becoming a faithful telephone correspondent, consistently inviting James to a game. James simply was not interested. NIU was just too close to home, and James needed to get away from some of his past pain and establish his identity. Moreover, Northern had yet to make an offer. By now I was pretty certain James would be skeptical of any school that tendered a just-before-midnight scholarship offer. Nonetheless, we discouraged no one, because until James signed a letter of intent we weren't going to send any suitors away cavalierly.

"Well, at least you've got a breather this week," I said, teasing Navy's Monken when he called. "You've had plenty of time to get ready for Notre Dame, and they couldn't even beat Boston College." Notre Dame, right near the top of the BCS rankings, had been upset at home by BC, soiling their hopes for an undefeated season.

"We've not only got Notre Dame, they're going to be angry," he said. I had asked Monken about the impact of Willingham as compared to Bob Davie in an earlier call. Ever the diplomat, he offered an interesting perspective. "It seems the kids are buying into his system more than they did with Davie. Sometimes it goes that way. Take Jim Fassel of the New York Giants. When he coached at Utah nothing worked. We used to beat him (when Monken assisted at Hawaii) 60–0. Look at Fassel now. His players love him and play all out for him in New York."

Navy was still struggling along trying to post its second win. The Midshipmen were an interesting odyssey. After simply destroying SMU 38–7 in the opener, they hadn't won since. Tulane, Rice, even Duke had beaten them. The game is so very mental. A victory over Northwestern in game number 3 might, as we had discussed, have put them over against the three other teams mentioned, giving them a 4–4 instead of 1–7 record, but when they fell to NU the downward spiral accelerated.

The conversation moved to the game with Buffalo Grove. "Coach, this is the one week that the name Zbikowski is not to be mentioned in this home," I said jokingly with James standing next to me waiting for the phone. "James has given me instructions that you are to remove him from the Navy recruiting list if that name is mentioned." With that, I handed a laughing Monken on to James.

Bruce Tall called Thursday night. I was ready for him. After exchanging pleasantries, we talked about the Buffalo Grove game.

"I would love to see him," said Tall. "In fact, our running backs coach (Pete Cordelli) is available but we used up our one game of seeing him live. I know some schools don't pay attention to that rule, but we do."

It was time to put the question to him. "Where do you have James on your recruiting list?"

"He's right at the top," said Tall. "I know we haven't offered him and I'm a little frustrated about it. In fact, we haven't offered any of the kids in my territory yet."

"That makes it kind of tough," I said. "James really liked Western, and you know we were there three times. James is like most kids. He wants to be loved, and now he's getting some other schools who've already offered him staying after him."

"Well, he's right at the top of my list," said Tall. "We are looking at three running backs and we haven't offered any of them. You know we do things differently here, and I would like to move things faster. But some schools will offer and take it off the table if they get a lot of early commitments. When we make an offer, it is real and we stand by it. We understand a kid can say no to us, but we will not say no to a kid we offer."

"I think you've seen he's a bigger, stronger kid than you saw last summer. In fact, he's always telling me how Fred Russell of Iowa was just 177 a year ago and now he's their main man at 192. So, he feels he can carry the ball."

"You don't have to convince me. I have no doubts about him."

"Do you think you'll be offering James?"

Hedging only a little, Tall said, "We should move on him very soon. Yes…we should be moving on him very soon."

It wondered whether if it were up to Tall—who was in his first year at Western—James would have been offered long ago. It appeared the barrier may be that Head Coach Darnell was committed to a conservative approach. In his desire to make each of his offers truly authentic, he just did not want to commit to a youngster until he was absolutely certain the kid was somebody he wanted. On one hand, this was an admirable approach to take. Darnell was not going to treat the prospective student-athlete like a commodity. In addition, Western had so much to offer in location and facilities that they could afford to be deliberate in their recruiting decisions. On the other, kids want to be wanted. Western, by arriving rather late to the party, was running the risk of either offering a youngster after the kid had already decided on another school, or at least appearing to be laissez-faire in their pursuit of a prospect.

A school's problem is intensified if the football team is having a losing season. A team like Bowling Green, for example, can play the hard-to-get game, at least a little. They can offer a youngster one of the most coveted of all gifts: an opportunity to play on a winning team and a likely trip to a bowl. Hence, they can intimate to the prospect that it is a privilege to be offered by the Falcons— a sort of gridiron version of "The few. The proud. The Marines." Western cannot. They need some "Jimmys and Joes" as soon as possible or Waldo Stadium may be filled with people dressed up like empty seats. A good way of doing that from where James and I are perched—as customers if you will—is to offer early and earnestly.

It may be time for Darnell, a coach I have a great deal of respect for, to take a page or two from his colleague Urban Meyer's book and get on the horn personally, and do it early and often. Paradoxically, it may be more useful to get Darnell on the phone simply *because* he doesn't offer early. A personal touch from a coach of his stature would perhaps offset his holding back the offer. Darnell is an interesting guy. Described consistently as "old school," he is impressive. Rita, a sophisticated, not at all naive African American woman, felt an instant sense of integrity flowing from him. She trusted him. He is a large, imposing figure. A man with presence. A prospect hearing his voice over the phone would be inclined to listen carefully.

In any case, the bane of every prospect's existence is that you just never know anything for certain. The whole process is one of matching the youngster's interest with what you perceive a given school's level of commitment is. Coaches lie, just as other people do. They are, technically, bound to nothing. An early offer can be rescinded. You are left then with a game, one of trying to read between the lines to determine what coaches are really stand-up guys. It is a game of handicapping where each school really is. And it goes beyond whether you feel a given school will offer genuinely or not. If, like James, you are more than a marginal recruit you want more than a scholarship. You want a scholarship to a program that will give you an opportunity to play. You don't want to be number 3 on a depth chart of three at your position. That may mean that you will never play a down at the university.

As for Western, perhaps they were just not that interested in James. That, however, seemed unlikely. He had gotten special treatment at their summer camp, the letters had come faithfully for months, and we had been told long ago that they did not offer early. Nevertheless, it was time for them to do something. Not unlike the couple that keeps dating for months but never really plans a future, it was time to define the relationship.

The Ivy League, nonscholarship Harvard stayed at it. Chad Klunder was persistent and effective. I was almost never there for the call, but James was fairly comfortable with him. Although the Ivy League plays IAA ball, it is very decent football. There are a number of NFL players, past and present, that have played in the Ivy. In fact, the Ivy League provides an interesting example of a college sports phenomenon: That the size or classification of a school or conference is not necessarily an accurate barometer of where it stands in the competitive jungle. A top-drawer IAA team could defeat a weak IA squad. You see this type of thing happen all the time in basketball. One year at North Park, our national championship Division III (nonscholarship) team, defeated Jacksonville on its own court by ten points in a year in which Jacksonville received a bid to the Division I big dance. In another, in which North Park did not even win its conference championship, the team lost by ten to a Northwestern squad that went to the NIT.

This football season, I counted ten IAA teams in Jeff Sagarin's Top 100 football power ratings (there being 117 IA teams). Penn, with only one loss, is from the Ivy and ranked eighty-second. Harvard is 127th. To put that in perspective, Penn is ranked above Indiana, Northwestern, Western Michigan, UAB, and Kansas. Harvard places ahead of SMU, Kent State, Tulsa, and UTEP. A limitation in the Ivy, however, is that there are no pure athletic scholarships in the league, and worse, there is no postseason. The champion does not enter the IAA playoffs. Nonetheless, Harvard stays at it, and the lure of the academic luster of the school was strong enough to get James to commit to an official visit on the weekend of December 7.

On Wednesday night, we sat in the kitchen late in the evening talking about the options. Much as we had talked over the past months I hadn't really taken his temperature on how the decision-making process is going. "Where are you at now?" I asked. "Who's at the top?"

"It's Navy and Bowling Green."

There are still plenty of decisions to make, but first there is Buffalo Grove.

28.

The Bison

"Hello, Ed? This is David Claerbaut, James Velissaris' dad," I said to Ed Zbikowski early the next week as he picked up the phone. "I don't know what's wrong with me, Ed, but I've got this terrific taste for Bison."

Ed laughed loudly, enjoying the trash talking of one middle-aged man to another. "Hey, how're you doing? I see you got a big one last week at St. Charles."

"Yeah, the team really played well. Hey, how is Tommy doing on his college decision?"

"More confused than ever. Iowa is in there big now."

The conversation turned to the upcoming game. We both agreed the return match was the way we wanted it. "This is the way it should be," said Ed. "Hey, if we aren't going to make it I would rather see Jimmy's team beat us than anybody. You had us beat pretty much the whole way last year."

"I agree on this end. With last year's game being a one-point cliff-hanger, it's good for the kids to settle it on the field a year later."

"Hey, if it ends," he said with a note of seriousness, "we can turn our attention to making the recruiting decisions."

"It's really good to talk, Ed. No matter what happens, all the best. We've got to get together after the season for a beer."

"You too. And definitely we got to have a beer together when this is over."

I was just so happy for James. Early in the week we talked about Buffalo Grove.

I was optimistic. "You can beat those guys," I said declaratively.

"They may be undefeated, but they have fewer quality points than we do," said James. (With playoff teams rarely meeting in the regular season, quality points—the total number of victories of a playoff team's opponents—are an important criterion in assessing the strength of a postseason foe.) "They haven't played a very tough schedule, and if we play the kind of offense we played last night, they won't be ready for us."

"My biggest fear, son, is that you guys are not going to believe you can take those guys. And you can. You had them beaten a year ago, and many of the same players will be out there Friday night."

Nevertheless, James was troubled. He came into the livingroom one evening and asked, "Why haven't I broken more runs?" This was just like James—no warming up, just right to the point. The fact was that he had not gained as many yards as the previous season and certainly had not delivered as many breakaway dazzlers.

"Three reasons," I replied, after giving it a bit of thought. "First, the holes just have not been there. How many games did you really have some openings?"

"Maybe two."

"How many last year?"

"Almost every game."

"Well, that's one reason. Another is that you have been focusing on becoming more of a power runner, breaking tackles," I said. "I talked to your brother Chris and he told me the biggest difference between you and Sean Brandt is that Sean tried to run away from contact. You will seek it out."

"He told me that, too."

"Another is that after two years, you aren't going to surprise anyone anymore. Every team is jacked up to stop you."

That seemed to satisfy him. Frankly, I did not want to make the matter James' fault, in large part because I didn't think it was. The holes had not been there as they had in the past, and with the rest of the offense occasionally sputtering, to stop James was to stop Glenbrook North.

Clearly, the season was bothering James. Another day he came into the living room, looked at me, and said, "I'm losing my confidence this year."

Somewhat taken aback, I asked why. Again, it was the lack of a breakout season. I went over the reasons I had mentioned earlier, assuring him also that college recruiters were impressed with his weight gain and power running. "Actually, gaining fewer but harder yards is probably working to your advantage with the colleges," I said. "They know you have breakaway speed, but now you're answering all the strength questions.

"Also, it may be a blessing very much in disguise that this isn't quite the season you had hoped it would be. Ever since junior football you've been winning championships. When you get to college you probably will endure some hard years. This is likely preparing you as well as anything."

Still, I felt badly for James, and I did wonder what it would take for James to break a few. Again, it was not as if he hadn't broken off some dandies—he had. They just hadn't come as frequently as in the previous two campaigns, years in which he was much smaller and not nearly the force he was as a senior.

There was, of course, the one reason we rarely talked about—his hamstring. Later James told me what a detriment the injury had become. "I would hardly practice at all the entire week, trying to rehab it as much as possible," he explained. "Then on game night I would rub heat salve into it and strap it up as tightly as possible."

The relief, however, was temporary. "I would feel fine through the first quarter, maybe the first ten minutes. Then it would feel as if the injury had just happened. There was just no acceleration. When I hit an opening, I couldn't create that instant daylight between myself and a defender. It's as if I was a six-gear runner who couldn't get beyond the fourth gear."

"How did you keep from popping it, while still playing?" I said, asking the obvious question.

"I was aware of it at all times. I could feel it, so I geared myself down. I just could not break into that final sprint. In the Highland Park game I broke a long one," he related as an illustration. "I saw the defender coming at me from the angle. Normally, I would just sprint past him at the last second, pushing it into that extra gear. I couldn't do that, so at the last instant I put a move on him and went by him."

There was yet another reason, and it came to me after thinking about it for several days. It seemed as if James was running differently in the middle of the field from the way he ran inside the ten. In midfield, he would run with his head down, focused on his mission to break tackles and run with power to gain those last few yards. When, however, he was ten or so yards from the end zone—where guys usually get stacked up—he regularly broke loose and scored standing up. The reason, I suspected, is that he ran near the end zone with his head up, surveying the field for an opening. Chris had noticed the same thing. I talked to James about it the next night, and he felt I may be right. I hoped the hypothesis would prove true against Buffalo Grove.

James had turned eighteen on November 2. Eighteen-year-olds are nothing if not resilient, and James quickly bounced back when later we talked about the game plan for Buffalo Grove.

"We're going with a no-huddle offense and no tailback," he said excitedly. "They've never seen that in scouting us." He took out a pen and drew an offensive set. James was very invigorated about the new look. I asked him if he had thought GBN would win against St. Charles North. "Yes, when I saw the change in the game plan I felt confident." Now he was confident again. The coaching staff was dialing it up even higher for the Bison.

I liked what I was hearing. "If you're going to be a good coach, you've got to beat teams that are better than you are," IHSA championship coach Ron Ellett once told me. "I beat a number of teams that were better than mine, and the only way you do that is through having a special game plan that they just aren't ready for." Apparently, the GBN coaches felt they were underdogs in the first two rounds—something I agreed with—and were coaching accordingly.

"What about the defense?" I asked. "Do you have any special strategies to control the Zibber?"

Whenever you talked about Buffalo Grove you had to talk about Zbikowski. I had spoken with Monken about him some time ago. "We're recruiting Zbikowski," said Monken then,. "He's really a great player." Even though he had had a less than brilliant game against GBN a year ago, there was just no question that Zbikowski was one of the premier high school gridders of 2002. Every coach I had talked with absolutely raved about him. I asked Monken to break him down as a prospect.

"He's a big, strong kid. He's a quarterback with a strong arm and just great speed." Speed was a major differentiating variable in the case of Zbikowski, who had been timed at 4.3 on the forty. Anyway, I probed the speed issue further, and Monken put in perspective.

"Do you know how fast most college quarterbacks are? You take a guy like [Phil] Rivers [the superstar passer from powerful North Carolina State]. He's probably around five on the forty. Zbikowski is so far ahead of the pack in quarterback speed."

It was unlikely that Zbikowski was going to wind up at Navy, but that they were recruiting him was a clear indication that the Middies were shooting for the moon, going for the best players in the country. Recruiting, like sales, is a numbers game. If you recruit conscientiously you are not going to get everyone, but you are bound to get some. Moreover, if you go after the very best, you are likely to get some of those.

As for any special wrinkles in the Glenbrook North defense, James had no answer. "I don't know. We practice with split squads. I do know that they don't have the running backs they had a year ago, so Zbikowski has to run the option more."

My thoughts turned to the time when wishbone offenses predominated. "The way you defend an option quarterback," I said to James, "is that you hit him every time you can legally do so. Even if you know he's going to pitch it, or has already pitched it, if you can hit him you do it. I know you watch ESPN Classic. You've seen those wishbone teams of the 1970s, haven't you?"

"Yes," James said quickly.

"I remember teams just hitting the quarterback over and over, every single time he handled the ball. At first it would have no effect, but by the third quarter you'd see that quarterback show the defense his hands. He'd raise his open palms at them, letting them know he didn't have the ball anymore, because he was getting tired of being knocked down. But they kept hitting him. Pretty soon his timing goes. He's pitching it early or even fumbling.

"This can really work against Zbikowski because he plays both ways. You keep hitting him and by the second half he's going to be sucking wind. The problem, I bet, is that too many teams think he's football's Jordan—they're in awe of him—and they stay away from roughing him up."

Quarterbacks don't like to be hit. "Do you know what is the most devastating play in football?" Lester Hayes, the great defensive back of the Oakland Raiders once asked me while seated next to me on a plane. "It's the sack. The quarterback doesn't know it's coming, and you hit him when he is just standing there. If you can get to a guy early in the game he is never the same."

Hayes went on to tell me of how he saw one of the Raider quarterbacks literally trembling on the sidelines from the aftermath of too many sacks. It wasn't so much fear as a sense of battle nerves that the quarterback was experiencing. "I felt sorry for him," said Hayes empathically.

"Who were the guys who handled the sacks best?" I asked.

"The great ones—Roger Staubach, Terry Bradshaw, guys like that. They just kept coming at you."

Although I had no desire to see Zbikowski injured, I hoped the Spartans could have a psychologically shaking effect on him with some hard hits.

In any case, few moments were more satisfying to me than those spent talking with my son about football and life. We would sit in the kitchen and go back and forth about the coming game, recruiting, or something else. What a gift to me at this point in my life! I was incredibly grateful to Rita for giving me such full access to him. So often birth parents protect their children from the stepparent, making a less than quality relationship a virtually self-fulfilling prophecy.

By Wednesday night, James had lost none of his optimism. "I told the defensive guys what you said," he told me, referring to my lecture on hitting Zbikowski at every opportunity.

"How are the guys mentally?" I asked.

"They're OK. We feel we can beat them. We know we had them down last year."

A victory would do wonders. Beyond extending, let alone redeeming the season, it meant GBN would occupy the number one seed in the brackets, and so would likely face-off against the lowest seed still standing in the quarterfinal round. On Wednesday I called Ivan and gave him and Ann a last-minute invite to the game.

"Man I would love to go," Ivan lamented, "but the weekend is really busy. We have a closing to go to and a wedding. I will talk to Ann and see if there is any way we could get there. I really would like to see that game."

Tim Larkin was going. "What time is the game? I'm going to call Todd and Rick from church and see if they want to go with me." I was heartened that those who knew James were rooting for him so intensely.

Truth be told I had not looked forward to a single game this season with the enthusiasm toward which I viewed this one. Other than the game against Niles West, on the weekend during which Ivan and Ann visited, I had trouble getting excited about any of the games. Somehow my mind kept pushing forward to the next four years for James. That is the difference between being a father on one hand, and a teenager on the other. I sensed how insignificant the 2002 season would likely be in the larger scheme of James' life. James, however, having lived less than eighteen years, did not see it that way. This was his *senior* year and he wanted to suck all the juice out of it.

I probably would have felt much differently had the team played better. But the three losses of this season equaled the total of the previous two (including the playoff defeats). There was simply no way to put a happy face on the 2002 season. The team had not performed well, and James was struggling through it with an assortment of injuries.

But now there was Buffalo Grove. Not often can one game transform a season, but that is exactly what this one could do. James was in a good mood and with high hopes. So was I.

Friday was unseasonably warm for November—in the fifties with little wind. I left with Tim Larkin about 6 p.m. for the game. Rita was giving her nephew Peter a ride from her downtown office. The stands of William Lutz Stadium were full, and the crowd had that playoff edge. With the starting lineups announced it was time to tee it up.

GBN would receive the opening kick. Scoring early figured to be important for a number of reasons. First, high school games often go to the team that scores first. That team makes a psychological statement in doing so and suddenly it has put its stamp on the game. In addition, Buffalo Grove was better known for its defensive prowess than anything. Therefore, putting one over immediately would be a substantial plus.

The kickoff went deep near the goal line, and amazingly on James' side of the field. He took off full blast up the middle with me shrieking, "Go, go, go." Suddenly, he was hit high in clothes-line-like fashion and he dropped as if he had been hit with an elephant gun. Before I could panic he was up and back to the huddle. GBN muddled along, but a long aerial from Kaspers to clutch Kyle Miller put the Spartans deep in Buffalo Grove real estate. There the drive stalled, but a thirty-yard-yard field goal by Marc Neuman gave GBN an early 3–0 lead.

I didn't like not punching it in, but three was better than zee. On this drive, however, the offense did not look all that imaginative. It was not a no-huddle enterprise, and James was often in the I. But it was early.

Not for long. On the first play from scrimmage, the Spartans had Zbikowski seemingly hemmed in behind the line of scrimmage on a would-be pass play. *Seemingly* is indeed the operative word. Zbikowski tucked it under and started darting around. Caroming off would-be tacklers in pinball-like fashion, he broke loose down the right sidelines for a sixty-five-yard touchdown. One play, 7–3. The disturbing feature of the play was that at least five Spartans had a clean shot at him and he rolled past and through them. At just 6-1, 190, he looked like a man among boys.

GBN went nowhere on the next drive, and shortly later the Bison struck again—14–3. I didn't need to see much more. With Rita constantly telling me to "shush" my "it's over" statements—she is James' mother and an ardent GBN rooter—I knew this was the last game of James' high school career. Buffalo Grove was better than we were, and worse, we were playing as badly and tentatively as we had played well and aggressively a week before. We were being beaten from the neck up and the shoulder pads down. It was 28–3 at the half—a half that ended fittingly on a fifty-plus yard pass that fell through James' fingers in a crowd of would-be receivers and interceptors. By halftime, I was becoming philosophical, and the talk turned to hot chocolate and popcorn.

Of course, I was secretly hoping for a second-half Spartan resurrection, but my left brain did not expect it and God did not grant it. The final score was 35–3, the worst beating I had ever seen James take going back to junior football. The Bison had held James to seventy-one yards on the ground. There was little consolation in James' having cleared the 1,400-yard mark for the season.

I was OK with it. The better team had won, and we were spared some wrenching down-to-the-wire loss that typified two of the last three GBN playoff eliminations. Most important, James left the field uninjured. Tim and I went down on the field as the two teams shook hands and then hastened in opposite directions. I saw Zbikowski about twenty-five yards away as he began to run off the field. "Tommy!" I yelled. He turned and I waved to him, knowing he would remember me from our times together at Northwestern and Bowling Green. Rather than just wave back, and he ran over to me thanked me after I congratulated him. We hugged and he parted for bigger and better things. I was happy for him.

Tim and I waited while Coach Whalen tried to console the troops and put a positive cap on the 7–4 season in the south end zone. Some kids listened intently, others appeared to be listening, and still others were sobbing. Whalen handled it well, given what had to be his own disappointment. When it ended, James got up, came over, and we hugged. The game, the season, and James' high school career were over.

29.

Days of Indecision

Saturday morning James was fine. He sat in the living room and began watching the Navy–Notre Dame game played in the Meadowlands. While we watched he said, "Were you disappointed that I dropped that pass at the end of the first half?"

"No, of course not. Besides, the game was out of reach already." I was disappointed for him, not in him.

"I wouldn't have scored on it anyway, because I was diving for it. It really came quickly. I looked up and it was right there."

James is very sensitive to his pass-receiving prowess. Several weeks ago, I told him that he would be wise to focus on his receiving skills in preparation for college. Unless he went to Harvard, he would almost certainly be used in the slot. At Navy, he would run and catch from the slot. At Bowling Green the focus may be more on receiving. In any case, he needed to become acclimated to dealing with a ball in the air. I know few people that put more pressure on themselves than James, and he was very conscious of any ball not caught.

"James, this is why I wish they had thrown the ball to you more often. Look at it this way. You are very familiar with running out of the I. You have done it literally hundreds of times. That is your comfort zone. Nothing surprises you there. That's how it is for Kyle [Miller, just an outstanding receiver] in pass receiving. He is used to seeing the ball in the air—the angle, the whole thing."

I was not just comforting James. That is exactly the case. James could see the field from the tailback position in his sleep. I suspect Miller could see the field similarly from the wide-receiving position. It is a matter of familiarity. This, for example, is why you may see an absolute dynamo of a running back or wide receiver be switched to defensive back in college. The sage college scout knows the skills are there even though the familiarity is not.

Coaching and practice have to fill the breach. In James' case, however, given his penchant for offense, the sooner he developed his hands the better.

When I was a teenager, Lombardi's Green Bay Packers ruled the football world. I remember the Vince Lombardi Show once featuring tight end Ron Kramer talking about pass catching. The most salient point he made was that the football should be caught with the hands—like a basketball or baseball—rather than allowed to float into one's arms or cradled against the stomach. It made terrific sense to me, and I never forgot it. I told James one of the best drills he could do would be to throw the ball back and forth at fairly close range with another person, gradually accelerating the speed of the throw, all the time catching it with his hands. Eventually he would be able to grab a veritable bullet in the air.

James left, leaving me to watch the game. I keep forgetting that he is now just eighteen, with his pants filled with ants. He will watch a football game when he is tired and winding down, but if he is alert his attention span will snap and he will be off to someplace else, even if it is on the phone with a friend.

Again, football proved so mental. Here was Navy, winless since the opener, with mighty Notre Dame down by eight, midway in the fourth quarter. Had the middies played at this emotional level in the rest of their games they would be talking bowl talk in Annapolis. Wait! Here come the Irish—a touchdown, a two-point conversion. You could feel the wind changing direction in the living room. The game ended with Notre Dame winning by a touchdown. I wonder what Monken—shown standing on the sidelines with his mod-looking sunglasses on—will have to say?

Bowling Green played later at South Florida. They won't be too full of themselves after being cropped by Northern Illinois last Saturday. It dropped them into second place in the MAC West and down to number twenty-five in the ESPN poll. South Florida, 7–2, is an independent and favored in the contest. You had to figure the reason Bowling Green would schedule a nonmarquee team like that on the road was to sell the "trip to Florida" perk to its recruits. Other than that, they were taking a needless chance at being handed another loss.

I was sleeping when Coach Chad Klunder of Harvard called

early Sunday evening. The Crimson really stayed at it. And they're having a banner year, having lost but one game and facing Penn for the Ivy League title next Saturday. The Ivy League can be a bastion of elitism, so I was concerned about Harvard. Academically, you would have to be a nimrod to knock it. Nonetheless, I taught sociology for eighteen years in colleges and universities, even having lectured at the University of Chicago medical school, and know what an impact such an environment can have on a person. James has plenty of intellectual horsepower. He is a clear thinker and rather independent of thought, so he may well resist the all too human temptation toward arrogance.

"Hello, is James there?" Now awake I recognized the drawl of Jeff Monken. We talked about the Notre Dame game. Monken, as would any coach, had the key game-turning plays etched in his brain. Of course, he lamented that had the Navy team played at a similar level throughout the season things might have been different.

"Coach, it's hard to feel sorry for you. Now you know what it was like at North Park."

We laughed and talked on. I asked him what was the largest number of losses he had ever suffered.

"Ten. It was a year at the University of Buffalo."

"Ten? Well, I guess I had you pegged all wrong. I thought it was all like those days at Millikin [Illinois, a Division III small college with a perennially strong football program, at which Monken played]." I asked him where he had James on the depth chart.

"He's number one among the slotbacks. We are talking to about five kids, but he is number one."

"Could you break that down for me?"

"James has great speed, is tough physically, and has a thirty-two ACT," Monken said, chuckling at the last item, "and he comes to us immediately."

It didn't register with me at the time, but so often Academy football recruits spend their first year at NAPS (Naval Academy Prep School), because they do not meet the qualifications of the Academy at the outset. There they can play a sort of junior varsity football as they ramp up academically, but they are not able to help the Navy program that year.

Then came the stunner. "Tell James if he wants to go to the Army–Navy football game, he needs to let me know soon. It's a home game for us in the Meadowlands, but I can't hang on to my tickets for very long."

Would he want to go to the Army–Navy football game? Does a rabbit like another rabbit? The Army–Navy confrontation was not a game. It was an event. I figured I might not see James for several days because I was going out to Detroit on business, so after signing off with Monken I wrote James a note about the invitation and put it on his bed. This was a wonderful opportunity and a sign of Navy's seriousness. Now he could experience it before making any decision. James wanted to go on his official visits with his decision made. We had talked about that before. "If I don't go with my mind made up, I will be swayed every place I go, and I won't know what to do," he explained the week before.

I understood. "You want to make an NFL decision. Make the call and only change it if there is indisputable evidence to the contrary."

He liked the analogy and smiled a smile of relief. "Yeah, that's it."

Now he was lying on his bed with the light revealing a furrowed brow. I knew he was troubled, so I sat down on the edge of the bed. "What's wrong, James? I know there's something bothering you."

"I've got to make a decision, and I only have three weeks."

I recalled our earlier conversation and felt for him. Now he had yet another problem. He had agreed to an official visit to Harvard for the weekend of December 7, the same date as the Army–Navy game. The game would be at Giants Stadium in the Meadowlands. He wanted to go and was trying to reschedule the Harvard visit. Because the Army–Navy contest was not part of an official visit, I would have to get James an airline ticket. Nonetheless, he said he would like to go, and I wanted him to experience that game to see how he felt about it. A week before he told me. "Playing in the Army–Navy game would be just awesome!"

I wasn't there for the Bowling Green call, but the big three were closing in. All was silent, however, on the Western Michigan front. Maybe the brain trust in Kalamazoo was heading in another direction.

I returned from my business trip to the Motor City and attended the Glenbrook North High School Fall Sports Awards Assembly. James was selected co-MVP of the team with Kevin Kaspers, was named all-conference, and was one of the school's Scholar Athletes. This latter achievement was especially gratifying. It marked a complete turnaround for him, from his early years of caring little and getting into a lot of mischief. There were people to thank for this outside of James. Foremost was his mother Rita, who simply never gave up on any of her children until they reached a certain standard of behavior. Another was a school counselor, Margaret Sullivan. Sullivan vigilantly watched over both Chris and James and never hesitated to call us if there was a problem we needed to know about. In fact, it became a standing joke between James and me that he could either hear from his mother and me about getting certain of his academic work done, or he could hear from Margaret Sullivan. There are not enough Margaret Sullivans in the nation's school systems.

After the plenary session was over, the various sports had group meetings at which the coaches handed out the varsity letters. Whalen is a good public speaker and handled his role in a classy manner. When it became the seniors' turn to receive their letters he spoke briefly about each of their contributions. When he came to James, he skipped over his records and talked about character. "What not a lot of people know about James, and what I am most proud of," he said, "is that James was banged up much of the time. He carried the ball 699 times for us over his career, and this year he played with a painful hamstring problem in addition to other injuries that might have kept other guys out. But he didn't complain. He didn't even mention it. That's what I will remember best about James."

After the event, James came over to Rita and me. It was a happy occasion for us. Our son had closed the books on a tremendous career, he was doing well academically, and he was healthy. With few places open later in the evening, James chose The Olive Garden. We ate in joy with lots of happy conversation.

The following Saturday was not a good day for James' football suitors. Harvard fell at Penn in the Ivy League title game, Bowling Green went down at South Florida 29–7, and Navy was squashed by a 4–6 UConn team, 38–0. Evidently, the Notre Dame game drained the midshipmen, because UConn came in with a power rating twenty-three points below the Irish, a team that had beaten Navy by just seven points. I also kept an eye on Western Michigan. They were routed at home by Toledo, 42–21. When I reported the Bowling Green outcome to James after church Sunday, he was somewhat relieved despite his fondness for the Falcons. "Maybe they won't pressure me," he said.

Monday night I approached James with a fresh recruiting scenario. "All the schools recruiting you have you in the slot," I said. "What if a school like Western Michigan finally decides you're their man in the 'I.' Then you would be able to be the running back."

Running backs have been drafted by the NFL out of the MAC, and James didn't have to put on much weight to reach the accepted size for a major college running back. Were he to redshirt his freshman year he could well reach two hundred by the time he began his eligibility. The issue was his long-term vision. James had a ready answer. "I would rather play in the slot. Navy runs the slotback. I am less likely to be hit as much there, risking injury."

Then he surprised me with his sense of big-time football pragmatism. "If I got hurt as a running back, the coaches would just put the next guy in and forget about me."

I was glad he felt that way. I frankly did not want him going for a hip or ankle replacement at forty because he had been taking hits for so many years. Better he play in the slot, where injuries were fewer and his risk of being forgotten was lower. For certain this seemed to pull the curtain down on Western Michigan. The Broncos did not feature the slotback very much, and they would have to do some hard selling to get James to decide in their favor this late after the interest we had shown them.

There was more. "I don't want to play defense, though, unless it's at a really major, Big Ten level." James had been used erratically on defense during the season, never really settling in. He opened the season being spotted at cornerback on third down and other obvious passing situations. Later he played free safety extensively. By the end of the season, to conserve his energy, he was on offense exclusively. The energy issue was interesting. Chris played both ways and so did Zbikowski. Yet James, who was in better shape than his brother had been, was too tired to make it go on both sides of the ball. There is no certain answer to this but I suspect it was mental. Chris has a laid-back temperament. He can pace himself. My guess is that Zbikowski can too. James is intense about breakfast. He is so focused, so wired in to almost any activity, that I think he simply burns out when he has to play the full game. His daily habits exhibit this. He can go nonstop on rather short sleep for several days, then sleep for hours on end. At certain points in the school year he would tell Rita he wanted to "get away for several days and relax." Unfortunately, that was not in the offing either of the last two summers. There was no way James would relax if it were at the expense of football.

Earlier James had cleared the December 7 date by postponing Harvard a week. He was running into potential conflicts. He wanted to visit both Bowling Green and Harvard. "I don't know if I can though," he said. "Harvard offered me the first two weekends in December. If I have to go to Bowling Green one of those two and see Army–Navy, I may miss Harvard." Monken told me the tickets were good until the weekend, so he had a little room to negotiate.

For me, I had just finished John Feinstein's *The Civil War*, a best-seller about the Army–Navy game. James had attended a Rotary luncheon at which a former Army captain, Jim Cantelupe, had been the guest speaker. He met Cantelupe afterward and the former Army star had given James a copy of the book. James showed it to Rita and me at dinner after the awards assembly. He proudly opened the book and showed us the inscription:

> *James,*
> *I hope you enjoy!*
> *Go Army—*
> *Beat Navy!*
> *Jim Cantelupe*

James then took out a pen and crossed out "Beat Navy."

30.

Working Through the Mix

"Hello, is James there?" It was Brian Murphy, a coach at the University of Wisconsin, calling on Tuesday night.

"No, coach, he's out now."

"I guess he keeps his own schedule," said Murphy.

"Now that the playoffs are over, coach, he is hard to predict."

"Are they out?" he asked.

"Yeah, they fell to Buffalo Grove and Zbikowski in the second round, just as they did last year."

"Buffalo Grove is out, too. Zbikowski got hurt, came back, then fumbled close to the opponent's goal on another hit at the end of the game." It was news to me. Just as the kids' interest in the playoffs faded once they were eleminated, my interest in the playoffs faded to black once my own kid was out. I guessed that Ed and I will have that beer sooner rather than later.

"How interested are you in James, coach. I'm coming right at you because I was an A.D. and I know how recruiting works."

He danced around the question, assuring me Wisconsin was interested.

"Come on, coach," I said, "you can get extra points with me by being honest. You guys are offering kids."

Murphy was deft. "I keep tunnel vision; I only focus on my own recruits. I really would like to see another tape of James later in the season. Coach Whalen sent me one earlier. What was his best game?"

Ultimately I wanted to clear that with James. I told him I would let James know of his request. We chatted a bit about the season and Murphy broke in, "Hey, what are you doing this weekend? You want to come up to see the Minnesota game?"

I really didn't want to. At this point, the drill would be the same. We would make the five-hour drive, perhaps meet the already preoccupied coaches briefly, sit in the autumn chill, and then return home. Though a win over the Golden Gophers would make Wisconsin bowl-eligible at 7–6, it wasn't Army–Navy and it was unlikely that James' attendance would help his cause. Things were too pragmatic for that.

"I don't know what is planned for the weekend, coach," I said, trying to wiggle out, "but look, you guys have been consistent in your contact with James so I feel free to come after you a bit. What side of the ball do you have James on?" I asked.

"Offense. Running back."

So much for d-back. No conversation with a major university is complete without discussing weight. Wisconsin, however, is not obsessed with big backs. A 190- to 195-pound "strong kid" is heavy enough to carry in Madison.

"How much did he weigh last spring?"

"He got up to 175. James is extremely conscientious, and we talked about how important being big enough to break tackles is."

"Well, I saw him in the weight room last spring," said Murphy, "and he looked good and thick."

As the conversation wound down I asked him the only real question. "When will you guys decide on who you'll offer?"

"I would say in the next two weeks. There are some schools that offer every one early, and some that wait till the last minute. We are in the middle, but fairly conservative."

We agreed that I would have James ask Coach Whalen to send a selected tape to Murphy. Murphy told us to "feel free to call him anytime," as he gave us his address and phone number.

I told James about the Badger call. He seemed pleased. It was, after all, the Big Ten.

"Maybe I didn't like them last spring, because it seemed they didn't like me," he mused. "You know, you talk to a girl and she says she's not interested, so you say, 'I never really liked her anyway.'"

The Wisconsin visit had been so different, and he had gone alone, something I didn't feel 100 percent good about. After two trips to a very receptive and solicitous Iowa football office, and two to a more neutral Northwestern, Wisconsin had given him the "Here we are, do you have what it takes to be a Badger?" feeling. It was something to think about, but even if the Badgers came in with an offer, we had to be skeptical. It was unlikely Alvarez and company were ready to hand him the ball the minute he hit Madison. More likely he would have to work his way up the depth chart, and then perhaps to a position he really did not want to play.

We talked about Buffalo Grove and Tom Zbikowski. James had heard about the game in greater detail. "I heard he turned it over four times and was really beside himself at the end of the game." James felt for him. He went on empathically. "Maybe I should give him a call. It's tough when you turn it over. I saw a game on tape in which he turned it over twice early and began hurrying after that. Two early ones and you're in quicksand." Perhaps James was reliving the Vernon Hills debacle.

"Hello, could I speak with James?" said the friendly voice on the phone. It was Bruce Tall of Western Michigan. I handed the receiver over to James anxious to hear what his Bronco status was to be.

"What did he have to say?" I hollered across the room to James the instant the call ended.

Anticipating my curiosity, James played cleverly: "He said they were no longer interested in me," and he shut the bathroom door firmly behind him.

He was more forthright when he emerged. "He said they are looking at several running backs and will probably decide within a week."

I liked Tall. He came off as a caring, decent guy. Unfortunately, Western had slipped substantially on James' list for two reasons. First, the recruiting delay concerned not only his status but also raised questions as to how good a program he would be entering. "I like the coach [Darnell] there, but it seems that whatever they're doing is not working," said James, referring to the team's 3–8 record at the time." The second was that the Western Michigan offense was less than ideally suited to James' skills as a slot or wingback. Most probably he would be dotting the "I."

Nonetheless, we were not going to look potential gift horses in the mouth, and if we'd learned anything at all it was that we would be wise to predict the unpredictable.

That Saturday the Division I regular season ended. Michigan fell to Ohio State in a bitter 14–9 contest in Ohio, putting the

Buckeyes in the BCS championship game. Navy was nipped late by an up-and-coming (6–5) Wake Forest team 30–27. Bowling Green tore into a hapless Eastern Michigan (What was going on there?) squad 63–21. Wisconsin outscored Minnesota 49–31, and Harvard (7–3) beat archrival Yale 20–13.

I thought of Lloyd Carr as Michigan came up short at Ohio State. Carr, despite our warm greetings, never called about James. No one from Michigan did. It was obvious why. Michigan plays a rather basic power offense and the Wolverines favor big backs. James would likely have had to tip the scales at two hundred-plus to be considered by Carr and company. Moreover, because James had spent so little time in a pass–receiving role, his skills there were not obvious enough for a team like Michigan to take a chance.

The Michigan case raises an interesting point. Elite programs like Michigan experience a trade-off. On one hand, they do not have to recruit "projects" (kids with talent that require much development like the youngster from Florida Bowling Green was looking at), nor do they have to take kids out of position if they don't want to. If they want a running back, they can recruit one. If they want a wide receiver, they can go after their player of choice. It is not that they will never convert a running back or wide receiver into a safety. It is that they don't have to. They are Michigan. Among the best. The top players want to play there. As was once said about Notre Dame under Parseghian, Michigan doesn't recruit; it summons. On the other hand, the pressure to win is immense. Carr has now lost twice in succession to Ohio State, a new and most unwelcome experience for him and the Wolverine faithful. The 2003 finale with Ohio State will now be larger than ever for Carr.

As the coach at Bowling Green said, a step down from Michigan, Ohio Sate, and company are the programs that often have to pick over what is left. These schools do often have an edge on a blue-chip prospect who is a native of their own state. Other than that, moving players to new positions and pursuing kids with the promise that they will play early (as a freshman or sophomore) are more frequently employed maneuvers. Of course, if and when these universities start developing a winning tradition, they can move to a higher level of selectivity. At the bottom, things can become more desperate. There will be a greater likelihood to take projects with a high upside and to recruit youngsters with the play-early lure in hopes of getting the win/loss corner turned.

Programs are evaluated based on expectations. At Michigan, Ohio State, Notre Dame, and Penn State, coaches are expected to win big and consistently. At the next level—Wisconsin, Purdue, and Minnesota, for example—there is an expectation of a plus-.500 season, but national prominence is hoped for rather than expected. Below this level (where Iowa used to be), at schools like Indiana and now Northwestern, there is a hope of victory, but hardly any strong anticipation.

All of this drives recruiting in a number of ways. First, many schools below the Michigan level simply do not go after the out-of-state megastars, realizing that to waste precious recruiting time pursuing these prospects could cost them more available athletes. Moreover, at every level there are the depth charts. A given school may be recruiting, say, three running backs and will have them ranked in priority order. Unfortunately, each of these three may be on any number of other schools' lists. Therefore, the coaches will make out a depth chart that goes well beyond three at the running back position knowing that they may have to go after number four through number six or beyond to get their three runners. This latter point is key. If a given blue-chipper receives say thirty offers, twenty-nine schools will not get him and everyone below this youngster will move up on each team's recruiting depth chart.

For the wary recruit, this knowledge should provide caution. While there may be great rejoicing in a young man's home to hear he is being offered by a truly major program, he must realize that should he be the third of the three running backs offered, he may have the sprint star's experience that Paul Saad told us about, perhaps never playing an important role at the school. This is why good recruiting below the elite level involves targeting certain "gettable" players, contacting them early, and courting them to the deadline. The courting process gives the recruit the sense that he is high on that school's depth chart and likely to play. To put this in the real world, suppose James is offered by Wisconsin or Purdue—both schools that have maintained contact. He will have to weigh those attractive playing-at-the-Big-Ten-level offers off against a Bowling Green, Harvard, or Navy that has given him reason to believe he will play at those institutions.

On Sunday afternoon a coach from Dartmouth, a school that is not new to the mix, called. I respected the coach for asking me politely if he had any real chance at James. "You are probably not at the top of the list, coach," I said as gently as possible. "Harvard has pursued James regularly and your program hasn't been that strong recently. That you have had problems with your athletic director doesn't help either." (The previous athletic director had engaged in some sort of unsavory behavior and made national news.) I didn't want to pile on, but I felt he wanted to know the truth.

Undaunted, the coach offered a counter: "Well, we're putting the program back together. We won the conference in 1996. We now have a new athletic director and things should be fine." I was sincere when I told him James had not made up his mind and he should feel free to dive in the water.

On Monday, I reached Mark Criner at Cincinnati. James had asked me to find out where the Bearcats were with regard to him. They had offered early out of nowhere, talked with him several times, then drifted away. This on-again, off-again behavior does nothing to strengthen a school's case in the eyes of a recruit. Youngsters like James are alert to secondary signs. Several times after GBN was eliminated, Gregg Brandon of Bowling Green left voice-mail messages about the Spartans' status in the playoffs. "Brandon doesn't even know we've been eliminated, and Monken (of Navy) knows more about our game with Buffalo Grove than I do," remarked James in passing.

As for Cincinnati, had they withdrawn the offer? What was going on? "We are very interested in James; he's a tremendous player," said Criner. "We still have two more games to play and if we win those we go to a bowl, so we are just really backed up in our recruiting."

Probably a half-truth, I thought. Criner was relaxed and talkative during our conversation, but you have to wonder how serious a program on the upswing, as this is, could be when no one even stayed in touch with James on the phone. Surely they did not treat all their recruits this way. If they did, the Bearcats program would be heading in a southerly direction quickly. To Criner's credit, he was aware that James had gotten bigger, perhaps having seen a tape of this season, but doubts lingered.

It didn't occur to me to ask him if the offer was still good, but he did tell me the team was looking for "running backs and d-backs" and that he would be calling James this week. We'll see. If he does, we will have to get more specific with him.

It didn't end with Cincinnati.

"Hello, is James there?" inquired the mellow voice. It was Butch Jones, back from the dead.

"No, he's out; what's happening coach?" Now I wanted something firm.

"Well, I wanted to find out where James is at in his recruiting choice, because we are seriously considering offering him." Jones talked slowly and calmly. He went on. "So far we have not offered any running backs, but now we have a senior we thought had some eligibility left but that is now in question. We have appealed to the NCAA and are awaiting their ruling. If it goes against him, we will be making an offer.

"To put it candidly, we didn't want to rip ourselves off by offering James when we may not need a running back, and I didn't want to rip James off by leading him on when we weren't sure we would need to recruit a running back, so I waited until now to talk with you."

I still liked Jones, but the scenario had problems for me. In the spring we had driven all the way to Mount Pleasant for a spring practice and then returned for a summer camp day, all at our expense. Throughout that experience Jones had led us to believe James would be considered for an early offer, something that would be determined by the end of June. Then we heard nothing at all from Jones and CMU until near the fall, as if no such consideration had ever occurred. All of this raised questions.

Didn't Jones know back in the spring that CMU would likely not offer a running back? If so, why did he not tell us so? Even more disturbing, why would he intimate the possibility of an early offer? And if he didn't know, and was sincerely concerned about being helpful to us ("Feel free to call me anytime if I can help you in any way"), why didn't he tell us something at the end of June?

Now, as the clock approached midnight here he was acting as if he had been doing us a favor all along.

Wanting to put nothing at risk, given that there were no birds tangibly in hand, and feeling we owed Jones nothing, I decided to sound encouraging. "He hasn't made up his mind, coach, and he will be home Sunday night, so that would be a good time to talk with him and see where he's at."

I probed Jones about other running backs they may be looking at. He was forthcoming. "We are looking at three kids and they're all top prospects."

I then sprung the trap. "Where is James on the depth chart?" Now I had him.

Well, at least I thought so. "We don't do things that way," said the smooth Jones, once again deftly slipping out of my noose. "We put kids in levels, and James is at the top level."

He asked me what I could tell him about James' current status. I told him about Navy, Harvard, and Bowling Green, reiterating that no decision had been made.

"Again, I don't want to mislead James. I think we'll know something between the seventh and the fourteenth—after he returns from Army–Navy and before he goes to Bowling Green. I wanted to find out where he's at to see if he would still be interested."

On Saturday, Cincinnati won its sixth game, enhancing their chances at a bowl. And untrue to his word, Criner never called.

So where did it stand now? Clearly, Bowling Green, Navy, and Harvard are right there. James has visits scheduled with the first two, and will likely visit Harvard in January. Cincinnati is a wild card now. I'd say it's even money that Western and Central will still come in, and a fair chance that Wisconsin will too. I have a sense it may not end here, once the names at the top of the depth charts disappear. Interestingly, Anthony Davis of the Badgers ran for 301 yards on 45 carries Saturday against Minnesota. James took sharp notice that Davis is maybe 195, a weight James almost certainly could reach by 2004, after coming out of a probable redshirt freshman season.

In truth, I would like more options for James. Certainly more choices can cloud the decision-making process, making it more difficult. James' case, however, is somewhat unique. Two of the three schools in hot pursuit of him are atypical institutions. Clearly, Harvard is a nontypical opportunity, given its Ivy League status—its heavy academic reputation without being able to offer athletic scholarships. Then there is Navy, a military academy that prides itself in its unusual status. This leaves James only Bowling Green as a more conventional higher educational institution playing Division I football. It would be nice to have another more typical school emerge from the darkness as an alternative to Bowling Green. Then again, late entries raise the depth chart issue.

I discussed the current situation and final strategy with Steve Helminiak and Mike Herbert. "Doc, there are three questions you should ask any school now," advised Helminiak. "One: Where do you have James—what position? Two: How many kids are you going to offer at that position? Three: If say, they offer five to be on the safe side, but are only going to take three, will James get a scholarship if all five accept?

"Those are the big three, Doc. Where will he play? How many will they offer at his position? And will he be offered officially if they all accept. You have a right to those answers."

Obviously, I could ask more questions—depth chart ranking, redshirting likelihood, and so on. But the key now was whether the school wanted James badly enough to take him if he accepted. If they were that certain of their interest, then he would likely get a good look—a fair chance—from the coaching staff the minute he stepped on campus.

As for James, the tension was showing and he had already had enough. I told him of my questioning strategy and he seemed relieved. "If any coach calls, you talk to him," he said, all but making me his agent. I was now prepared, set for the final phase, and I was looking forward to it.

Former Cy Young award winner Bruce Sutter once told me the reason he liked to be a closer was "because what you do out there will probably determine the outcome of the game, and either way, it will be over soon."

What these schools did would have much to do with the outcome of James' college choice, and it would be over soon.

31.

Avon Calling

The light on the answering machine was flashing when I got home from church. "Hi, this is Coach Klunder. I'm going to be flying into Chicago tonight. Tomorrow I'll be visiting Glenbrook North and I would like to stop by your home in the evening to talk with James about going to Harvard."

I was a little put off by the message. I had never spoken with this coach, and now with no real advance notice, he seemed to be inviting himself over for coffee and poundcake the next evening to talk with James about one of the most momentous decisions he will ever make.

It was also very inconvenient. I was going out of town the next day and so would not be able to attend this little confab. Had this been someone from Navy or Bowling Green I would not have minded. After all, I had visited both schools and talked many times with the coaches involved. This was different. I had never exchanged more than twenty-five words with Klunder, and I had not left any shoe prints on Cambridge soil with James.

I relayed my angst to James. "Oh, I thought you knew this was the week coaches visit the schools and make home visits," he said matter-of-factly. "I'm sorry."

James will probably never rival President Reagan as a great communicator. Because I knew Wisconsin was going to visit GBN in the coming week and had had many discussions with a variety of coaches, he assumed I would realize home visits could well be in the immediate offing. In any case, I called Klunder on his cell phone and he graciously offered to try to catch an earlier flight to Chicago and meet with Rita, James, and me that evening.

At 7:15 he was at the door.

Chad Klunder, thirty-ish, a large, athletic, pleasant man, stepped in. We exchanged greetings. He explained that during this recruiting period the NCAA allows unlimited phone calls, but only face-to-face visits with the kid one day per week. This meant that Klunder could not visit Glenbrook North in the morning, because it would be construed by the NCAA as a second visit in the same week. Later James puckishly suggested that Klunder would have been wiser to come over at 12:01 a.m. and then stop at GBN later in the morning, assuring everything transpired on the same calendar day.

While Rita was still in the kitchen I asked Klunder how he wound up at Harvard.

"When I finished college, I became a graduate assistant strength coach at the University of Minnesota for five years, the last one under Glen Mason, who is there now." Klunder went to Harvard following a colleague from Minnesota who put in the word for him.

Rita joined us. James was not yet home.

"My only concern about James visiting Bowling Green in two weeks," said Chad, "is if they take him aside and tell him that his scholarship offer is good, but that he better decide now, or within a week, or they will offer it to someone else. They may say, 'We need an answer in a few days or it may not be there for you.' I've had that happen to me."

It was interesting that throughout the discussion with Klunder, Navy never came up. He seemed concerned about Bowling Green turning up the steam. I asked him about the year-round regimen in Division IAA.

"We send the kids home for the summer. We trust them to work out on their own. These are good kids. They'll follow the workout book we give them when they leave."

I was thankful to hear James' key in the door right about then. Of course, Klunder had come primarily to see him. Financial aid soon came up, what with Ivy League schools not offering scholarships. Rita was particularly concerned about Harvard's possibly factoring in my financial statement with hers in assessing James' financial-aid status.

"It's done case-by-case," said Chad. "The most important thing is to get your financial information in by the end of the coming week."

James listened with interest as Klunder uttered the secret

words, "Everything is need-based, and Harvard makes it feasible for any qualified student to get in."

Then a little pressure. "We've got thirty spots open in football. Once things are full we can't help a kid."

Then, looking at James, he laid it on a bit. "You're the top guy on our board. Tailback guaranteed. You could play tailback as a freshman with us." Later he repeated the appeal. "You are an impact player for us. On top of the board."

Harvard had enjoyed recent success under Head Coach Tim Murphy. "Every kid from this year's graduating class has a championship ring. We've won thirteen of the last fourteen games in the Ivy League."

Klunder also made clear that the door to the NFL was ajar. "Matt Birk, number 78 for the Vikings, is a two-time Pro Bowl center from Harvard." Klunder estimated that about three or four kids a year get shots at the NFL. The point was clear: Get a Harvard education and put nothing at risk for the NFL.

"Each year 20,000 kids apply to Harvard; only 1,600 get in," Chad explained. "We take about thirty a year in football. Now if a kid gets hurt or even quits, it doesn't affect his financial-aid status. If you quit at a IA school, your scholarship will be taken. For the kid who gets injured at Harvard, he is still part of the team and can use our sports medicine facility."

When asked about the Fellowship of Christian Athletes status at Harvard, Klunder was ready. "Our offensive coordinator, Jay Mills, goes to the national meetings." Jay Mills? The name was familiar, banging against something in my memory bank. Several days later I looked him up on the Internet. It was the same Jay Mills from Gerry Faust's Notre Dame staff I had interviewed for the head coaching position at North Park sixteen years ago. He had made a very good impression.

"You can't lose going to Harvard," Klunder pressed on. "You go to Bowling Green and don't like it, you can't get in to Harvard. We don't take transfers and we don't redshirt.

"Besides, Urban Meyer is a great coach, but he may not be there in four or five years. You can't go to a college for the coach. You've got to go for yourself."

Then more. "You may go to a place with a big stadium with a

big-screen TV, but will you like the people?" This was smart selling. Klunder was covering the possible unspoken objections related to Harvard not being a 1A program by answering them out
front.

Rita asked about a typical day at Harvard. "Classes begin at
9:00. Two or three a day. Four per semester. Football meetings are
at 3:00. Practice from 4:00 to 6:00. Everyone lives on campus at
Harvard because apartments are too expensive. Freshmen are in a
dormitory, the rest are in houses. You eat in your own house.

"In the off-season there is mandatory lifting. In the spring,
there are twelve practices for IAA schools [fifteen allowed at IA]."

I asked about the offense my old pal Jay Mills was running
these days. "It's a one-back, spread offense, about fifty-fifty pass
and run," Chad replied.

With all the questions answered, Klunder made one more appeal. "We see the best kid on the first night. You come to Harvard
and you'll be the man. You'll be an impact player."

Klunder had done a solid job. He hardly descended the steps of
our home, however, and the telephone rang. "Hello, this is Jeff
Monken of Navy. Is James there?"

Monken was calling not only to confirm James' attendance at
the Army–Navy game, but also that he would receive a special
high–security pass to go down on the field with the players before
the game. The privilege extended only to James, I would have to
stay in the stands because "the president [George W. Bush] will be
there and security will be extra tight."

Euphoria reigned in the Claerbaut home due to the strong appeal from Harvard, followed by an invitation to join the Navy
players on the turf of Giants Stadium in East Rutherford, New
Jersey, before the kickoff of the 103rd Army–Navy classic, played
in the presence of the president.

I couldn't help but look back, filled with a parent's joy over
how far James had come. Less than two years before he had decided to let go "the destructiveness" he had been engaging in,
born of the pain of a shattered family. He had counted the cost,
made a series of academic and athletic commitments, and mus-
tered the discipline to see them through. Now he was being re-
warded with the opportunity to attend two of the most exclusive

higher educational institutions in the nation. And he had the humility not to gloat.

A few days previous I called Paul Saad from the Detroit area to see what was going on with his son, Nick. "His team didn't win the state championship," said Paul, "but he had another great year. In Michigan they pick an All-State team, and then above that, a Dream Team. Nick made the Dream Team."

I was happy for both of them. Paul is a quality guy, and his son seemed to be a solid kid. I had felt badly last summer at Central Michigan when Nick had not gotten any early offers. I asked Paul about recruiting.

"He has been offered by Central," said Paul, "and he has several other visits scheduled. Ultimately, Nick also received offers from Western Michigan and Toledo. In both cases he could go either as a running back or defensive back.

I was particularly interested in Central. "At what position?" I asked, to determine whether Butch Jones had been telling me the truth about not having offered a running back.

"As an athlete—no special position—he could go at running back, tight end, or d-back."

"How big is Nick now?"

"Six-two, 215." This is more of a tight end, linebacker, or secondary body type, I thought. Jones had passed my informal polygraph, but just barely.

I spent a good bit of the three days following Klunder's visit on a business trip. Nothing new occurred on the recruiting front in my absence. It was just as well. I was busy enough—amid my consulting—trying to make travel arrangements for James and my trip to New Jersey at week's end. I was home only a few hours on Wednesday night before the phone rang. "Is James there?" It was a man with a Southern accent.

"May I ask who's calling?"

"This is Paul Johnson, head coach of the Naval Academy."

We chatted briefly, with Johnson's wanting to know where things stood with James.

"You're right at the top," I said. "Let me tell you this, coach," I continued, trying to move away from having to be any more specific about James' intentions, "I was an athletic director in a previous professional life and I can tell you that Jeff Monken has done the best job of anyone recruiting James."

"Jeff not only follows 'em up when he recruits them, he keeps an eye on them when they get here," Johnson drawled.

Just then, James came through the door and I gave him the phone. Johnson reconfirmed the arrangement for the Army–Navy game. "Be sure to have your identification, because security will be very tight for you going down on the field with the president there."

The conversation continued with James offering happy but cryptic responses to Johnson's questions. "I want you to know, we are looking forward to seeing you here, James. You are a top choice for the slotback position."

When the conversation ended I quickly asked James what Johnson had said. "He said, 'It was a pleasure recruiting you but we aren't interested,'" James spoofed. My thoughts returned to one of my conversations with Steve Helminiak in which he emphasized that head coaches reserve their calls for the blue-chip prospects. Here was Johnson, not seventy-two hours from the Army–Navy kickoff, taking time to call James. Clearly, James was central to their plans.

No word from Western Michigan, Central Michigan, Wisconsin, or Cincinnati, although the latter has an ESPN windup game at East Carolina Friday night. Gregg Brandon did call and we confirmed his visit to Bowling Green the second weekend in December. It had been a tough finish for the Falcons. A month ago they were 8–0 and ranked sixteenth in the country. Since then the team had dropped three of four, finishing with a strong but somewhat disappointing 9–3 log, and out of the bowl picture.

On Thursday I talked with Steve Helminiak about the current state of things. "Schools that push for December visits are serious," he stated. "Those that come later in the month, trying to get you there in January, don't have you at the top of the board. Those that don't contact you until January have you at the bottom of the list."

Well, James was apparently on the top of at least three lists—those of Harvard, Bowling Green, and Navy. He would visit Bowling Green next week and Harvard in January. Now it was time to beat Army.

32.

Beat Army

James and I had planned to leave for the Army–Navy game early Friday morning, enabling me to give him a tourist's day in New York City. Unfortunately, the East Coast was blasted with snow on Thursday, resulting in delays and cancellations for the airlines. We were bumped back to a 2:00 p.m. departure to Newark International Airport from Chicago's O'Hare.

We landed about 6:00 p.m. Eastern Standard Time, and not surprisingly James was famished. After getting our rental car and navigating around northern New Jersey, we found an Olive Garden restaurant and hour and a half later. There we waited forty more minutes to be seated. By now, James and I were laughing at our misadventures. Ravenously hungry, James all but swallowed his soup in several gulps and then proceeded to pick at my salad with his fork as he awaited his entrée. The pasta dish was hardly set before him before he had wolfed it down. At dinner I did manage to ask him where he was with his recruiting choices. We decided his position best resembled an inverted triangle, with Harvard and Navy at the top and Bowling Green below.

We then left for our hotel some thirty miles west with me listening to oldies on CBS 101.1 FM and James directing me as he charted our journey on the rental car map. We were in the room less than an hour before James asked, "Want something to eat?" When James asks you if you are hungry he is really saying he is hungry. With that we ordered a large pizza and cinna stix to be delivered to the room and watched what would be an incredible NBA game, one in which the Lakers would emerge from a thirty-point third-quarter deficit to beat Dallas by a bucket in regulation. I dozed off several times during the latter stages of the game, only to have James rouse me from my slumber to see the thrilling finish.

Saturday, December 7, dawned bright and clear. We were both

concerned about the possibility of arctic temperatures at the Meadowlands. Extreme cold would be most unwelcome, given that James had to be present two hours before game time to meet the Navy coaches and players on the field.

We arrived at Giants Stadium just before 10:00 a.m., only to find the parking lot already well populated with tailgaters devouring barbecue foods and imbibing in liquid refreshments of a malt and barley nature. Getting our tickets at the Will-Call was easy. Getting James on to the field was not. There were no signs indicating where recruits should go, nor were there any directions in the packet that came with the tickets. We began walking as close to the entrance of the stadium as we could, looking for someone to direct us. I saw the Stadium Club and headed for it.

"This is my son. He is a naval recruit. He is supposed to be down on the field with the coaches and team, but we can't find anyone to direct us," I pleaded to the security guard.

"Go inside. To the left is where the reception for the Navy people is being held. To the right is Army. Someone from the Navy should be able to help you." With that, we entered the Navy party, an event sponsored by the secretary of the Navy as it turned out, and I began looking for someone to whom to plead our case. It's never difficult for a football recruit to get cooperation from someone associated with the school recruiting him, particularly if that person is a football fan. Hence, I was not surprised when an official at the party said, "Follow me." He took us through the kitchen of the Stadium Club to a service elevator, instructing us to go to the bottom floor and ask an attendant outside the team's dressing room.

When the door opened, a troubled attendant greeted us. "You are not supposed to be down here. Do you have credentials?" she asked with concern. I explained the situation as calmly as I could to her, and with reluctance she said, "Follow me." "This is off-limits; I could get in trouble," she said as we walked on the concrete floor of the oval corridor that collars the Meadowlands. Just as we reached the Jets dressing room, the door opened and out walked Head Coach Paul Johnson. "Coach, James Velissaris!" I shouted. He greeted us warmly and, after hearing our plight, went inside to get instructions for us. No sooner did he go in before Jeff Monken exited. "Coach, James Velissaris!" I shouted again. Over

Jeff came, and he and some of his associates resolved the dilemma. We had to go back outside to the Will-Call area and look for a marine in uniform. He would have James' credentials.

We went back up and out, found the marine, and James was on his way through the west tunnel down to the field. I, now chilled and relieved, headed back to the Stadium Club. Making certain my "Guest of James Velissaris" badge was pinned on my running suit, I regreeted the guard at the outside door and, acting as if I knew where I was going, once again crashed the Navy party. There I visited with several of the guests milling about. I talked with one convivial alum, Peter Jenkins, and his wife, Mary Stalnaker. "Here I am an Annapolis graduate. What will happen if anyone asks me what I do now?" Jenkins said.

Taking his bait, I asked Jenkins what he was currently doing for a living. "I'm a professor at West Point," he said with a healthy laugh. "I teach thermodynamics." His wife, also a professor, taught civil engineering at the University of Colorado. Given that the two were Navy fans, they welcomed me enthusiastically after I identified myself as the father of a recruit. I stayed in the warmth of the Stadium Club for as long as I could, aware that it would be a lot colder in my seat.

Our seats were in the southeast side of the end zone, only five rows from the field. I looked down on the field where the two teams were warming up; then up several tiers to the upper deck of Giants Stadium, where the seats were filling up just as they were everywhere else. It is difficult to capture verbally the pulse of the Army–Navy experience. What was clear was why John Feinstein felt compelled to write *Civil War*, his book on the subject after witnessing the event. We sat in the Navy section with the masses of uniformed midshipmen, dressed in navy blue all around. The Army cadets, decked out in their gray uniforms, were on the other side of the same end zone. Cheers and chants rang out from the sections as the stadium clock ticked down to kickoff.

James had bought a now cold hot chocolate for me, having waited patiently for me after leaving the sideline. I asked him how it felt being on the field before such an event. Earlier, when I asked him if he was excited, he merely nodded his head, so I was not surprised when the extent of his description was, "OK, it was good." With the stadium clock down to thirty minutes the teams left the field through the west tunnel, and soon the face of President Bush appeared on the Verizon Wireless Jumbotron. Bush ceremoniously marked the occasion. When he concluded with his "and may God bless the United States of America," the crowd cheered.

The significance of the date—December 7, sixty-one years to the day since the bombing of Pearl Harbor—was not lost on either James or me. Nor was the matter of safety. Here we were, sealed into this huge stadium just outside of New York, not many miles from what was the World Trade Center less than fifteen months ago, with the president somewhere in attendance. What better way for a group of terrorists to mock the United States than to wreak tragic havoc at this event? Although I comforted myself with the remark "There will be no safer place on the globe than the Army–Navy game" made by a friend from New York several weeks previous, I was still uneasy.

With the teams off the field, I watched the clock tick off the seconds. The last thirty or so minutes before the start of a sporting event, with teams off the field (or floor), are loaded with anticipation and suspense. The clock methodically ticks down toward zero as you stare at an empty playing surface, surrounded by masses of passion-filled fans, all waiting for their respective teams to re-enter the theater and for the confrontation to begin. The tension was broken when the Navy chaplain offered the benediction, citing the "act of aggression" sixty-one years before. At 13:56, the Navy chorus sang the national anthem. For the next ten minutes, the only thing that moved was the stadium clock. With about five minutes left, Army—the visitors in this one—ran onto the field to the roar of their partisans. At 3:25 Navy emerged from the tunnel, and now all that was left was the coin toss and the kickoff.

Army won the toss and chose to receive. The teams lined up. On the far side of the field the Navy kicker spotted the ball. Not more than thirty-five yards in front of us stood Army wide receiver William White, waiting at the goal line for the kick. The ball sailed end, over end appearing ever larger as it headed on a near direct line toward James and me, bouncing once before White took it and ran it back near the forty. Army went three and out. Navy, after breaking off some solid runs, threw an incomplete pass on third down at about the fifty. It appeared they would be punting. But wait! A flag had been thrown, and when the ruling was roughing the passer, the Midshipmen had life. With 8:32 left in the first, quarterback Craig Candeto snuck over the goal below us and with the PAT it was 7–0 good guys. Late in the quarter, Army countered with a field goal, but when Navy punched in another score on the first play of the second quarter it was 14–3. Two more midshipmen touchdowns followed another Army field goal, and at the half it was 28–6.

James and I warmed ourselves inside the Stadium Club at the half. Under ordinary circumstances we would have left in the third quarter of what eventually became a 58–12 blowout. But this was the Army–Navy game, and James wanted to see the postgame tradition of unity. It was impressive. Within minutes of the final gun, the euphoric midshipmen joined their Army foes and stood in front of the cadets section for the playing of the Army's "Alma Mater." Then the two teams cooperatively stood before the midshipmen for their "Blue and Gold." Although the moods of the two teams were clearly in contrast, the reverent respect shown by both for one another's role in the nation's defense was something that stays in one's memory.

That night, back in Chicago, James and I talked about the game and how dominant Navy had been. "If Navy would have played this well in a number of other games they would have been six and six and perhaps headed to a bowl," I said. "They beat SMU, and could well have beaten Duke, Northwestern, Notre Dame, and Wake Forest. Monken's preseason goal of getting to a bowl doesn't seem so far-fetched when you look at it that way."

James agreed.

"They really do have to tighten up on special teams defense," I said, noting a number of lengthy Army kickoff returns.

"They lack guys with the athletic quick step," explained James. "On Big Ten teams there is about that much difference in talent between the first and third strings," he stated, holding his thumb and index finger about an inch apart. "They would have guys like me on the return teams to get down there before the return man can accelerate. When you get to the mid-major level, though, the spread is like this." He held his hands about nine inches apart.

That is exactly the case. Butch Jones had lamented to me about the injuries that had beset the Central Michigan squad. "We had a strong start," he said to me on a phone call a while back. "I hate to make excuses, but we got clobbered by injuries and that took us down."

"We ran out of gas," was Gregg Brandon's summation of Bowling Green's late-season decline. Though Brandon may not have been referring to physical injuries, the lack of depth on teams at this level results in some rather heavy physical and mental burdens being placed on a team's top players.

The night for us was not about injuries or excuses. James and I had taken our last father–son unofficial trip together, and we were home safely. It had been a year—a wonderful year—but the hard part for James was still ahead.

The decision clock was ticking.

33.

Twists and Turns

"Hi, this is Coach Klunder of Harvard." Chad Klunder of Harvard was nothing if not persistent, calling regularly even in our absence. On Monday afternoon he had left a message about "stopping by" again on Wednesday night to see James. It seemed a bit much. Not two weeks before he had suggested a short-notice meeting with the family, necessitating the arrangement of our schedules on the same day to accommodate his visit.

"You're not helping your cause, coach," I said, being more blunt than I perhaps should have been. "You're pressing too hard."

"You never know; I was hoping to see . . . "

"I'm telling you, you're not helping your cause," I repeated, sorry for my abruptness. "James is feeling plenty of pressure and he is very well aware of Harvard. You guys are right there," I said, trying to sound a bit more mellow. "We are flattered by your interest, and we are well aware of the benefits of Harvard."

Then he switched gears. "Well, I can see James at school Wednesday, but Coach Murphy, our head coach, will be out next weekend, and he wanted to stop over, say, Monday and meet the family and talk with all of you."

"Monday is the night Navy is coming over," I said, feeling irritated.

"Well, maybe Coach Murphy can come before or after, or if not, then maybe Sunday night."

Clearly, things were heating up. First it's Klunder on a Wednesday and then Murphy the following Monday with the right cross. The problem was not the visits themselves; it was that Klunder seemed to be all but mandating the dates. It's important to note that Klunder was doing all the right things. Getting into the home, working the parents—especially the mother—can be incredibly advantageous. Ed Zbikowski definitely knew this and was careful to keep coaches out of his living room.

"Why is that necessary?" I asked with annoyance.

"Well, he is the head coach, and he does want to meet the recruits and their families," Klunder explained. Of course he did, and of course that was most appropriate, although neither Paul Johnson nor Urban Meyer had darkened our door. "James is really feeling the pinch," I explained. "In fact, he sometimes asks me, 'You talk to the coaches,' because it is wearing him down."

Klunder seemed to understand. He was only doing his job and he was doing it very, very diligently. Many a coach would like to have someone work as conscientiously as Chad Klunder had on James. In fact, Klunder was performing the way I have trained salespeople around the country to perform. Because of his efforts he had pushed a IAA school right into the thick of the recruiting battle. In addition, when you contrast his efforts with that of some of the other schools, there was really nothing to complain about. I was simply feeling crotchety, but I didn't want to be discourteous. I reassured him I would get the message to James and we would call him back shortly. We did and arranged for Coach Murphy to come by Sunday night.

I wondered what was going on at Bowling Green. On Monday ESPN claimed that Marvin Lewis, the celebrated defensive guru of the Baltimore Ravens, had been offered the Michigan State job and that an announcement of Lewis as head coach could come any minute. Well that's it for Urban Meyer and the Spartan green and white, I thought. An hour or so later the update came. Lewis had informed the Baltimore organization that he was not going to East Lansing. Maybe now Michigan State will be dialing an Ohio area code.

On Tuesday night, while James was out, Gregg Brandon of Bowling Green called. "Maybe you've seen it in the media, I don't know, but Coach Meyer has received some offers from other schools. They're pressing him pretty hard. We should know something in a day or two, but we have to put the visit with James on hold for now."

"I had been hearing a lot about Urban and Michigan State," I said.

"For awhile it looked like it would be Michigan State but he's probably pretty far down on the list, now." A few late-season losses will do that in the pragmatic world of big-time college football.

"What are the schools?" I asked.

"He's been offered the head coaching positions at Utah and Wyoming."

"Utah and Wyoming!" I exclaimed. "He doesn't want to go there, those are parallel moves. Urban is thirty-eight and a guy on the rise. The next move should be to a really big-time, Big Ten–level program."

The instant I stopped talking I realized I had gone a bit over the line, suggesting what Urban Meyer's life direction should be, so I switched gears. "Gregg, a lot of guys call here, some I like and some I don't like. I like you and feel comfortable with you, so I'm being candid." I went on. "I think you coached at Wyoming and that's great country . . . "

"I did," he confirmed.

"But you also coached at the top level and you know the difference."

"That's for sure," he affirmed.

"What's the attraction of those schools?" I asked.

"Well, they're offering a lot of money for one thing. Also, when you win seventeen of twenty-four games in two years the way we did here and you don't get to a bowl, well it's pretty tough."

Gregg Brandon was dead right. Bowling Green had once made it to number sixteen in the ESPN poll this past season. Although they dropped three of their final four, they closed the books at 9–3. A year ago, one ranking had them finishing as the twenty-sixth best team in the nation with an 8–4 record. Meanwhile, Cincinnati of the Conference USA just finished 2002 with a 7–6 record and a bowl bid.

"What about you, Gregg?" I asked. "You've got to get a shot at the top spot there."

"I'm sure going for it if it opens," he said.

"Well, you should. You're forty-six, just the right age. You've got top-notch experience and you're offense has been among the best in the country. You would give the program the continuity they need. They don't want to start all over and risk sending the program back to where it was when you guys came."

"Thank you, I appreciate that," he said humbly.

We talked a bit more and parted warmly.

This is what stinks about big-time football. Probably forty of those kids at Bowling Green came directly or indirectly because of Urban Meyer. Now he could be gone but they can't transfer without penalty. Furthermore, you've got to figure a good bit of his staff will move with him. These players are sheep without a shepherd, and no one cares.

On Wednesday afternoon I checked the Internet. There it was. Urban Meyer had accepted the head coaching position at Utah. A week before, he insisted he was staying put at Bowling Green.

That night Edgy Tim called, wanting an update on James' recruiting adventures. I filled him in, telling him it was Navy and Harvard. We talked about the cleanliness of the recruiting process.

"Tim, we've been at this for a year and not only has no one approached James illegally, I haven't heard of any skulduggery anywhere. I know you are in and around this business constantly. Is it really that clean?"

"It's really gotten a lot better. Face it, the high-profile programs are really watched closely and the penalties are so severe, why take a chance?" he answered.

He went on. "There is more attention, more eyes and ears than ever before tuned in on recruiting. All those Internet sites, scouting services, and recruiting buzz in the media have had at least one positive effect. You can't get away with much. For example, if a school says they're recruiting two running backs and then goes after four, it gets out."

"I also think that with the big money involved," I offered, "no one wants to see someone get an unfair advantage. So if anyone sees you get an illegal edge, you will probably be turned in."

"Exactly, you can't hide especially if you are in a high-profile program."

"It used to be operated like what they called the 'blue code,'" I said, "in which honest policemen would not inform on a corrupt one. Now it seems just the opposite."

"It's almost 180 degrees. It may not be a coach or anyone in a program that will get the word through to the NCAA, but illegal recruiting gets reported."

Was it ever different! Bear Bryant that admitted he had paid players in the 1950s, justifying such dishonesty by claiming he had to "meet the competition." It does seem that the temptation to recruit illegally is greater in basketball, where a single blue-chipper can turn a program, as opposed to football, a game requiring a small army of solid performers. That certainly seemed to be the case in Chicago in the 1980s and 1990s, when I was at North Park.

Because we had enjoyed national success there, we were in regular contact with Division I coaches and were cut in on the larger basketball grapevine. For awhile, the word on the street was that to land a topflight Chicago kid, you may have to ante up to the tune of five figures to the youngster's mother, his coach, and maybe a school administrator if his grades were a problem in need of fixing. Every bit of it was hearsay. It always is, because that stuff is never talked about publicly. Nonetheless, it seemed more than curious that for a number of years virtually every single hot prospect from the Chicago public high school system went to Illinois. Not Purdue, not Indiana, not Iowa, not Michigan. Illinois. My daughter, Rochelle, who graduated from Illinois, knew a number of the players. "Every player on the starting five had a Chevy Blazer from the same dealer," she told James and me, laughing. "Isn't that a coincidence? And even though some of them came from poor families, they all had spending money." Moreover, there were regular thinly disguised charges leveled at Lou Henson and particularly his right-hand man, Jimmy Collins.

Again, no one knows, but the rumors were persistent. It seems more than accidental that when Henson left Illinois in the mid-1990s the school turned to Mr. Clean, Lon Krueger, to take over the coaching reins rather than Collins. And once in the saddle, Krueger and Illinois did not get another Chicago city recruit.

Anyway, I was encouraged by our experience with the integrity of the recruiting process. An industry it was and is, but a less dishonest one.

What has not been so honest, though not in a corrupt sense, are the actions of Cincinnati. In a word, I found their lack of responsiveness annoying. Here is a school—one of two—that back in July extended an early "official" scholarship offer to James. Because no offer is actually official until the school tenders the paperwork to the youngster to be signed no earlier than the first Wednesday in February of his senior year, one can only infer that *official* is intended to denote integrity of intent. In other words, the school's offer is made in good, sincere, faith—one that will be honored when signing time comes should the youth decide to attend the institution. If that is the test of *official*, then it seems Cincinnati may have flunked it. Not only has Mark Criner, our contact person, not called when he said he would, I left a voice mail on the telephone of Head Coach Rick Minter, the person who extended the "official" offer, and he did not respond either. Indeed, I was happy to see Cincinnati fall to North Texas in its bowl game, finishing the season with a power rating in arrears of Bowling Green.

What is so irksome about Cincinnati's moral negligence is that it exemplifies what is wrong about big-time college recruiting. Because James has other opportunities and because he has family to support him, the seeming withdrawal of the Cincinnati's offer is likely of little material consequence to him. But what if he were from a one-parent, indigent family, had only that one offer, and was founding all of his future plans on the belief that he would be going to Cincinnati?

And there have to be kids in exactly that circumstance with various schools.

Iowa, though not as guilty of misleading James as Cincinnati, is also not high on my honor list. No school recruited James more intensely than did the one in the cornfields. Not only did James receive mail weekly and sometimes more often than that, every one either telling him of their interest in him, or why the Hawkeye program ought to be his first choice, but both his mother and I received Mother's and Father's Day cards. Moreover, he was urged to attend—at his own expense—the school's junior day, spring practice, and summer camp. We attended the first two, only to be showered with professions of interest, and near-scholarship pledges. Then suddenly all contact ceased. Make no mistake, we never felt that Iowa owed James an offer. They promised none and should not be held to extending one. What is upsetting, is that after a blizzard of mail and a flood of verbal encouragement, the school did not have the class to send James a letter stating that although their staff believes that he has Division 1 ability, they have but x number of offers to grant to running backs and that his position on the depth chart suggests that he may not be receiving one from Iowa. A simple correspondence of that nature would have made all the difference. It would have given James' relationship with Iowa, and the coaches that courted him, a sense of integrity. But no such letter came. He was dropped with all the sensitivity with which a fickle teenager ends an alliance driven by puppy love. Again, for James none of this had much impact. But what about the kid who counted on Iowa to be straight with him and believed in Kirk Ferentz and his staff?

It's an industry, as Ed Zbikowski would say.

When James came home he said he had met with Coach Klunder at GBN. Klunder had told him that he had to take his academic responsibilities with utmost seriousness because the staff had to push through some resistance to get him accepted. The problem was not his ACT. It was his class standing, something that had suffered due to his woeful freshman performance. By the end of the academic year James had repaired that problem by all but acing nothing but college-prep, advanced placement courses, driving his GPA skyward.

Later, the Dartmouth coach called. Apparently he had talked to Coach Whalen, who had inexplicably mentioned the provisional nature of the Harvard acceptance. Also an Ivy League school, Dartmouth had another view. "We've looked at your scores, James, and you are well within the range of acceptance." James was not terribly interested in Dartmouth, given its football struggles, but he kept the door open to future conversation.

James also learned that Harvard was recruiting the top running back from nearby football power Maine South. "I played against the kid on weekends during the summer," James said. "He's bigger than I am and though not as fast as I am, very fast. It's OK that they are recruiting another tailback, but when Klunder was here he mentioned he was recruiting another player in the western suburbs and left out the kid from Maine South. Plus he made it sound as if I were the only tailback he wanted."

This kind of stuff troubled James. The fastest way to get James to write you off is to lie to him. Now he was wondering about how truthful Chad Klunder had been. "When Coach Murphy comes Sunday I'm going after him on the recruiting stuff."

I suggested he do it carefully. Instead of telling Murphy about the Maine South youngster, giving him a chance to construct a quick defense, we decided to ask open-ended, who-else-are-you-recruiting and are-you-recruiting-other-tailbacks, questions.

Time was running out, and the game was becoming one of separating the good guys from the bad guys.

34.

A Twin Bill

Tim Murphy, a tall, lean, balding man in his fifties, has been the head coach at Harvard since 1994. His two previous head coaching stops were at the University of Maine and Cincinnati. He left Cincinnati after an 8–3 season, having completely turned around a moribund program in his five-year tenure in the Queen City. Murphy's program at Harvard had taken an upward turn over the past two seasons. After going 33–37 after his first seven campaigns, he had led the Crimson to an undefeated 9–0 mark in 2001, and had followed that with a strong 7–3 finish this past season.

"We are looking for the best football players we can get who are excellent students," is what Murphy led off with as he sat on our living room couch facing James. His style is low-key and slightly nervous.

"Every four-year player who has graduated has played on a championship team since I have been there," he said softly. "Harvard is the only Division I program to accomplish that.

"We have excellent students at Harvard. Ninety-eight percent of our students graduate, and the rate is higher among our football players. The reason is the school's selectivity. Each year only 1,500 of 2,000 applicants are admitted. And of those 18,000 or so who don't, 12,000 could have made it. There just was no room. If you work, you'll make it," Murphy said, looking at James.

"How much do you know about Harvard?" Murphy asked James. James answered briefly, highlighting what he knew of the school's academic reputation.

Murphy then addressed the issue of James' seemingly provisional status. "Your class rank is not high, but your counselor [Margaret Sullivan, I am sure] filled in the reasons." He then asked James what courses he was taking this year. James rattled off a series of advanced placement classes—calculus and the like—that met with Murphy's approval.

"I grew up in a blue-collar background and was the only one in my family to go to college," he explained. "I was recruited by only one school and went there. I decided I wanted to be more savvy about higher education.

"Take a good look at Harvard. When you ask people about the best college in America, what do you think a lot of them would say?" asked Murphy almost rhetorically.

"The bottom line is that the perception among many is that Harvard is the best college in America. I would guess you have a vision for your life—a great job, the ability to live where you want to live, and being able to make a great life for you and your family. Harvard gives you a credibility and respect that money can't buy. Our kids take pride in that.

"You have to ask yourself, 'Do I see myself at Harvard?' God forbid, you hurt a knee and can't play, would you still want to be there?"

He went on to football. "We play a great level of football and can win championships. We will be in the hunt every year. We have had eleven guys sign NFL contracts in the past five years. They could have gone to Notre Dame or Stanford, but they went to Harvard. You see, at Harvard I don't have to worry about kids academically. We want kids who are serious about football. We know our kids are serious about their academics."

"How many running backs are you recruiting?" I asked, leading toward the question of where James actually stood in the Crimson's plans.

"Six, for two spots. James is our number one guy. If he doesn't commit, then we move to the next guy."

I asked him if James would start as a freshman. I cared less about whether or not James would start than how well Murphy's response cohered with his placement of James at the top of Harvard's list.

"It would be difficult to start as a freshman. I couldn't promise that," he said.

"Why would it be difficult if he is your top guy? Do you have a returning starter at running back?"

"No, our tailback graduated. But James does have to prove he can learn our system as a freshman. I can tell you this, he is probably the most gifted guy we have recruited since I have been here. He will start if he earns the opportunity."

He turned to James. "You are our top choice. In fact, you are our top priority on the offensive side of the ball. At Harvard our kids are every bit as serious about football as my kids were at Cincinnati. The difference in the level of football between IA and IAA is overall speed."

That is why Harvard wants James. He brings IA speed to a IAA program. There was nothing Coach Murphy said that was not consistent with that of Coach Klunder.

He then moved at erasing the elitist stereotype attached to Harvard. He told the story of a recruiting venture in Nebraska. The youngster he had recruited came from a small high school—twenty-onekids in his graduating class—that played eight-man football. Initially, the youngster told Murphy he was not interested in Harvard. He didn't fit there.

"Here I had flown two thousand miles and then drove three hours to see this kid, and he tells me he won't even consider Harvard. He was going to Nebraska. It wasn't as if this were Dallas or Chicago where I could move on to another kid, so I wasn't going to give up that easily. I told him that most of our students are normal kids. They come from public high schools and get financial aid to afford to go to Harvard. I gave him an airline ticket and said, 'Here, visit us. You've got nothing to lose.'"

Of course, the story has a happy ending. The youngster visited Boston, liked Harvard, graduated, and went on to the NFL.

Murphy asked James what schools he was considering. "Harvard and Navy," was his response.

Murphy questioned James about his interest in the Naval commitment. Interestingly, Murphy had apparently sought the Navy job at the end of his undefeated 2001 season. I rummaged through the archives of the Internet and pieced the story together. Murphy had interviewed for the Navy position near the end of

November of 2001. The Academy sealed the deal with Johnson in the first few days in December, and Murphy then issued a public statement dated December 7, indicating that he was happy to be at Harvard. (Coaches are perpetually on the move. By the 2003 season, Chad Klunder had moved to Notre Dame and Bruce Tall to West Virginia.)

He then moved toward his conclusion. "There's nothing other schools can offer you that Harvard can't, but there are things Harvard can offer that other schools can't. You will never be sorry you chose Harvard."

We then watched the team's highlight film, narrated by NFL Films' Harry Kalas.

James was scheduled to visit Harvard January 3. Final recruiting decisions had to be made by January 10. "But James may not have a decision by the tenth," I said, knowing Navy would come later.

"It has to be the tenth," said Murphy becoming more animated. "We can't hold out any longer, because if James does not commit we need to move to the next kid. If we wait beyond the tenth, there could be no one left."

I didn't buy Murphy's position entirely. What was particularly telling is that he never asked the only logical question: How much more time might James need? Without doubt, a school cannot wait too long on getting commitments from certain kids, because indeed they can be gone. Nevertheless, we are talking about one prospect here—one—who faces unusual circumstances. If Murphy would be honest with those below James, telling them that he may have an opening at tailback but needs just a bit more time, I doubt the entire Harvard program would be thrown into trauma.

James was less concerned. He said he would have a decision by January anyway. We went on to clarify the financial-aid picture to whatever extent possible.

Monday night belonged to Jeff Monken and Navy.

The atmosphere was much smoother and free-flowing than it had been during the Harvard visits. Not only was James more comfortable with Monken than anyone else who had recruited him, Monken had already spent several hours with James at GBN that afternoon.

Early, Monken made his case for the Naval Academy. "James, with a thirty-two ACT you can hang and bang with the best of them academically. You can also hang and bang with the best in football. Why not go to a school where you can do both? As for us, you're exactly the type of kid we wanted at Georgia Southern and Hawaii."

I asked Jeff about the difficulties of recruiting for Navy. After acknowledging the special challenges, Monken made a summary statement. "If every kid you recruit decided to go to Navy, you'd know you're recruiting the wrong guys."

We talked about the five-year postgraduate military commitment. "A lot of guys will serve two years and then go to graduate school—law, medicine, or something else—and then come back to serve their remaining three years," explained Monken.

With Rita not yet home, I decided to move the conversation immediately to football. "What are the rules about going to the NFL?"

"Two years. You go to camp when drafted, and the team holds your rights for two years. Then if you make the team, the Navy waives the remaining three years of your service. But it's a long shot. Less than 1 percent of all high school players will ever go to an NFL camp."

Monken was headed to Buffalo Grove. Naturally, the discussion moved to Tom Zbikowski.

"I think he's more confused than ever. He's visited Nebraska, Iowa, and Notre Dame," said Jeff, obviously on top of the situation. "He canceled his visits to Boston College and Arizona State. He has not eliminated Navy."

I told him about my conversation with Ed in which he said kiddingly that I wouldn't be rid of him for another five years if both Tom and James went to the Naval Academy.

Monken emphasized his mission. "We are going after guys like James and Tom Zbikowski for a reason, and we are going to get good players. And Navy will do whatever it takes to be sure our guys will graduate."

I asked how many slotbacks Navy was recruiting.

"We got probably ten, and you [James] are in the top three.

There is a super prospect in Los Angeles and a kid in Florida who is really fast. He has a rocket booster up his keister.

"Let me tell you how we decided on where the guys were. I made a highlight film of all ten and studied it. Then the staff looked at it."

"How many starting slotbacks are coming back?" I inquired.

"Both slots are returning. No matter how physically gifted James may be, those guys have twelve games of major college experience and know our offense. Each week I get together with all the slotbacks. We talk about life, their girlfriends, school—everything—and where they are on the depth chart."

Jeff then went on and talked about NAPS, the Navy prep school in Newport, Rhode Island. "It's for freshmen only, is less regimented, and weekends are free. The team plays ten games and is coached by members of Coach Johnson's staff, so they learn the offense."

He then suggested NAPS as a possibility for James.

This was something neither James nor I wanted to hear at this point. It was hard enough for James to bite down on the five-year service commitment without adding yet another year of undergraduate education. Besides, Monken had talked of James "playing early" and having a thirty-two ACT, something I took to mean he would need no preparatory training for the Naval Academy.

I pressed the issue of whether James could play on the varsity as a freshman.

"It will be difficult," said Monken. "Physically I have no doubt about James. None. If he can learn the offense, he'll play. We have no one as fast as James. Physically, there is no question James can help us," he said, repeating himself. "But the offense is really complex, like nothing you've ever experienced, and you have to know it. Once you know the offense you'll play."

"Could you send me your playbook or something so I could study it before I came?" James asked.

"It wouldn't do much good. There are so many variations in each play that you wouldn't get it that way. You have to play it to learn it, and it's not easy."

If Monken was steering James toward NAPS I did not like it. I didn't remember him raising this possibility before. Rolling it out now was doing nothing for his credibility.

The subject moved to Coach Johnson. "Our head coach, Paul Johnson, is just great," said Monken. "He was offered the Hawaii job before June Jones took it, and he turned that down. He was a finalist for the job at North Carolina State. He turned down an interview at TCU because he was busy with N.C. State."

"I can't understand why he didn't stay at Georgia Southern for another year or two," I said, "win another IAA title or two, and then nail a top-drawer job."

"Paul Johnson is one of the most competitive people I know. He plays Ping-Pong as if it is the Super Bowl. I am confident we are going to win. He sees the Navy as a great challenge and he is going to get it done. You know when people tell you that you can't do something it makes you want to do it more."

He went on. "We've come a long way already. The team you saw play Army was not the same team you saw play North Carolina State. It takes time when guys have to learn a new offense, learn a new defense, and work with a new coaching staff. But we will get it done. Our coaches believe. Buddy Green left being the defensive coordinator at North Carolina State to join Coach Johnson's staff. Kevin Kelly was defensive coordinator at Marshall and took the job as linebackers coach for us, and Ken Nuimatalolo served on John Robinson's staff at UNLV before coming here. They all believe in Coach Johnson.

"Coach Johnson is the most respected option coach in the country. Face it, you don't get to zero and ten overnight, and it won't turn around overnight. It'll be a process. But it will happen."

Rita joined us and the talk moved to the academic experience. Monken had done his homework well. He was thoroughly versed in the entire Naval Academy experience and presented it well. Much of it I had heard while visiting three months previous. He highlighted the nightly mandatory study hall, the 7:1 faculty-student ratio, the 80 percent graduation rate, and the Academy's location with fifty colleges within an hour's drive.

It was late when he left. There was much to think about. Navy, with its military orientation, was in a class by itself. The five-year commitment had pluses and minuses, depending on your point of view. But you could feel the football program coming, and it was big time.

35.

Road Trips

On Tuesday afternoon, just before Monken's visit, James burst into my office. "I've made my decision. I don't want to discuss it now, but I'm going to Navy. I've thought about it and prayed about it and it feels right. I am a football player who is a good student. I want to play Division I football. Besides, there are a lot of advantages in going to the Navy."

I was surprised. I thought the vote was going to Harvard. "You should have seen your face when I said I was going to Navy," James said later. "You really looked surprised."

James talked about Harvard. "I didn't feel as close to any coach as I do to Monken." Perhaps this was due to having spent more time with the Navy assistant. Besides, he was leaning to a IA school. Again, I had no problems with non-IA football as such. I had been the athletic director at a Division III school, and Chris—perhaps a better all-around athlete than his younger brother—had been recruited at that level. Nonetheless, Harvard would not be playing Bowling Green, Navy, or Notre Dame.

So it was Navy.

Maybe.

After Coach Monken left, I could see James was troubled. The NAPS possibility and the service commitment were giving him pause. His mother and I kicked it around with him for a while. When James went to bed I sensed he was not at all resolved.

Gregg Brandon got the job at Bowling Green. That reopened a door. Brandon called.

"I'm really happy for you, coach," I said.

"Thank you, I'm really excited." It was clear that Brandon had dearly wanted the position. To his credit, it was the players who clinched it for him, going to the university and urging his appointment.

"It had to be you, and you've earned it," I said. "You have major college experience and were a prime force behind that offense."

He was appreciative. We then discussed James and scheduled a visit to Bowling Green for the weekend of January 17, the week after the Navy visit.

All remained quiet on the Cincinnati front. No call from Rick Minter, Mark Criner, or anyone else. This is the kind of stuff that leaves prospects and their parents with less than fond feelings about major college recruitment. Schools like Cincinnati send a clear message of hypocrisy: while they profess great concern for the "student-athlete," their actions indicate they have no interest in that youngster at all the moment they determine he will not be a contributor to their football success.

Meanwhile, James said nothing for days. Then one evening I invited him to go out to eat. "I really don't want to talk about my decision," he said, as if he had not been radiating avoidance for days.

When we got to the Ruby Tuesdays restaurant, I pulled out his allowance. "Will this buy me some information?" I said with a grin as I extended my arm across the table with the bills aimed in his direction.

He laughed. "I don't want to go to the military," he said almost defiantly.

I surprised him by saying nothing. Over and over I had been saying to him that he needed to look at the five-year commitment carefully and ask himself if he saw it as a positive, a negative, or a neutral matter. "There are people who see it each way," I had said.

The discussion went on without resolution. Clearly, the official campus visits would likely resolve the issue.

The first one was to Harvard. Each student is allowed a maximum of five official visits by the NCAA. Each visit is paid for entirely by the school. This includes airfare, meals, and lodging. Many if not most athletes take fewer than the maximum five if only because the schools are not interested in funding visits unless they feel they are very close to landing a youngster.

With James and his mother having left a day early for Boston, I picked up the ringing phone in a sleepy state early Friday morning. "I know you are at Harvard this week," the voice said, "but this is Coach . . . "

"James is already there, coach," I said groggily, thinking Coach Klunder was trying to locate him for his visit beginning that day.

"This isn't Harvard calling. This is Coach Walsh of Dartmouth," the voice said emphatically.

Not certain whether I was more embarrassed or amused, I got off the phone quickly and headed for Boston's Logan Airport to join James and Rita in Cambridge, Massachusetts.

It was a cold, crisp Friday evening when Coach Garvey picked me up along with several recruits and took us to the Michael C. Murr Center, a building that houses the tennis and squash courts and the strength and conditioning facility and highlights Harvard's athletic tradition with a time line and other displays. I met Rita there, along with the other parents and recruits.

The next stop was Annenberg Hall, the freshman cafeteria. The building had apparently once been a church, and the architecture indicated it. It was fun to see, firsthand, how the students were fed at Harvard. James, now with his host (each recruit is assigned a host who is a member of the team), a pleasant young man named Rodney from Indianapolis, ate separately with the recruits and their hosts, while the parents occupied a section of their own. After dinner, James headed for the dormitory. He was impressed.

"It was really nice—two bedrooms and a common room—like a really nice apartment. We hung around and watched the Ohio State–Miami national championship football game."

The digs were even better for the parents. Lodged at the Cambridge Hyatt Regency, we spent the evening eating and drinking on the Harvard tab and watching the game at a reception held in one of the hotel bars. Unwinding with the coaches and other parents was a genuine highlight and established some pleasant bonds among the group. My informal poll revealed, not surprisingly, that most of the other kids were (a) very good students, and (b) being recruited by other non-Division IA programs.

After breakfast the next morning, the coaches took the parents and recruits to the football offices housed in the stadium complex. The hallways were adorned with photographs of the Harvard teams over the years. I looked for the pictures of the teams on which Robert and Ted Kennedy had played. Several of the key pictures had been removed, but I did see a photo of Bobby as a Harvard football junior.

Our family meeting with Coach Murphy was, in a word, uncomfortable. Rita, James, and I sat on the sofa in his office, facing him. Murphy graciously reiterated his interest in James and then asked if we had any questions. None of us had any. I was hoping that would be it, and we could leave.

Of course, Murphy homed in on me. "Mr. Claerbaut, how do you feel about James going to Harvard?" I knew Rita was favorable toward Harvard, and that James seemed to be enjoying his experience at the school thoroughly, all of which would accentuate my position on the perimeter. Nevertheless, Rita wanted me to be candid.

I raised a football question or two and mentioned that Harvard had been the only school to remark about other schools. Murphy indicated that such was not their intention. All in all, Harvard had made no false claims—it was everything it purported to be—and so the subject moved to how I could best cooperate with the financial aid application.

The meeting closed with happy handshakes all around and Murphy tactfully thanked me for my honesty. Wanting some space, I had James and Rita attend the weight room presentation without me. It was unlikely I would hear anything new were I to attend.

After lunch, I went back to the hotel for a nap while Rita went on a tour. James returned to the dorm also for a nap. Later he saw a basketball game between Harvard and Dartmouth.

Needing to get back to Chicago for a Sunday morning commitment at my church, I headed for the airport in the late afternoon, unfortunately having to miss the Saturday evening bash, a dinner to be held in the rotating dining room on the top floor of the Hyatt Regency from which one can view the Boston skyline. Each coach spoke at the sumptuous steak dinner, with Murphy once again welcoming the throng and promoting the university's bene-fits.

I didn't get out of the airport.

An equipment malfunction throttled my plans, and so I headed back to the Hyatt, arriving well after the meal was over. I stopped in at the reception in the bar where the parents and coaches were watching the NFL playoff game. As for James, it was back to the dorm and a bit of partying with the hosts and some other students who dropped by.

"I really liked Harvard," he said. "I had not decided for Har-vard but I was surprised at how much fun I had. The kids were not arrogant, as I had been led to believe they would be, and of course they really help you feel the special nature of Harvard—the Harvard Square and that kind of stuff. You really feel the effect of being at a famous institution."

Indeed, the coaching staff did do an excellent job at staging the event. Ever careful to stay within the NCAA guidelines (they couldn't bring me back from the airport on the ill-fated Saturday night venture), they were very, very much on top of things. When I returned home I sent Coach Murphy an e-mail message apolo-gizing for my part in the rather awkward meeting in his office and commending him and his staff on what was a first-class event. To his credit, Murphy sent a warm reply within twenty-four hours.

While at one of the informal get-togethers I thought of Bruce Tall, now at Western Michigan. Tall had left Harvard, where he had been the defensive coordinator, the year before. I asked one of the new coaches about Tall's defection. His answer provided an insight into the life of an assistant.

"Coach Tall has a family," said the coach, "and let me tell you it is very expensive to buy a house and live here on an assistant's salary." I had never thought of that, but say an assistant pulls in maybe $60,000 to $80,000, depending on rank and seniority. A coach could buy a palace in Kalamazoo for what he might pay for little more than a garage in Cambridge.

Money is important, something that Brandon had mentioned likely played into Urban Meyer's decision to move on to Utah. So is the opportunity to win. One coach explained what figured to have been Meyer's (and coaches' like him) logic. "Look at it this way," the coach said. "He's had two big years at Bowling Green but the Big Ten hasn't called. Now, if you're Meyer you're saying to yourself, 'Hey, with Marshall and Toledo in the MAC, we could slip a bit, then the phone may not ring at all.' The MAC is not the Mountain West and he can win at Utah. He will have one huge problem there, however."

"What's that?" I asked.

"He will have to do totally out-of-state recruiting. There are very few Division 1 players in the state, and most of them are Mormons, and you know what Utah school they will be attending," the coach said, obviously referring to Brigham Young.

In any case, thinking of Tall and watching the dutiful nature of the Harvard staff, I gained a newfound respect for the life of the assistant. The pay is uneven and the demands high. This would be but the first of three weeks of campus visits for these coaches. They would work brutal hours, lugging recruits and parents back and forth in vans from the airport, squiring a group of teenagers around on the campus, and then entertaining the parents in the hotel bar late into the night. All of this without one shred of certainty that any given youngster is going to commit to the university in pursuit of him. And this, of course, is the coaches' *off-season*.

"It must be tough," I said to Coach Garvey on one of our van rides back to the hotel. "You really got to sell the school to these kids."

"We've got to recruit them or we don't eat," was his honest reply.

I was tired. No sooner did I get back from Harvard early Sunday morning than I was arranging to fly to Detroit on business the following afternoon. I was hoping to beg off of the Navy visit, having been there before. Rita, however, is a trooper. To be fair to the process, she wanted to go, and so we did.

Although we all flew to Annapolis on Friday, I arrived on a later flight from Rita and James. Coach Monken was at the airport to pick me up. "I owe you an apology," I said almost instantly upon shaking hands with him.

"Why?"

"I jumped on you a bit about NAPS on the phone some time ago, and James later told me you had told him about the NAPS possibility right from the outset of recruiting him. He had forgotten that."

"No problem," Monken said. "I met with the admissions people and James is good to go direct [to Annapolis] his first year, based on his grades and academic abilities."

We talked about recruiting, and I gave him an update on James. "If he had to decide right now," I reported, "I think it would be Harvard. He had a good time there, and this is the military."

Monken was not rattled, though he did seem surprised after what he took away from the home visit with us a few weeks previous. "This is a big weekend for him. He should know what he wants when it's over."

The experience at Navy was similar to that of Harvard. There was a host, a young man named Bronston from Houston, lots of time with other recruits, and plenty of football talk. A principal difference, however, was that James stayed in the Sheraton, the same hotel at which the parents were lodged. I asked Monken about that, and he explained that most schools put recruits up in hotels.

"I guess Harvard wanted to show off their student living quarters," Rita sagely observed.

A highlight occurred on Saturday afternoon while I was heading to Washington, D.C. in a rental car to pick up Rochelle. The youngsters and their families were taken by van to the stadium. There they would encounter some first-rate promoting.

"When we entered the stadium, the jumbotron was announcing the players' names and numbers, along with their heights, weights, and high schools in alphabetical order over the loudspeaker," said James with amusement. "'James Velissaris, 5-10, 175 pounds, from Glenbrook North.' They kept recycling the names and some of the guys were really impressed."

From there the group headed into the locker room for another sales job. "In the locker room they had Navy jerseys hanging up with our names and numbers on them," James explained with a chuckle. "It was kind of weird, but I guarantee you they got two or three guys right there."

There was more. Under each jersey was a laminated, large-pocket size card, providing a profile of the player. This is what James' card said:

22

#22 BILL INGRAM: Was inducted into the College Football Hall of Fame in 1973 . . . scored a school-record 21 touchdowns in 1917.

#22 JAMES VELISSARIS: With his ability and the explosiveness of Navy's spread offense, Velissaris is a threat to break Ingram's record of 21 touchdowns in a season . . . a candidate for the Doak Walker Award, which is given to the nation's most outstanding running back.

"Then on a table in front of each locker was a bunch of equipment and apparel, all of it personalized," explained James. "It jumped out at you. You see the Nike endorsements. Every cleat you could possibly imagine; every helmet you could possibly imagine; every shoulder pad. It's a lot different from a standard pair of shoulder pads for every position like you get in high school. My high school helmet popped off about five times in the middle of a play. My shoulder pads in my sophomore year were too small for me and popped out of place in the Maine West game.

"You should have seen the sight," he said to me with a grin. "All the kids putting on those jerseys and having their parents taking pictures."

On Saturday there was a dinner at the hotel. Rochelle joined us there, and James was eager to see her. She stayed the night with Rita and me at the hotel, giving us time to be together. As with Harvard, for the recruits the evenings included some partying with some other students present, although the group was racially mixed. Rita, Rochelle, and I went to a reception for the families in one of the hotel suites.

On Sunday morning Rita, James, and I met with Coach Paul Johnson in his office. Johnson has a very laid-back Southern style about him. His office is crowded with trophies and he sat under a photograph of the 1996 Aloha Bowl game that Navy had won 42–38 over California, his final year as an assistant at the Academy.

"You've seen our program, James, and you know we really are high on you. We want you here," Johnson drawled. "Do you have any questions?"

He had none.

"Well, what is your impression now that you've seen things up close?"

"It's different from what I thought. It is not as restricted as I thought it would be," James replied.

"In a lot of ways it's not much different from any other college. As for the military service, very few graduates are ever in actual combat." He went on to tell of one of his former players, a young man from the South who initially wanted nothing to do with military life.

"After visiting here, he came. And after his five years he re-upped," said Johnson with a chuckle. "After serving that hitch I asked him what he was going to do. He told me he was going to leave. He had a wife and family and it was time to get on with civilian life." Johnson used the example to make two points. First, not every reluctant midshipmen finds the life unpleasant, and second, people can move on with lifetime military benefits.

"Where do you stand, James?" Johnson moved in. "Where do you think you'll be going?"

"It's either Harvard or here," said James, without tipping his hand.

"Well, you know we want you. And we will win. Coaches like Coach Green from North Carolina State, Coach Kelly from Marshall, Coach Nuimatalolo from UNLV—all of us would not be here if we didn't expect to win."

Johnson played down the learning curve for a first-year player.

"I'm not going to promise you, you will play. Beware of any coach who tells you that you will play. You probably can't trust him," Johnson said firmly. "But I will tell you this. We will play the best players, and if you are the best, then you will play. The offense isn't that hard to learn. You basically do one of three things on each play.

"You will get a chance to play some football next year, even if it's with the JV team. We had a freshman last year who started playing there and then moved to the varsity. So you will play some football."

The conversation wound down with Coach Johnson shaking hands with each of us. There was no special pressure but a clear "I hope to see you here, next year" concluding air.

After meeting with Johnson, the three of us and Rochelle went to church in the spectacular Navy chapel. From there it was off to D.C. to take Rochelle back, and then a return to drop the rental car before Monken brought us to the airport.

On the ride to the airport, Monken showed his competitiveness, leaning on James a bit. He asked why James was still considering visiting Bowling Green if it was between Navy and Harvard. James said little, a certain indication that he was not comfortable. Monken pressed on in his slow, deliberate style. "You know the football situation here, James," he said. "You have to ask yourself if the military is for you. Yeah, it will be tough, but anything worth doing is going to be tough. You know that."

James had heard an amusing story about Monken's intensity from one of the hosting players. One day at practice after Johnson dispersed the players to their position coaches, the slotbacks couldn't locate Monken immediately. After looking around they saw him way on the other end of the field off to the sideline. The players sprinted up to the coach, wondering why he was not on the field. Monken gave them his reason. "We played so badly the last game, we don't deserve to be on the field," he said. "You guys have to earn your way back on."

"He's tough," said one player, "but he will make you better."

James, however, had enough intensity for one day. He was relieved upon getting to the airport. "You've got to figure he's a bit frustrated," I said to him softly, referring to Monken. "He thought he had you a month ago, and now he's still not sure."

That seemed to mollify James. But the decision was still pending.

36.

The Decision

James firmed up his thinking on the plane ride home to Chicago. The decision was not easy. As Coach Whalen said so well to me a few days later, "Harvard, Navy, and Bowling Green are three very, very different schools to pick from."

James focused on the Harvard/Navy matter. "I thought about what my brother Mike had said to me recently," James later told me. (Mike was out from California, spending several months in the Midwest plying his versatile and incredible skills managing a construction project for Rita and me.) "He talked to me about having to chase your dream. I am blessed. I don't have to chase my football dream. It is being offered to me. So many people would kill for that."

James had talked extensively with Rochelle that last day at Navy. It had crystallized some of his thinking. "I realized when I talked to Rochelle why I didn't know what I wanted to study—major in—because all I knew my whole life is that I wanted to play football."

He noted the investment in the Navy program. "When I saw the renovation of the stadium [going from a 35,000 seating capacity to an enclosed 50,000] I had a flashback of the North Carolina State experience. It was a full house—big time. The fans had to know they were going to get beat by a team like that, yet the place was still packed."

There was still the academic allure of Harvard. Murphy and his staff could not have extended a clearer welcome to James, nor could the visit have been improved upon for James, Rita, and me. They had done well in promoting the academic and social advantages that Harvard had to offer. The Crimson had also enjoyed considerable football success over the past two seasons and could boast of alums in the NFL. "That some of the players there were recruited by Division IA schools was also appealing," James remarked. Nevertheless, the football was not at a top level. "Now that I think about it, though, I don't know how many actually had been offered."

A major pull toward Cambridge had been the less restrictive life of the conventional college student as opposed to those attending the academies. That, however, changed during the weekend at Annapolis. "Experiencing a bit of life off the base on the weekend nights showed me the social life off the base was the opposite of what you would expect." James also liked the comfortable racial mix. "There was not the expected racial pairing among the guys or the girls at Navy."

Then there was money. "Rochelle talked about how hard it is to be in a situation in which you end up owing money and being in debt [something she faces upon graduating from law school]," he explained. "Both Harvard and Navy are topflight schools, but I will be able to avoid any debt once I get out of the Academy."

After having weighed the factors, he had decided.

It was Navy.

"I think you should cancel the trip to Bowling Green, then," said Rita once she knew of his decision. "It wouldn't be right to visit there when you know you will not be going to the school." She was correct, and James took it off the board.

James moved quickly and quietly. He rose early the following Monday morning and headed to Glenbrook North. There, he used Coach Whalen's phone to inform Coach Monken that he would be a Midshipman.

By 2:30 my phone rang.

"Hi, this is Coach Whalen. Congratulations."

"Thanks, Coach," I replied, happy and surprised to hear from Whalen.

"James called Coach Monken from my office this morning," he said. "Boy, this is just great. What a tremendous opportunity for James! I am so happy for him."

"Coach, I knew it was Navy, but I didn't know he would make the call right away," I said. "I know it was really weighing heavily, and I guess he needed to get it over with."

We talked about a few other things, including how the spread offense seemed right for James. We also talked about some near misses with other schools, including Wisconsin and Western Michigan, neither of which called.

"I think they had to extrapolate a bit, imagining James in the slot, since he played in the tailback position here and they weren't 100 percent certain," was Whalen's analysis. It made sense.

I appreciated Whalen's call. It was a quality thing to do.

"Hi, is James there?" It was Edgy Tim, on the case within hours of the news breaking.

"No, he isn't home yet."

"I see he declared for Navy," said Tim. "This is just fabulous. Congratulations! What an incredible opportunity!"

There were other calls. The *Pioneer Press*, a division of the *Chicago Sun-Times* that had covered James for the past three years, interviewed him on the phone. Head Coach Paul Johnson also called, congratulating James and welcoming him to the Academy.

My voice mail at Argus contained congratulations from Steve Helminiak and Mike Herbert. I called Ivan and Ann, and they were thrilled. "Let's drive out there in the fall," was Ivan's sentiment. "I would love to see him there." A dear friend of mine, Jeff Cummings, who graduated from Navy, insisted he meet James soon. "That way I won't be a stranger when I take him out to dinner during my trip back for my reunion this fall."

A week later a handwritten card came for James. It was from Coach Monken.

> *Dear James,*
> *I just wanted to congratulate you again on your decision to attend Navy.*
> *We couldn't be more thrilled to have you "aboard."*
> *We are looking forward to this coming fall. You are going to have an unbelievable experience here over the next four years. You made a great choice!*
> *Talk to you soon.*
> *Go NAVY! Beat Army!*
> *Coach Monken*

There was one other personal note.

James,
Congratulations on your decision to attend the Naval Academy. What an exciting choice.
The combination of your discipline, work ethic, and athletic ability . . . I know you are going to have great success.
It was a pleasure and an honor to have the opportunity to recruit you.
Best of luck!
> *Sincerely,*
> *Bruce Tall*

Later, Tim Murphy of Harvard sent a letter of congratulations and best wishes to James. I was happy to see that. I wanted no ill feeling with the Crimson. Then there was Ed Zbikowski. Tommy was soon to decide for Notre Dame.

Congratulations! I heard about Jimmy," he said. "Isn't this just terrific? Think of it, with Tommy at Notre Dame, they will play against each other for four more years."

Ed had been just wonderful through this. I was really happy for him and Tommy. Ed and I had a celebratory lunch together in mid-February. But on this call his focus was on "Jimmy." "I'm just so proud of Jimmy," he enthused, "and what an opportunity. He will really be set when he gets out of there."

There were still things to do, all in advance of the first Wednesday in February, the "national signing day," when recruits can sign the official scholarship letters of intent. Not the least of these for James, was to be nominated for the academy by a member of congress. An applicant must submit a transcript of his grades in addition to an ACT or SAT score, along with three letters of recommendation and a personal essay on leadership to the member of Congress. Rep. Rahm Emanuel of Illinois graciously consented to nominate James.

On February 5, at three in the afternoon, James signed his letter of intent with Navy. No press was present, because quite a bit had been made of James' decision when it first became public.

Nonetheless, a reception—beautifully arranged by Rita—was held in Athletic Director Coach Bob Pieper's office at Glenbrook North. With family and friends looking on and flashbulbs popping, James signed the document. It read:

THE UNITED STATES NAVAL ACADEMY

On this *5th* day of *FEBRUARY* in the year *2003*, I, *JAMES VELISSARIS* do hereby commit to attend the United States Naval Academy at Annapolis. I understand that a full Offer of Appointment will be forthcoming upon completion of my outstanding Admission requirements. I further understand that I will receive full room and board, full medical and dental benefits and a monthly allowance. Upon graduation from the United States Naval Academy with a Bachelor of Science Degree, I will be commissioned as an Ensign in the United States Navy or a Second Lieutenant in the United States Marine Corps.

The document contained three signatures, those of David A. Vetter, dean of admissions, James, and Head Coach Paul Johnson.

It was a classy thing for Pieper and Coach Whalen to turn the signing into a celebration at James' high school, given that it was not a media event. There was media noise on the East Coast, however, and Coach Whalen ably contributed to that. In an Annapolis paper, touting the high quality of Navy's recruiting class—and citing James as one prime example of the "haul"—Whalen was quoted. "There's a lot of kids in our area who say they run a 4.4. James is faster than all of them."

"The kid can flat out fly," Whalen added. "He's the fastest player I've ever coached, and that's not even what makes him such a great back. His greatest attribute is that he's incredibly quick and has an ability to see the hole and hit it. I can't wait to see him play in that double-slot attack that Navy employs. He's going to run wild."

James and I especially appreciated his mother for putting together the food arrangements for the reception and adding so many of her own, distinctive decorative touches to mark the occasion.

It was a fitting end to our journey.

The journey had ended so differently from the way it had started. At the outset, Iowa, Wisconsin, and Western Michigan seemed out front. Navy had been eliminated early, Bowling Green not heard from, and Harvard not even considered. Now, fifteen months later, it was Navy.

"Funny how things turn out," James said to me in one of our times together.

"How's that, son?"

"When you took Chris and me to Notre Dame a few years ago, I was hooked. I wanted to play at Notre Dame. Now I will. Only I will be running out of the visitor's tunnel."

A wise man, George Gion, had lost his wife late in life. He told me the first year alone was excruciating, the second year less painful, and then after that—he said with a warm, wonderful smile—"it's just memories."

For me the recruiting adventure was really just a means to a greater end—building a bond with a son. The next few years should, indeed, be very exciting. After that, however, there will always be the memories.

Epilogue

Induction into the Naval Academy was July 1, 2003. The weather was warm but comfortable that day. It started with a picnic lunch as well as a stirring and informative orientation for the families of the new Plebes. Rita, Rochelle, and I could hardly wait for the induction ceremonies on the steps of Bancroft Hall that evening. At about 5:45 p.m. the new inductees marched to their seats for the induction. The oath, a solemn vow with a presidential-like ring, was to be administered in 15 minutes. Rita was snapping pictures and all of us were trying to identify James among the marchers. It was impossible, given the distance and the identical attire of all the inductees.

After the new Plebes shouted "I do" enthusiastically upon taking the oath, the families were directed to various spots alphabetically designated to greet and say a temporary goodbye to the new Plebes. Rita, Rochelle, and I went to "V" and waited eagerly for James.

He did not appear. "Velissaris?" It was the voice of Marine GySgt. Blair E. Greentaner, a vital, ruddy-complexioned man with a friendly manner.

"Here."

"Your son is all right," he said. "But he will not be joining the Navy."

During the summer James had continued his workouts and protein and carbohydrate intake, making it past the 180 pound threshold that the larger schools set as their standard. He had made it, just a year late. His hamstring, however, did not improve despite rest and more rehab. An MRI in the spring determined that he had a slight tear.

For James, this was a difficult reality. As with so many other teenage athletes, it was the first time his body betrayed him. Despite second thoughts about his future he continued his rehab process, this time under the guidance of professional sports trainers. By summer, some healing had occurred and he had learned how to protect himself against further injury.

I spoke to one of his trainers about preventing reinjury. "James simply has to be aware of muscle fatigue in the hamstring," he explained. "Particularly as he recovers, he needs to stop when he experiences soreness or fatigue."

"Once recovered, will he be more prone to reinjuring the hamstring than, say, an athlete who has never experienced a tear?" I asked.

"No, but he must continue to work on his flexibility when he warms up," the trainer answered.

James was zealous and optimistic about his workout routine. In the late spring he conducted a Christian camp, focusing on football and life skills in an intense, largely Puerto Rican inner-city Chicago neighborhood. His brother Chris assisted him. The camp went so well the junior high decided to have a football team in the fall. Time was ticking down to his July 1st inductions day into the Navy.

After church on June 29th, James and I left for Chicago's O'Hare Airport, bound for Baltimore-Washington International Airport and the U. S. Naval Academy. His mother had taken an earlier flight. We got there after nine in the evening and drove the rental car to the hotel at which we would be staying until his induction on July 1st.

"I'm excited," I said to the tired James. "How do you feel?"

"I'm a little down."

I wasn't surprised. Sunday had been a day of goodbyes for him. He had parted with the people at the church who liked him, his girlfriend, and his brother Chris. On the previous Friday night his mother held a family and friend farewell get together for him at his sister Christine's home. He had not yet said any hellos to new classmates, teammates, or coaches.

Monday night there was a reception for the football recruits and their parents. Feeling the reality of football around the corner—practice would begin in eight days—energized James. After the meeting, James, Rita, and I walked around the yard (campus) and watched some of the 7-on-7 games being played by high school camp youngsters on some of the practice fields. James knew his way around the yard, pointing out buildings and other items of interest. We then drove to the football stadium and there James and I took Rita on a private tour of the structure, which was in the process of renovation and the addition of 20,000 seats. James and I went down on the field and felt the tightness of the grass.

"It always seems shorter when it is enclosed," James said to me with a smile, referring to the difference between an open-ended high school field and a wraparound college or NFL stadium, with the field encapsulated by stands.

We headed back to our room for final preparations, realizing that in less than twelve hours—7 a.m.—James was due to report to the academy for the induction process, culminating with the taking of the oath of office at 6 p.m. Rita left to pick up some food and James went downstairs to run.

"My hamstring is still tight," he said to me when he returned to the room. "I don't know what to do."

I asked him how far he had run. He had done a mile or so at a rather rapid, six-minute clip. "When was the last time you ran that far?" I asked.

"It's been awhile."

"Well then you have to expect it to be sore," I said, wanting to assure him.

"I guess you're right."

James was concerned about going all out in basic training of Plebe Summer in two days, risking a serious reinjury. His trainers in Chicago and the sports people at Navy felt full recovery was just a matter of time—a month or so—therefore he was encouraged not to call attention to the injury with the induction medical staff. By doing so, he would risk not being permitted to start Plebe Summer. He was conflicted. He didn't want to be dishonest with the medical staff in the morning, yet he had reason to believe he was in the kind of condition that would enable him to get through the running aspect of Plebe Summer without reinjury. With football starting in about a week he could work under the supervision of the sports medicine staff, people who specialize in rehabbing hamstrings and other common athletic injuries.

I urged him to call Coach Monken, one of the Navy coaches. James does not like to operate under a cloud when it comes to key matters and I felt he could get closure that way.

"I don't want to irritate him," James said, not wanting to be an extra burden to Monken.

I assured him that the coach who had recruited him so consistently would want to know and help him. He called the coach and talked briefly. He said nothing to me after the call.

The next morning I drove Rita and James to the academy for induction and Plebe Summer. Plebe Summer runs about six intense weeks, after which there is an August weekend of celebration for the graduate and his family. James was already looking forward to that event and had given his mother some preferences for the occasion. I returned to the hotel to complete the checkout and then left for Washington D.C. to pick up Rochelle, who had taken the day off from her law school internship at the Department of Justice to attend the events for James.

"Dad, James is going to be a man of honor. In fact, he already is a man of honor," she said, referring to his character.

There are no words to capture the surprise among the three of us when Marine GySgt. Greentaner delivered the news about James.

"Follow me and I will take you to him," said the officer softly.

We asked what happened. Greentaner told us that after going through the preliminaries, James had changed his mind a few hours before the private swearing in and signing of the oath, about three hours before the formal ceremony. James had asked, "Is this it?" referring to the finality of the oath.

"Yes it is," he had been told.

"I really can't sign this," he said.

Rita, Rochelle, and I were escorted to a building adjacent to where the ceremony had taken place. We spoke together and separately with him. His pain was palpable. If ever a parent was more concerned for his child than himself, this was the time. He looked at me.

"I'm sorry I let you down," he said several times. He had known how excited I was about his going to Navy and he wanted me to be happy and proud. I felt heartsick that he had carried the burden of the expectations of others at the expense of his own feelings.

For James it was about honesty, a value by which he measures himself and others. He had struggled privately with his decision for months. He had had second thoughts throughout. Sometimes he shared his doubts; sometimes he did not. His hamstring was not ready, and he did not want to deceive anyone as to its condition.

Far more important, however, he knew that he would not have sought admission to the academy were he not a football recruit. He was not going for the right reasons. In that context he felt he could not, in good conscience, take the oath of office.

He had looked carefully at the oath he was required to sign. He had not seen it before this day. It read:

> *I, James R. Velissaris, having been appointed a midshipman in the United States Navy, do solemnly swear (or affirm) that I will support and defend the Constitution of the United States against all enemies, foreign and domestic; that I will bear true faith and allegiance to the same; that I take this obligation freely, without any mental reservation or purpose of evasion; and that I will well and faithfully discharge the duties of the office on which I am about to enter; so help me God.* </ext>

"I could not take an oath like that before my country, and especially to God," he told me the next day, "knowing that I had come to the academy primarily to play football rather than serve my country in the Navy like the rest of the Plebes had. It would not be honest."

He had been clear about the military obligation. The coaches had never been dishonest about that. The importance of the primary obligation to the country, however, was something James felt he had been in some denial over and also something that was understandably not focused heavily upon in his recruitment as a football player.

Four different navy and marine officers met with him almost immediately. After hearing his reasons, each told him had done the right thing in not signing. After several coaches took a somewhat different approach in talking with him about it, suggesting that he may be experiencing last-minute jitters and he may be making too much of the signing, he was even more certain that was now doing the honorable thing, despite the embarrassment that might follow.

It was not a matter of whether he could succeed at the academy. Other than the tender hamstring, he would have been perhaps the most fit of any Plebe heading into Plebe Summer. Academically, he had finished high school on top, with many of his classes at an Advanced Placement, college prep level, and the Ivy League had been in pursuit of him. Emotionally, he had endured far worse than the discomforts of military life. Nor was it a question of respect for the Naval Academy. He admired the academy and what it stood for, and had been honored by their pursuit of him. It was a question of integrity. On the yard, and fully apprised of the life he was committing to enter, he had been staring the oath in the face. That inner voice told him he could not take the oath with full honesty.

When Rita reviewed for him the consequences of his decision, James said, "If I never play another down of football, I am still doing the right thing." After words and hugs from Rita, Rochelle, and I, officer Greentaner took James away to get him released. We waited in The Drydock, the academy's version of a student union. Eventually the officer returned with James.

"All set to go," he said kindly. "It was a tough decision for your son, but you have to be proud that he wanted to do everything with integrity."

Greentaner could not have handled it better. "He was even better in private with me than he was with the family present," said James.

James was still a civilian. There were still a few college options open and James planned on pursuing them. Though he felt very badly about any negative effect this awesome and lonely decision to turn away from the wonderful opportunities of the academy had on others, he trusted God that things would work out.

The hamstring will heal fully and important life lessons have been learned.

After hearing the painful details the following day in Chicago, I said, "I am proud of you, son. You did the honorable thing."

We hugged warmly, father and son. It was time to move on.

On July 14th Harvard returned James' inquiry and made the same package available as before. James accepted.